MW01035162

BISON
BOOKS

VENEZUELAN BUST, BASEBALL BOOM

Andrés Reiner and Scouting on the New Frontier

Milton H. Jamail

University of Nebraska Press | Lincoln and London

Library of Congress Cataloging-in-Publication Data
Jamail, Milton H.
Venezuelan bust, baseball boom : Andrés Reiner and scouting on the new frontier / Milton H. Jamail.
p. cm. Includes bibliographical references (p.).
ISBN 978-0-8032-1571-9 (pbk. : alk. paper)
1. Reiner, Andrés, 1935– 2. Baseball—Scouting—Venezuela. 3. Baseball—Scouting—Texas—Houston. 4. Houston Astros (Baseball team) I. Title.
GV865.R422J36 2008
796.3570987—dc22 2007033162

Set in Scala by Bob Reitz. Designed by A. Shahan.

Contents

Illustrations

Preface

In 1987 when I began to do research on baseball in Latin America, I read anything I could find on the subject in both English and Spanish and interviewed every current and former player from the region I could locate. I soon discovered that baseball was the most popular sport in Cuba, the Dominican Republic, Nicaragua, Panama, and Venezuela and also had a long history in Mexico, Puerto Rico, and the north coast of Colombia. I also realized that the definitive history of baseball in the Caribbean region that I envisioned writing was neither possible nor necessary: the subject was much too complex, and other scholars and serious journalists were also working on the topic.

In the early 1990s I focused my research on Cuba and Venezuela. Not much was written about contemporary baseball in either country, and both were coming onto the radar screens of major league scouts. In 2000 my book, *Full Count: Inside Cuban Baseball*, a look at baseball in post-1959 Cuba, was published. The focus of this book is Venezuela, and to a much lesser extent Colombia, Nicaragua, and Panama.

I first went to Venezuela in 1986 to attend an academic conference and was intrigued by this fascinating country. I returned to Venezuela in May 1990 to write a six-part series for the *Houston Post* on the Astros' Latin American scouting program. I stayed in contact with those in the Houston front office in charge of Astros' scouting and also communicated with other major league organizations concerning their interest in searching for players in Venezuela. And I closely monitored the progress of the increasing number of Venezuelan players in U.S. professional baseball: 75 percent of the 214 Venezuelans who have played in the major leagues made their debut after 1988. Clearly Venezuelan baseball had become more important to professional organizations in the United States.

While Venezuela is not actually a "new" frontier for baseball scouts, it is a country that had been on the back burner until Andrés Reiner opened the Astros' facility in 1989. In the early 1990s it became apparent that the Astros were the front runners in this Venezuelan scouting boom, and I began to write about the accomplishments of the organization in opening the market for the recruitment of major league baseball players. Portions of those articles that first appeared in *Astros Magazine*, *Baseball America*, and *USA Today Baseball Weekly* are herein included.

In addition to examining Andrés's vision of scouting and development, *Venezuelan Bust, Baseball Boom* also includes a brief overview of the origins of baseball in Venezuela, explores the role of the Houston organization in scouting in Latin America since its inception in 1962, and traces the progress through professional baseball of several of the prospects signed out of the Astros' academy.

The book is the product of a seventeen-year conversation with Andrés Reiner. I traveled with him throughout the Caribbean on over a dozen occasions and observed the manner in which he carried out his project. I saw scouting reports on most of the players he signed and reviewed his correspondence relating to the academy. Between 1990 and 2005 I went on scouting trips and attended ballgames and tryouts from one end of Venezuela to the other with several of his scouts (in particular Rafael Cariel and Orlando Fernández), and just hung out with coaches and instructors at the Astros' academy near Valencia.

Being with these scouts and coaches was such a pleasure that I found it difficult to end to my research. I wanted to continue to tag along with Andrés as he crisscrossed the Caribbean Basin and beyond, and to accompany Rafael Cariel on the road to El Dorado.

Venezuelan Bust, Baseball Boom

1

Venezuelan Bust, Baseball Boom

Mr. Reiner's Dream

On August 2, 2005, the Houston Astros sent an e-mail message to the other major league organizations announcing that Special Assistant to the General Manager Andrés Reiner would be leaving the organization at the end of the season. Reiner, who had worked for Houston since 1989, was the architect of the Astros' Venezuelan academy. In the seventeen years since the organization opened its facility in Venezuela, twenty-two players signed by Reiner had reached the major leagues. Seven of them, including 2004 and 2006 American League Cy Young Award winner Johán Santana (Minnesota), 2005 All-Star Game Home Run Derby champion Bob Abreu (New York Yankees), Freddy García (Philadelphia), Carlos Guillén (Detroit), and Melvin Mora (Baltimore) are still active in the major leagues. Only two of them play for the Astros.

Reiner's resignation was a shock to many in the baseball industry, but his departure had been in the works for well over a year. After GM Gerry Hunsicker resigned in November 2004, Reiner knew his days with the Astros were numbered. He was convinced that the Astros' front office was incapable of making the changes he believed essential and felt that if he stayed he would, in effect, be endorsing what the club was doing. In late February 2005 he submitted his letter of resignation, citing "philosophical differences" with the current management of the club. He agonized before making that decision and had to summon up the inner strength that had carried him through tough times in the past. But once Reiner decided to leave, he told me he felt an inner peace.

Andrés Reiner was born in Hungary on November 16, 1935, and immigrated to Venezuela in late 1946. He played soccer as a child in Budapest but lost his left leg in an accident. "It was because of my English class that I lost my leg," Andrés told me. In Hungary his father, István Reiner, insisted that he study English when he was seven years old. Andrés was about ten and on his way to class one winter day when he tripped—his school bag got caught on the train—and the train hit him. The accident put an end to any hope of following in his father's footsteps as a professional soccer player.

István Reiner was born in a part of Hungary near Zagreb, now in Croatia. Selected to the Hungarian national soccer team thirteen times, the senior Reiner later went into banking and was the head of the Bank of London's operations in Budapest before operating an import-export business in the Hungarian capital.

In 1946 with the Communist Party on the verge of taking control in Hungary, the family decided to immigrate to the United States. István Reiner, through a government official who was a former soccer teammate, arranged for the family to receive passports to leave the country legally. But they would not be allowed to return, and the export business would have to be forfeited to the government.

The visas to the United States never materialized. The family, however, was able to obtain visas to Mexico and with them traveled to Paris, where they were allowed to stay for ninety days while arranging passage to Mexico. While the Reiners were in Paris, the newly elected Mexican president, Miguel Alemán, cancelled all visas for foreigners. Andrés and his family were stuck in Paris and at the end of ninety days would be sent back to Hungary.

Mr. Reiner inquired about obtaining a visa for Uruguay, but the process was slow. Then someone told him about a man in a café who every afternoon sold visas for another South American country.

"I was eleven at the time and had learned a little French so my father asked me to go with him to the café," recalls Andrés. "The man was the consul for Venezuela in Paris, and he was selling visas for four hundred dollars each." István Reiner purchased visas for the family. "On the way home my father said, 'Andrés, let's go to a bookstore, buy a map, and see where this country is.'" Forty-five years later, it was Andrés who put Venezuela on the map of Major League Baseball.

In 1946 only three ships made the voyage from France to the French Caribbean and on to Venezuela. Andrés remembers the consul explaining how they might get passage on the ss *Colombé*. The consul had sold visas—and passages—to a group of Italians but thought they would have a difficult time getting to the port at La Havre because of the possibility of a rail strike in Italy. The consul could not assure the Reiners passage on the ss *Colombé* until the Italians were no-shows and the ship had actually set sail. Andrés and his family made their way to La Havre, the Italian rail strike did occur, and the passengers didn't show up. So with Andrés and his family sitting on shore with all of their possessions, the ss *Colombé* set sail. When the ship was about a half a mile out, it sent back a small boat to pick them up. They were finally on their way to Venezuela. Andrés recalls that after a little more than a week at sea, the ship docked on the Caribbean island of Guadeloupe. After stops in Martinique and Trinidad, the ship landed at the Venezuelan port city of La Guaira. The Reiners soon settled into their new home in downtown Caracas.

When they arrived in Venezuela, Andrés spoke no Spanish. Within six weeks, he was sent to school where the instruction was exclusively in Spanish, and as he puts it, "I survived." But he was clearly a stranger in a new land, learning a new language and adapting to a new culture, and was often referred to as *musiú*—a term Venezuelans use for foreigners, especially those who are white and don't speak Spanish.

Andrés wondered why soccer wasn't played in Venezuela, and on his way to school, he noticed that many of the boys carried something made out of leather. He asked his father and older brother what this strange thing was, but neither knew. It was, Andrés later ascertained, a baseball glove. His classmates played only baseball in school, and he soon joined in. But Andrés quickly discovered that due to his physical limitations (he now wore a prosthesis) as well as his unfamiliarity with the game, he could only be a pitcher. He also found that if he arrived with a baseball, he would be one of the boys picked to play in the sandlot games. He never turned up without one and soon fell in love with baseball. And like most young boys in Caracas, he spent countless hours playing *chapitas*—the Venezuelan equivalent of stickball—where the batter uses a broom handle to attempt to hit a bottle cap.

He remembers attending his first professional game in Venezuela at Estadio San Agustín in late October or early November 1947. There was a doubleheader every Sunday at the stadium—starting at 9:30 a.m.—featuring the four teams in the league, Vargas, Venezuela, Cervecería Caracas, and Magallanes. Andrés showed up at 7:30 a.m. for batting practice and was particularly intrigued by the Vargas team that featured the battery of pitcher Don Newcombe and catcher Roy Campanella, both Negro League stars who went on to play with the Brooklyn Dodgers. Other Negro League greats such as Sam Hairston, Bob Dandridge, and Ray Welmaker; Cuban sensation Lázaro Salazar; and Venezuelans Alejandro Carrasquel and Alfonso "Chico" Carrasquel were also players who made a lasting impression on Andrés in his early years. This combination of playing and watching, along with his desire to discover the attributes of a successful ballplayer, would greatly aid Andrés in the pursuit of his dream almost forty years later.

I first met Andrés in 1990. After reading in a Houston newspaper that the Astros had opened a new baseball facility in Venezuela, I contacted Houston scouting director Dan O'Brien and asked if I could visit the academy. O'Brien explained that it was run by Andrés Reiner and gave me his phone number in Valencia.

I called, introduced myself, and began to explain that I was a sportswriter.

"I am familiar with your writing," interrupted Andrés, having read a story I'd written about another Astros scout, Julio Linares. I told Andrés that I had an assignment from the *Houston Post* to write a series on the Astros' involvement in Latin America and asked if he would have time to visit if I came to Venezuela.[1] He responded that he'd be happy to show me around and would meet me at the Valencia airport. "I'll be the one wearing an Astros cap." When I arrived in late May 1990, he was.

In the ensuing sixteen years, I returned to Venezuela more than a dozen times to visit Andrés and have accompanied him on scouting trips to Colombia, Nicaragua, and Panama. I met him in Cuba during the Baltimore Orioles visit in 1999 and in Mexico during the 1997 Caribbean Series. I have sat with him at games in Round Rock, San Antonio, New Orleans, and Houston. I've interviewed him about the progress of his program at least twice a year, often more frequently, and speak with him at least once a month. I now call him a friend—a good friend. And I have often thought whether I could write in a dispassionate way about him. Could I be fair? After some deliberation, I decided that Andrés's story was an important one to tell and that I was the best person to tell it.[2]

"I have spent my life in baseball, even when I had my own business," Andrés told me when we first met in 1990. Whether operating a jewelry store, a construction business, or a bowling alley, he devoted all of his free time to baseball. During the 1960s he worked as an instructor in the minor leagues of Venezuelan professional baseball. In 1970 he helped establish the Criollitos—the foundation of youth baseball—in Valencia, a major industrial city one hundred miles west of Caracas. That same year Andrés worked with a group that moved the Magallanes club of the Liga Venezolana de Béisbol Profesional (Venezuela Professional Baseball League) from Caracas to Valencia—akin to taking the New York Giants out of the Polo Grounds and relocating them to San Francisco. During the early 1980s while living in Houston, he recruited prospects in the United States to play for Magallanes during the winter. But it was only in 1989, when the Astros hired him, that baseball became a full-time business for Andrés. Finally, he would have a job he really loved.

Andrés is not the sort of person one would imagine as a scout on the frontier of baseball. He is bilingual and bicultural, and while fluent in English (albeit with a slight Hungarian accent), his preferred language is Spanish. He is happiest having dinner with his wife at home and listening to classical music or taking a respite from baseball to travel in Europe. His refined, conservative nature and gentle demeanor would seem to make him unsuitable for scouting in Venezuela. The search for talent there is old style, just as it was in the United States before the free-agent draft began in 1965. In Venezuela, the competition must be outhustled and outworked. And when Andrés is looking for players, evaluating talent, or negotiating with the parents of a prospect, he is a tiger, both feared and respected by opposing organizations. The competition is well aware that Andrés and his staff will comb the countryside in search of players and can often convince parents into signing with the Astros for less money.

He is much more comfortable dealing with the baseball world in Venezuela than he is navigating the complex internal politics of the baseball industry in the United States. Andrés is an exceptional judge of baseball talent, but he is also keenly attuned to trends in Venezuela's economy, and he believed that the downturn in the economy in the early 1980s would result in an upsurge in interest in careers in major league baseball. He had a vision: to establish a baseball program that would scout, sign, develop, and prepare players to compete in the United States. Andrés was convinced that Venezuela was to be the new El Dorado in the search for baseball talent. His only problem was convincing a major league team to think likewise. In 1984 he explained his plan to create an academy for the production of baseball players to several major league organizations including Pittsburgh, San Francisco, and Houston. All turned him down.

With the Astros, Andrés presented his plan to Bill Wood, who in 1984 was the organization's director of minor league operations. The two had become acquainted in 1982 when Andrés was living in Houston. How did Wood react when this man who had never played professional baseball presented him with a scheme that appeared to be less than practical?

"Andrés and I had a relationship based on his assistance in placing players in winter ball, so it wasn't as if he came in cold," recalled Wood, now a scout with Cincinnati. "I knew he had an association with baseball. He sold his premise very well, and it struck a chord in my mind. I felt like the Houston ball club was failing in our approach to our Latin development program," explained Wood. "We just weren't developing the players. I thought we were behind severely in the Dominican, and it would be really expensive to catch up there."

"So this was a whole new beginning when Andrés explained his idea to me. He sold me on the idea that if we took this approach in the way he suggested, we really would have an edge on people. He said nobody else was approaching it this way and that we could establish ourselves much the way that the Dodgers were in the Dominican Republic. And that just really appealed to me," Wood said. "He did a great sales job to a willing buyer. It was Andrés's idea to do it right in Venezuela—build an organization there that could lead to something big. And I thought that it was a good plan."

But in 1984, Wood was not able to act on Andrés's proposal. "I told him, 'If you don't sell this idea to someone else, there will be a receptive ear here in the future,'" said Wood. When Wood became the Astros' GM just before the 1988 season, he decided to take a chance. He called Andrés and asked him to update his proposal. Andrés laid out his revised vision—complete with budget—in a four-page single-spaced letter to Wood, explaining that in the years since his first discussion with him, he had carefully thought about the proposal.

"I am more convinced than ever that my project is the best and only way to get really good prospects out of Venezuela," wrote Andrés.

Andrés believed that Venezuela had the potential to produce as many major league players in the next five years as it had in the previous forty years (it actually took eight years to accomplish this). Not only was the current generation of players bigger, but due to the economic situation, much more likely to be interested in careers in professional baseball. The petroleum-based economy of the 1960s and 1970s had caused parents to encourage their sons to pursue their studies. When the economy turned sour, parents of young men began to view careers in professional baseball as a long-term investment strategy.

Andrés pointed out that scouting in Venezuela in the late 1980s was superficial and without any overall plan or strategy. For the most part it consisted of a scout covering a small area close to where he lived. Once or twice a year, a scouting supervisor from the United States would come in, work out a few prospects for a couple of days, and sign a player or two. He went on to explain that unlike the Dominican Republic or Puerto Rico, which are very small, Venezuela is a big country—slightly larger in area than Texas. It could take a scout up to eighteen hours to get from one part of the country to another by car. Andrés also noted that because of the organization—or lack thereof—of Venezuelan amateur baseball at that time, the players to be scouted would be both technically and physically poorly prepared.

"The conditions are perfect now to make some investment in money and labor to put a good scouting network together," Andrés concluded. He then laid out the three basic points of his plan:

= Maintaining a very simple instructional camp with the purpose of improving the candidates both physically and technically. This would allow a better evaluation of the players and lower the risk of making mistakes.

= Dividing Venezuela into three geographical scouting zones.

= Hiring a supervisor or coordinator loyal to the organization. The supervisor would live in Venezuela and direct the day-to-day activities of the facility. In addition to the supervisor, Andrés suggested two coaches, three zone scouts, a trainer, and a physician trained in sports medicine.

Andrés also included his budget. For the first year he asked for $73,300—which included all salaries and expenses. It was revised downward by the Astros with the supervisor's salary lowered and one zone-scouting position eliminated, bringing the total operating cost to approximately $60,000. When shown the budget fifteen years later, Bill Wood admitted being embarrassed that it was so abysmally low.

The advantage of such a comprehensive scouting program, the first such endeavor by any major league organization in Venezuela (Pittsburgh operated an academy in Caracas in 1955, and Toronto had a small facility in the 1970s), would be that a team would have its own network scouting in the country on a daily basis. Prospects would be brought to a facility, receive instruction, and be evaluated. This would enable the organization to have a good idea of the talent and make-up of players, resulting in fewer players being released. Although it was not an issue at the time, Andrés was introducing the concept of combining aspects of both scouting and development. Most, if not all, baseball organizations go to great lengths to keep the two separate.

Andrés believed that the players trained in the academy would develop a loyalty to the organization and thus sign for less money. He saw the Venezuelan market value for players as between $3,000 and $6,000, with only a few exceptions. At the time, the highest bonus ever given to a Venezuelan player was $40,000, and the players who had received this amount could be counted on one hand.

"Dear Bill, if you want to put this project in progress, I would like to be the supervisor or coordinator," Andrés ended his letter.

On July 12, 1989, Andrés signed a contract with the Houston Astros to work as a scout for an annual salary of $8,000. Less than a month later, he began to develop the program outlined in his plan. Using his contacts in the business, baseball, and university communities, Reiner opened the Academia de Béisbol de los Astros de Houston, and his dream was now en route to becoming a reality.

While the Astros and other major league teams go into the international market as a cost-saving measure, the reality is that the baseball industry is forced to recruit players overseas because there aren't enough quality players being produced in the United States. Whether this shortage is the result of the sports talent in the United States being spread too thin (baseball has to compete with football, basketball, and soccer for the top athletes) or because there are too many other options for young men (television, the Internet, video games) is really irrelevant. To be competitive, all major league organizations participate actively in the Latin market. Most teams focus on the Dominican Republic, a few on Venezuela.

Houston was the first club to venture into Venezuela in an organized and systematic way. Before Andrés and the Astros opened the Venezuelan pipeline, few in the baseball industry understood the talent-producing potential of the South American country—and with good reason. Prior to the mid-1980s it was difficult to interest many young men in professional careers in the game, even though baseball is the national sport of Venezuela.

"I remember telling my friends that I was going to play professional baseball, and they asked me, 'How are you going to make a living?'" recalls Al Pedrique, former major league manager and now Special Assistant to the General Manager/Latin America for the Astros. In 1978 when Pedrique signed a minor league contract with the New York Mets at age eighteen, it was indeed an unusual career path for a young Venezuelan man.

Venezuela was the richest country in Latin America, and with the enormous revenues generated from its petroleum boom during the 1970s, it went through a spending frenzy. Venezuela Saudita—Saudi Venezuela—was the term widely used. Part of the bonanza meant that almost any qualified student could obtain a grant to attend a university overseas. Why play baseball when the opportunity existed to study abroad on a government-paid scholarship?

For centuries residents of what is now Venezuela had been aware that petroleum resources were located in their territory—it seeped out of the ground near Lake Maracaibo—but it was not until petroleum-based products began to be in demand in the United States in the 1860s that Venezuelans viewed the substance as a commercial product. In the early 1890s Venezuela was still a predominantly rural country that depended on its coffee crop to earn foreign exchange, but by the early 1900s the British and Dutch began to exploit the oil fields. On a December day in 1922, an oil well on the eastern shore of Lake Maracaibo gushed 100,000 barrels into the air and put Venezuela at the forefront of leading petroleum producers.

"By 1928, Venezuela exported more crude oil than any other nation and ranked second in world output," writes Stephen G. Rabe in *The Road to OPEC: United States Relations with Venezuela, 1919–1976.*[3] It was during the boom of the 1920s that U.S. companies became dominant. For the next fifty years, Venezuela enjoyed a prosperity that few of its residents could have dreamed of. By the early 1970s, with the formation of the OPEC (Organization of Petroleum Exporting Countries), oil prices on the world market quadrupled, and Venezuelans imagined they lived in a magical place where oil revenues would provide almost everything for everybody. But average real incomes in Venezuela peaked in 1978, midway through the oil boom, and for the overwhelming majority of the population, they have declined ever since. In 1983 approximately 75 percent of Venezuelans were still considered middle class. Twenty years later, more than 60 percent of the population lived below the poverty level. How did such a drastic shift occur? The main reasons were Venezuela's almost complete dependency on petroleum for over half a century and the extremely high external debt incurred during the oil boom of the 1970s.

A precipitous drop in the price of petroleum in the early 1980s and the subsequent devaluation of the Venezuelan currency—the bolívar—on "Black Friday," February 28, 1983, sent shockwaves through the economy and led to a drastic shrinking of opportunities for the vast majority of Venezuelans. The situation led many parents who once hid bats and gloves from their sons to now encourage them to play baseball. And play they did. By the late 1980s, spurred on by the success of native sons Tony Armas, Bo Díaz, Ozzie Guillén, and Andrés Galarraga, there was a renewed interest in young men signing professional contracts to go to the United States to play the sport.

No matter how bad the economic situation is in Venezuela or how visionary the scouting program of Andrés Reiner, significant quantities of baseball players can only be found in a country that has a long, rich tradition of baseball. Although a young man's dream of striking it rich in baseball is a motivating factor in the increased signings, other equally important elements help explain why Venezuela produces so many quality players: baseball is the sport of choice of young men, and it is played year-round. Recent surveys show that 75 percent of *criollos*—native-born Venezuelans—selected baseball as their favorite sport, and no one in Venezuela ever gets bored watching or talking about it. So while in the United States the World Series has to battle with *Survivor* for television viewership and the slow pace of baseball has skewed support of the game to the over-fifty crowd, in Venezuela baseball enjoys a popularity comparable to that in the United States in the 1950s when the sport was in its heyday.

An ideal place to get a glimpse of the depth of the love of baseball in Venezuela is the Salón de la Fama/Museo de Béisbol in Valencia. A sort of a mini-Cooperstown, the museum was the idea of, and a tribute to, Carlos Daniel Cárdenas Lares. I met Carlos Daniel at the Caribbean Series in Puerto La Cruz in 1994, only a month before he died at age twenty. Although muscular dystrophy confined his body to a wheelchair, it did not hamper his devotion to the game. In 1990 when he was only sixteen, Carlos Daniel wrote *Venezolanos en las grandes ligas*, a book that detailed the careers of the fifty-five Venezuelans who had played in the major leagues.[4] His collaborator on that volume, Giner García, is a Venezuelan journalist and baseball commentator whom I would come to know very well during my visits to Venezuela and in our work together for *Baseball America*. In 2005 García was named executive director of the Salón de la Fama.

The Fundación Cárdenas Lares, the foundation run by Carlos Daniel's family, built the museum. The family owned the land on which the Centro Sambil, an upscale shopping mall on the northern edge of Valencia, is located. The family gave the shopping center developers the land, and in return the museum was placed in the very center of the mall. It is quite impressive. The mall itself is in the shape of a diamond, and the entrances are Home Plate (in English), Primera Base, Segunda Base, and Tercera Base.[5] The center of the museum and the shopping mall is a sixty-foot-high fiberglass baseball covered in white canvas with red stitching. Inside the ball are statues of the members elected to the Salón de la Fama, which opened in the summer of 2003.

I had spent more than a decade going to games in Venezuela, talking to players, scouts, and team owners and reading the history of the sport in the country. I was well aware that baseball was both the national sport and a national passion, but it was only after I spent two afternoons in the museum in 2003 that I truly understood the intensity of the love Venezuelans have for the game.

Although baseball was being played in Venezuela as early as 1895 and the first player to reach the big leagues, Alejandro Carrasquel, made his debut with the Washington Senators in 1939, it was a contest in 1941 that really solidified the nation's fascination with the game. Venezuela's unexpected victory over Cuba in the championship game of the 1941 World Amateur Baseball tournament, highlighted in the museum, fixated the country on baseball.

"This was as important for us as winning a gold medal in the Olympics," Giner García told me.

The 1941 win created an atmosphere in which baseball flourished, and in 1946, the Liga Venezolana de Béisbol Profesional was inaugurated. Andrés arrived in Venezuela only months after the league started, and he and professional baseball have literally grown up together in his adopted land.

2

It's Their Game Too

The Origins of Baseball in Venezuela

On October 29, 1941, five Venezuelan planes dropped their payload on the Cuban gunboat nearing the port of La Guaira. It was not a battle in a conflict between the two countries but a celebration of Venezuela's unexpected victory over Cuba in the championship game of the 1941 World Amateur Baseball tournament. Roses fell from the air, and sixty small boats approached the ship offered by the Cuban government to carry the Venezuelan team home from Havana. The players were overwhelmed by the warm reception on the sea, but nothing could prepare them for the size of the crowd and enthusiasm of the fans waiting to greet them when they disembarked. Government offices, businesses, and schools closed, and more than 100,000 people—one-third of the population of Caracas—lined the twenty-mile-long highway between La Guaira and the capital city.

Arriving in Caracas, *los héroes del 41* were welcomed by President Gen. Isaías Medina Angrita at the national palace and then met by another throng of adoring fans at the Estadio Nacional where Andrés Eloy Blanco, a beloved writer, poet, and politician saluted the team in the name of the people of Venezuela. Blanco was the perfect person to connect baseball with the spirit of national unity evoked by the victory. In 1918 he had played baseball for Los Samanes, one the country's most popular teams, and in 1928 was jailed for his involvement in the student movement against the dictatorship of President Juan Vicente Gómez. Blanco began his speech with references to ancient Greece, the early Olympic games, and then fast-forwarded to the Spanish conquest in the sixteenth century. He continued by describing decisive battles in South American history as bases on a ball field. This grand historical overview was then linked to the victory in Cuba by a team composed of players from all regions of the country as a symbolic unification of the soul of Venezuela. Finally Blanco directed his remarks to the members of the team:

"Thank you, in the name of the Venezuelan people, for this enormous feeling of joy."

Only a week earlier, on October 22, La Tropical Stadium in Havana was packed for the tie-breaking game between Cuba and Venezuela that would decide the best amateur team in the world. Both teams had finished the tournament with 7-1 records. Cuba had dominated the event in previous years and was unprepared for Venezuela's challenge. Before the contest the Venezuelan manager, Manual "Pollo" Malpica, gathered his team in the clubhouse, asking them, "You are going to be playing against 27 players, four umpires and 30,000 fans. Does anyone need a pill to calm their nerves?"

Venezuela was at a standstill with nearly everyone fixed on the radio transmission from Havana, and when pitcher Daniel "Chino" Canónico defeated the Cuban team to capture Venezuela's first amateur championship, the country erupted in celebration.[1] It was not just a triumph; it was a *hazaña*—a heroic feat. The victory over Cuba in 1941 was selected in 2000 as the *Hazaña del Siglo,*—the most important sporting event of the twentieth century—by the country's association of sportswriters. The 1941 game is, without doubt, the defining moment in the sports history of the country. It served to consolidate baseball as the *deporte rey*—the dominant sport—in Venezuela. "The Venezuelans' passion for baseball reached unimaginable heights after October 22, 1941," reads a caption in the Museo de Béisbol.

It was an unforgettable day for Cubans as well. The loss had broken the Cubans' aura of invincibility.[2] Andrés Eloy Blanco in his address spoke of two champions in the Havana tournament, the victorious Venezuelans and the Cubans. "If anyone should smile with satisfaction over the Venezuelan victory, it is Cuba," Blanco told the crowd, "because it was Cuba that taught us how to play this marvelous game."

Cubans did indeed play a crucial role in the early development of baseball in Venezuela. Emilio Cramer went to Caracas in the early 1890s and established the La Cubana cigarette factory. Cramer and other Cubans spent endless hours in the Plaza Bolívar in the center of Caracas discussing baseball and were soon joined by Venezuelans, some who had seen the game on a visit to the United States, and by at least one U.S. citizen living in Venezuela.[3] Out of these gatherings, El Caracas Base Ball Club emerged in the spring of 1895. Cramer—who did not play on the team—later in 1895 organized the Carlos Manuel de Céspedes Baseball Club, named after a hero of Cuba's independence struggle against Spain. The club was "an all-star team that played exhibition games for the express purpose of raising revenues . . . to support the Cuban war effort," writes historian Louis Pérez.[4]

It is a common misconception that the Marines (or other branches of the U.S. military) introduced baseball to the Caribbean region during frequent interventions. It was in fact Cubans who were the pioneers of game in the area. Students returning home from their studies in the United States first took baseball to Cuba in 1864. Cubans, some refugees from the war of independence from Spain and others who worked in the sugar or tobacco industries, then carried baseball with them to the Dominican Republic in the 1880s and to Puerto Rico and the Yucatán region of Mexico in the late 1890s, as well as to Venezuela.

The first baseball game in Venezuela was played on May 23, 1895. We know the exact date of the game because one of the participants commissioned a photographer to capture an image of the players. A photo of El Caracas Base Ball Club appeared in the August 15, 1895, edition of a local publication, *El Cojo Ilustrado*. A note on the origins of baseball in the United States and an explanation of how it was played accompanied the photo.[5]

While there is much literature in Venezuela on the origins of baseball there, some of it is misleading or misinformed. The publication of an essay by Javier González in *La enciclopedia del béisbol en Venezuela* in 1997 was the first authoritative account of Venezuelan baseball history.[6] González also wrote the script for an hour-long film, *Venezuela al bate: Orígenes de nuestro béisbol (1895–1945)*, released in

2002, which provides an excellent overview of the roots of the game in Venezuela.

I had the opportunity to spend several hours with González in July 2005. Although I found his pioneering efforts in rescuing the history of Venezuelan baseball through writing and film to be very illuminating, he was even more impressive in person.

González, in his early fifties, is a librarian, a scholar, and devoted student of Venezuelan baseball. He is the first person to systematically and seriously pursue the origins of baseball in Venezuela. Over the past twenty years, he has combined his academic training (he has degrees in history and library science) to attempt to correct many of the errors in historical accounts. During his time working at the Hemeroteca Nacional—the country's newspaper and periodicals library—he was able to comb through material that few researchers in Venezuela were aware of or had access to. Although González explained that 183 books about baseball have been published in Venezuela, "the older histories were not written by professionals, so the author might accept as fact something that was told to them in an interview."

At the time, González was the director of the Salón de la Fama/Museo de Béisbol. In its own way, the Venezuelan baseball museum is equally impressive as the National Baseball Hall of Fame and Museum. Opened in 2003, it is vibrant, accessible, and exudes a passion for baseball. The first level is devoted to the history of the sport with the main focus on Venezuela. The second level features an interactive section designed for younger fans, and the third floor houses the Hall of Fame.

The vast majority of the space in the museum is, however, devoted to baseball in Venezuela. There is a photo of the 1895 Caracas team and one of the original bats used in the first game. On May 23, 1895, the twenty-two members of El Caracas Base Ball Club split into two groups—red and black—and played to the delight of 2,000 fans. In the summer and fall of 1895, they faced each other every Sunday. In September of that year, grandstands were constructed and improvements made to the field El Stand del Este, Venezuela's first baseball park. The message here is that baseball took hold and became the dominant sport in Venezuela, unusual on the South America continent where soccer prevails elsewhere.

It is likely, explained González, that Venezuelans had played rounders, described by Paul Dickson as "an ancient British bat and ball game from which baseball is partly derived," since at least the 1870s.[7] The British introduced rounders, tennis, and soccer to the present state of Bolívar during their mining adventures in the 1860s and 1870s.[8] The transition from rounders to baseball, with the help of the Cubans, was relatively effortless.

There is some debate about the social backgrounds of the founders of Venezuelan baseball. Cramer, the Cuban who helped form the original El Caracas Base Ball Club in 1895, told reporter Jess Losada in 1941 that most of the members of the club hailed from wealthy families who put up money to import bats, gloves, and balls.[9] I had always assumed that those responsible for baseball in Venezuela were the sons of the elite returning from their studies abroad. But historian González argues that many of the players were from more modest backgrounds and not exclusively from the aristocracy as has been often stated. He does point out that it is fair to say that folks with the big bucks in Caracas were avid supporters of baseball.

"I researched the class background of every player in that first game in 1895," González told me. "Among others, there was a fruit vendor, a cigarette factory worker, and the son of the owner of a brewery." His source was a directory of the city of Caracas listing residents by profession, and his research shows that there were no U.S.-educated Venezuelans in the founding group.

González also is quite certain that 1895 is the year baseball comes on the scene in Venezuela. "In February 1895 there is a note in a Caracas newspaper reporting people playing baseball on Sunday afternoons, and the first organized game is played in May. I looked at all the newspapers in 1894 and there is not a single mention of baseball. Because there was so little to write about at that time, I believe that if baseball was being played, it would have been reported," explained González.

Baseball expanded between 1895 and 1899 and was played in Valencia, Coro, and Maracaibo—cities west of Caracas. There was a momentary lull in play in 1899 due to the political unrest after a coup by Cipriano Castro. By 1900 El Caracas, as the El Caracas Base Ball Club came to be known, had quit playing, and about the same time a group of youngsters who had learned the game from members of El Caracas started their own team, Sucre. Yet another a new team, Club Caracas, was formed around the same time.[10]

Shortly after the turn of the century, another Cuban, Emérito Argudín played a prominent role in the development of Venezuelan baseball. Argudín arrived in Venezuela in 1898 to study after classes at the University of Havana were suspended during the Spanish-American War. Argudín not only was the best player in Venezuela but also taught the sport, and in 1902 founded the country's first baseball magazine, *Base-Ball*, and published the first rulebook, *Reglas del Base Ball*. That same year, Sucre, Club Caracas, and a new team, Miranda, squared off in the first championship series. Playing with Club Caracas, Argudín was the series MVP; won the Triple Crown (leading the league in batting, home runs, and RBI); led in runs scored, walks and stolen bases; and was the best defensive shortstop. Considered the first star of Venezuelan baseball, "He was," writes González, "the Andrés Galarraga of the beginning of the 20th century."[11]

In the early 1900s Venezuela was a rural country with strong ties to Europe. In fact, it was a blockade of Venezuelan ports by Great Britain, Germany, and Italy that brought U.S. ships to patrol off the coast. In 1902 the new Club Caracas played two games against the crew of the USS *Marietta*, a navy gunboat docked at La Guaira. The *Marietta* had previously seen action in the Spanish-American War in Cuba in 1898, landed at Bluefields, Nicaragua, in 1899 in defense of U.S. interests, and subsequently operated off the coast of Honduras in March and April 1903 while U.S. Marines landed to protect the U.S. Embassy at Puerto Cortés.

On October 19, 1902, U.S. sailors defeated Caracas 16–13 despite two home runs from Emérito Argudín, in the first-ever game between a local club and a foreign team. Caracas won the second game one week later, 27–17. In the Caracas victory, Argudín again hit two home runs. These encounters inspired a tremendous interest in baseball in Venezuela, and soon ten teams were founded in the city of La Guaira alone.

In 1903 San Bernardino, a club composed of many of the original El Caracas Base Ball Club members was founded, and within two years had become the best club in Caracas. According to González, this was the first baseball team composed primarily of the sons of the aristocracy. The same year, teams were formed in cities along the coast to the east of Caracas, all the way to Carúpano.

In 1907 when Caracas-based San Bernardino played a game with Vargas, a team from La Guaira, the country's first major rivalry began. San Bernardino represented the big city and the ruling class, while Vargas carried the banner of a small town and the working class. When Vargas went to Caracas to play a game, fans gathered in a park in La Guaira where, on a huge blackboard, a man with a piece of chalk recorded the progress of the game as received by telephone.

The San Bernardino–Vargas rivalry helped to generate a serious and passionate fan base, inspired a song, "Base Ball," to which Venezuelans danced, and gave rise to the publication of a magazine, *The Base Ball Herald*, and eleven team publications. As it was in Cuba, baseball became more than a sport—it was a symbol of modernity and progress.

Baseball references also entered the vocabulary. "In 1908, Cipriano Castro, after eight years in power, didn't make it to the ninth inning of his government, and Juan Vicente Gómez is the new manager of the team," the narration in the video *Venezuela al bate* informs the viewer.

In 1910, the San Cristóbal Base Ball Club was established, becoming the first Andean baseball team in the country, and by 1915 there were over one hundred baseball clubs scattered throughout Venezuela. Also in 1910, Los Samanes baseball club began to play. While it was composed of sons of the elite, it was also drawn from those families opposed to the regime of President Juan Vicente Gómez. The games of Los Samanes assumed a political nature; some players were openly antigovernment, and a couple of them were arrested for signing a manifesto against Gómez. But the Los Samanes club also played a role in expanding baseball even further into the less affluent sectors of Venezuelan society. "Baseball was surrendered to the popular classes," writes Judith Ewell, after the Los Samanes club was defeated by "some of the younger tougher street teams that began to dominate."[12]

In 1917 Magallanes, which would become one of the most popular and enduring teams in Venezuela, played its first game. That same year a Puerto Rican team, the Borinquen Stars, played to sell-out crowds during a more than two-month stay in the country. At the end of 1918, a "Spanish Fever" epidemic hit Caracas leaving 20,000 dead, including some ballplayers, and the government temporarily closed public stadiums. And although baseball started up again in 1919, it really did not get back into full swing until the end of the 1920s.

The ticket booth at the entrance to the Museo de Béisbol is an exact replica of one at the Estadio San Agustín, which opened in Caracas in 1928. Along the wall on one side of the booth is a floor-to-ceiling photomural of the stadium. Directly behind is a mural of a pastoral scene at Estadio Los Samanes in 1914. Further along in the exhibit area is an intriguing photo of the Crisfield Crabbers, one of the two teams that inaugurated the new ballpark in 1928. Other than the two games in 1902 played by the crew of the USS *Marietta*, no baseball team from the United States had visited Venezuela before Crisfield did. Where was Crisfield, I wondered? And how did this team get to Venezuela?

The Encyclopedia of Minor League Baseball explains that Crisfield is located on Maryland's eastern shore and that the Crisfield Crabbers were the 1927 champions of the Class D Eastern Shore League, which was composed of ten teams in Maryland and Virginia and operated from 1921 to 1928.[13]

I decided to make a trip to Crisfield and visit the library or possibly even meet some old folks who had heard about the trip. The three-hour journey from Washington DC, took me past Annapolis, home of the U.S. Naval Academy, over the Chesapeake Bay, and down the Delmarva Peninsula to Crisfield, near the border with Virginia. I had formed a mental image of Crisfield as a resort town with charming old buildings and cobbledstoned streets. No way. That is Annapolis. The only similarity between Annapolis and Crisfield is that they both face Chesapeake Bay.

On the way into town, I passed by the old Customs House (now the survey office and post office) and got the impression that this had been a vibrant port city in the past. And in fact it was. In 1910 the Crisfield's Customs House had included the largest registry of sailing vessels in the United States. By the 1880s Crisfield had become known as the "Seafood Capital of the World." It was and continues to be a town centered on the "watermen," the people who fish and trap crabs in the bay. Today this is clearly a very economically depressed area, and the largest employer is the nearby prison. "Even some of the watermen are working there," one local resident told me.

In the public library, I combed through every page of every issue of the weekly newspaper, the *Crisfield Times*, between January and June 1928. There was no mention whatsoever of the Crisfield Crabbers' trip to Venezuela. While the tour had little impact in Crisfield, it was important in Venezuela where it was chronicled in the local press.

After three weeks of games against local teams in Puerto Rico, where they inaugurated the Stand Escolar de Caguas, the Crisfield Crabbers arrived at the port of La Guaira on January 18, 1928. The series in Venezuela was to begin on January 20, but intense rain postponed the opening game until January 29.[14] On that day Crisfield lost to Santa María 3–1 in the inaugural game at Estadio San Agustín. When I looked at the box score of the game, I was intrigued by one name: Paul Richards. Could this possibly be the same Paul Richards who went on to become the general manager of the expansion Houston Colt .45s in 1962? A review of Richards's file at the National Baseball Hall of Fame and Museum in Cooperstown revealed that it was. Richards, from Waxahachie, Texas, played with Crisfield in 1926 and 1927, when at age eighteen he led the league in home runs with twenty-four. He played in the major leagues between 1932 and 1935 and again between 1943 and 1946. Richards managed the Chicago White Sox and Baltimore Orioles for eleven seasons during 1950s and early 1960s. (He returned to manage the White Sox for one year in 1976.)

Crisfield won the second game on January 30 against Santa María, 9–4, and one very prominent citizen of the United States was in attendance, although he did not arrive by ship. Charles A. Lindbergh flew his own plane, the *Spirit of St. Louis*. Lindbergh, who eight months earlier in May 1927, had flown from New York to Paris on the first nonstop transatlantic flight, was scouting routes for commercial airline companies in Latin America. He was also serving as a goodwill ambassador to express the U.S. government's support of president and dictator Juan Vicente Gómez.

"In the 1920s, as the interests of the U.S. oil industry and Venezuela became intertwined, the United States bolstered the regime of Juan Vicente Gómez," writes historian Stephen Rabe.[15] By 1928 Venezuela was the second-largest producer of petroleum in the world after the United States and was the leading foreign source of petroleum for the United States. Petroleum had put Venezuela on the world energy map and squarely on the radar of the United States.

Lindbergh had flown nonstop from Washington DC, to Mexico City in December 1927 and continued through Central America to Colombia and then on to Venezuela before flying to Havana and back to the United States. It was the last flight of the *Spirit of St. Louis*, now on display at the Smithsonian Institution's National Air and Space Museum in Washington DC.

Crisfield went on to split a doubleheader—the first ever in Venezuela—with the 29 de Julio team on February 5 and defeated Los Criollos del Royal on February 14. The team ended its tour with a 3-2 record and spent almost a month in Venezuela. Shortly after the Crisfield team returned to the United States, baseball was put on the back burner in Venezuela as political unrest accelerated and the regime of Juan Vicente Gómez became more repressive. Many student leaders, including Andrés Eloy Blanco were imprisoned, and the 1928 baseball season was cancelled.

Between 1930 and 1945, there were frequent national tournaments and an increased number of foreign players. Venezuelans became accustomed to seeing the best talent from the Dominican Republic, Puerto Rico, the U.S. Negro Leagues, and Cuba, including three of that country's all-time best players: Martín Dihigo, Ramón Bragaña, and Manuel "Cocaína" García. García pitched the first no-hit, no-run game in the history of Venezuelan baseball in his debut in 1932. Mr. García, whom I had a chance to meet in 1990, pitched another no-hitter in the 1932 season and also won the batting title that year with a .371 average. Other imports included Tetelo Vargas from the Dominican Republic, Pancho Coímbre and Pedro "Perucho" Cepeda—the father of Orlando Cepeda—from Puerto Rico, and Negro League stars Josh Gibson, Satchel Paige, and Roy Dandridge. The importation of world-class players not only generated excitement among fans but also helped to improve the quality of Venezuelans who played alongside them. Slowly Venezuela was becoming an important baseball power. The win in Havana in 1941 put baseball on the center stage in Venezuela, and titles in the World Amateur championship series in 1944 and 1945 help solidify its hold.

During the 1930s and early 1940s, the line was often blurred between professional and amateur players. The imported players were clearly professional. Some Venezuelans were paid, while others received a percentage of the ticket sales, and still others were given merchandise. In November and December 1945 the American All-Stars, a team composed of Negro League players including Jackie Robinson and Roy Campanella, played a series of games in Venezuela against local teams. According to international amateur baseball regulations, all Venezuelans who competed were ruled to be professionals. This directive paved the way for the founding of the Liga Venezolana de Béisbol Profesional that began play in 1946; the same year Andrés Reiner first set foot in Venezuela. Wanting to fit in his new country, Andrés began to learn about baseball. He didn't have much choice; it was the newly crowned king of sports, and it was impossible not to be seduced by it.

Although Andrés's apartment in Valencia is only a few miles from the Museo de Béisbol, he had never visited it until I convinced him to go with me in July 2005. Upon entering, he was immediately transported back in time.

The first permanent museum exhibit of photos, jerseys, gloves, and bats is titled "*Cuatro gigantes, una leyenda.*" The four giants were Alejandro "El Patón" Carrasquel, the first Venezuelan to play in the major leagues; his nephew, Alfonso "Chico" Carrasquel; David Concepción; and Andrés Galarraga. The legend is Luis Aparicio, the only Venezuelan in Cooperstown.

Andrés remembered seeing all of them play. "I saw 'Patón' pitch every Sunday in the late 1940s and early 1950s," he said while studying a 1939 photo of Carrasquel in a Washington uniform. "The first time I saw Aparicio in a game was 1954, and he was playing left field for the Venezuelan national team," he added, viewing a youthful photo of Luis Aparicio. Observing the very small rudimentary glove used by Chico Carrasquel with the White Sox, he commented, "With that glove, he made the All-Star Team." Next up is a display on David Concepción, the player every Venezuelan believes deserves to be in the Hall of Fame. "No one can imagine how skinny Concepción was when he first started," continued Andrés.

As we moved along from exhibit to exhibit, Andrés was clearly touched by the photos of players he had seen over the past fifty-eight years. He recalled details from games in the late 1940s, 1950s, and the 1960s and outstanding performances of Venezuelans and outstanding import players such as Lázaro Salazar, Luis Tiant, Phil Niekro, Bob Gibson, John Gibson, Roy Campanella, and Don Newcombe.

What really attracted his attention, however, was a photo of Roy Welmaker, a Negro League player who first came to Venezuela with the American All-Stars in 1945 and who became one of Andrés's favorite players during the winter of 1948–49.

"He was one of the idols of our professional baseball," said Andrés.

During the 1946 season Welmaker, then thirty-two years old, pitched in 25 of the 30 games that the Vargas team played (they only played twice a week). The left-hander completed 17 of the 20 games he started, posted a 12-8 record with 139 strikeouts in 193.2 innings and 2.81 ERA to win the triple crown.

"You can see what kind of players played here," said Andrés. "Today, you don't see the quality of baseball they played, nor the desire with which they played."

When we left after two hours, I asked Andrés for his opinion of the museum.

"It is very impressive," he said, quickly adding, "but it made me sad. I am old. I have seen all these guys play."

Even though the museum tour made Andrés nostalgic, it clearly also revived positive memories. As we stood in front of a photo of the Estadio San Agustín in the late 1940 where he had seen his first baseball game, I noticed that Andrés began to move his feet and dance along with the rhythms of the music from that period playing in the background.

The Liga Venezolana de Béisbol Profesional is composed of eight teams, and plays a 62-game schedule from October through January. In addition to the "eternal rivals" Caracas and Magallanes, with its home stadium in Valencia, teams are located in Maracaibo (Zulia), Barquisimeto (Lara), Puerto La Cruz (Caribes), Maracay (Aragua), and on the Isla de Margarita (Bravos, formerly Pastora), with the La Guaira team based in Caracas. The champion represents Venezuela in competition against the Dominican Republic, Mexico, and Puerto Rico in the Caribbean Series held each February.

Players from the United States go to Venezuela to get more experience and hone their skills. Venezuelan fans still talk about young men who spent their winters there, including Don Baylor, Dave Parker, Pete Rose, Bob Gibson, Orel Hershiser, and Barry Bonds—the last two invited by Andrés to play with Magallanes.[16]

Some native players also need at bats and innings, but other Venezuelan major leaguers have an extra incentive: a self-imposed obligation to play before the home crowds. One of those is New York Yankees outfielder, Bob Kelly Abreu. Abreu certainly did not need playing time when he returned to the Venezuelan league in 2004, and the $150,000 premium on his life-insurance policy, which he paid out of pocket, was more than three times the salary given to him by the Caracas club.

When Abreu was born in 1974, his father took one look at the infant and said, "This kid is going to be a major league baseball player when he grows up so I'm going to give him a name that people in the United States can understand—Bob Kelly." At least that's the way Abreu remembers hearing the story. "I asked my mom and she told me that there was an American named Kelly who played winter ball at La Guaira," Abreu, one of the first products of the Astros' Venezuelan academy, told me when we first met in 1990. He is not sure where the Bob comes from—and it's Bob, not Roberto. Among his friends, he is known as Kelly, or by his nickname—Comedulce, "Sweet Tooth."

In the Museo de Béisbol there is a photo of Pat Kelly. Few baseball fans in the United States would recognize the name. Kelly, born in Philadelphia, played for parts of fifteen seasons in the American League with Minnesota, Kansas City, Chicago, Baltimore, and Cleveland and posted a career batting average of .264, definitely not a Hall of Fame number. But in Venezuela, the left-hand hitting outfielder was a star. The caption in the museum exhibit reads that he was one of the best import players over his four seasons—one with Magallanes and three with La Guaira—in Venezuela between 1968 and 1973. In the winter of 1968–69, Kelly and his Magallanes teammate, Clarence "Cito" Gaston, dominated the league. Gaston won the league batting title with a .383 average and led in RBI with 64 while Kelly hit .342 with 45 RBI. They each had 11 home runs.

Kelly and Gaston thus became the first members of the *Poder Negro*—Black Power—era of the Magallanes team: African American import players who hit for power. In later years, the group included Don Baylor, Bob Darwin (who some Venezuelans believe could be the inspiration for Abreu's first name), Jim Holt, Willie Horton, Harold King, Mitchell Page, and Dave Parker. Venezuelan sportswriters coined the term *"Poder Negro"* after the incident at the Mexico City Olympics in 1968 when Tommie Smith and John Carlos raised black-gloved fists in a Black Power salute and lowered their heads while being awarded gold and bronze medals, respectively for their performances in the two-hundred-meter dash. Black Power was also a political movement in the United States and elsewhere during the 1960s. But for Nelson Abreu, Pat Kelly was just a famous ballplayer who provided the inspiration for naming his baby boy.

On my first visit to the museum in 2003, Pedro Caro, a young man in his mid-twenties, gave me a tour. I brought along Rafael Cariel, the Astros scout who, along with Andrés, signed Richard Hidalgo. Cariel never made it to the major leagues, but is a hero in Venezuela for his game-winning hit in a Caribbean Series victory for Venezuela in 1979. I introduced Cariel to Pedro Caro who was speechless. Caro is a Magallanes fan and was familiar with Cariel's career. After recovering his composure, he took us on a three-hour walk through the museum. Nearly at the end of our tour, Cariel, Caro, and I ascended the stairway to the third level—the baseball dome at the Museo de Béisbol where carved wooden statues, each two and a half feet high, of the fourteen members of the hall are displayed. Behind the statues are a half-dozen baseball-themed sculptures, the last of which is a larger-than-life shortstop fully extended and diving for a ball. The shortstop is wearing the number 13, the number used by David Concepción, Ozzie Guillén, and Omar Vizquel. Rafael Cariel pointed out that the glove was on the right hand, making the shortstop left-handed. There have been very few left-handed shortstops and definitely not Concepción, Guillén, or Vizquel.

"*¡Coño!*" was Pedro Caro's response. "*Coño*" is a multipurpose word whose connotations can run from vulgar to sexual, to disgust, to excitement through admiration, surprise, or in this case amazement.

"*¡Coño!*" was the very word Rafael Cariel used when he discovered Richard Hidalgo. "When I saw Richard for the first time, my eyes almost popped out: what a body, what an arm, what an ability to play baseball!" recalled Cariel.

It was the fall of 1990 and Hidalgo was still living in Guarenas, the urban development just to the east of Caracas in what can best be described as a tough neighborhood, in the highrise public housing project, Urbanización Menca de Leoni.

Cariel immediately called Andrés and then visited Hidalgo. He was nervous about entering the housing project but understood that you don't get ahead in the scouting game by being timid. He located the apartment—Block 34, First Floor, No. 8—and spoke with Hidalgo's mother, explaining that at the academy in addition to improving his baseball ability her son would be given English lessons and taught skills that would help him become a man. He assured her that the Astros would take good care of him. Initially, Hidalgo's mother was apprehensive, then Cariel asked her to come outside and motioned for her to look up at the sky.

"Up there is a God who looks after black people like us," Cariel told her. "Richard has the opportunity to take you out of this housing project."

Richard's mom thought for a moment and said, "Take him." Her son went to the Astros' academy on December 1, 1990, and on July 2, 1991, a few days after turning sixteen, signed a contract with the Astros, received a signing bonus of one million bolívares ($27,500) and bought a new home for his mother. "It was a gift that fell from the sky," Hidalgo recalled in 2000.

I have followed Hidalgo's career since he was signed. I first met him at the Caribbean Series in Puerto La Cruz, Venezuela, in 1994 and visited with him both in the United States and Venezuela during his journey through the Astros' minor league system. After he arrived in the major leagues in 1997, I often spoke with him in Houston. I have also followed his career with Magallanes, where in 1997 he was selected as the MVP of the Liga Venezolana de Béisbol Profesional championship series against Caracas. During that series, I behaved like those fans back in La Guaria in 1907 waiting for the results of the San Bernardino–Vargas game to be posted, but instead of following the play-by-play progress on a blackboard, I used the Internet.

With 25,000 fans screaming incessantly at the league championship game between Caracas and Magallanes in 1997, the roar of the crowd at Estadio Universitario in Caracas was deafening. But to Hidalgo it was like a listening to a symphony.

"I felt like I was on the field by myself. I didn't hear the crowd," Hidalgo told me. "Oh, I could hear the noise, but it sounded far away. I was very focused and just told myself what I needed to do." He must have said the right things. Hidalgo hit .600 in the final series, with 12 hits in 5 games and was named MVP of the Venezuelan league finals.

It is difficult to imagine a bigger stage in Venezuelan baseball than a Caracas-Magallanes game in Caracas, but a Caracas-Magallanes game in the finals of Venezuelan professional baseball definitely takes it up a notch. Magallanes is rather like the New York Yankees—people love them or hate them but always pay money to see them play.[17] The rivalry with the Caracas team dates back to 1942 when Cervecería Caracas, the predecessors to the Leones, first took the field.

"After each game in the finals I would prepare for the next one by breathing deeply and relaxing, and imagining the next game in my head," explained Hidalgo. "When you are relaxed, you can do whatever you need to do."

Hidalgo may have been one of the few people in the country who was relaxed. It is said that physicians never schedule surgery the day after a Caracas-Magallanes game, and Venezuelan presidents seldom give televised speeches that would conflict—or worse—preempt a game. When Magallanes plays in Caracas, attendance is more than twice that of any other home game, and ticket prices are almost doubled.

"It would be difficult to explain the atmosphere at a Caracas-Magallanes game. Because to really understand it, you have to experience it," Humberto Acosta, baseball columnist for *El Nacional,* one of Venezuela's leading dailies, told me. "I believe it would be as difficult as,"—Acosta begins and then, carefully choosing his words—"describing baseball to a man from Africa who has never heard of, much less seen, a game. Baseball is a complicated sport with lots of rules. How would you explain a stolen base? How would you explain this dynamic aspect of the game? Because he has not grown up with the game, it would be hard for him to understand."

"This is how it would be for the average North American baseball fan to understand what he would see at a Caracas-Magallanes game. *Un Caracas-Magallanes es la fiesta que es el juego mismo*—the essence of baseball itself," said Acosta.

It doesn't get much more exciting than a Caracas-Magallanes game. *Baseball America* lists it as one of the must-see attractions in baseball, and I have been fortunate to see three of them: regular-season games in 1991 and 2000 and a playoff game in 2006.

An electric feeling was palpable in the air at the Estadio Universitario on November 23, 2000. A near-capacity crowd of 20,000, surprisingly evenly divided between fans of both teams, waved banners, screamed, blew whistles, and blasted air horns. Salsa music and an occasional recording of a roaring lion accompanied the clamor over the loudspeakers. The cacophony produced a constant, almost deafening din that started well before the first pitch and built throughout the game. Unbelievably, the noise level got even louder when players such as Caracas outfielder Bob Kelly Abreu, or Magallanes right fielder Melvin Mora, another Astros' academy product, came up to bat or when an outstanding play was made.

The fans, nearly all of whom wore game jerseys or team caps, were not neatly compartmentalized into separate sections but sat, or more often stood, elbow-to-elbow throughout the stadium. When Mora hit a ball that looked as if it might be a home run, everyone in the stadium appeared to be cheering for the ball to clear the fence, but when the Caracas right fielder made the catch at the warning track, a more ear-piercing roar of delight emanated from the Caracas fans.

"I think sometimes the fans wear two caps to the game," said manager Phil Regan. Regan, who at the time was in his second year with Magallanes and had previously managed the Caracas club for most of the 1990s, continued, "Whichever team wins, that is the cap they wear out of the stadium."

"The Magallanes-Caracas game is the most incredible baseball game I have ever seen," said former Houston Astros third baseman, Morgan Ensberg, who played on the Caracas team in 2000. "The atmosphere is very similar to the final game in the College World Series. In fact, it's just like the last out of the College World Series, but here it goes on for the entire game."

For the Venezuelan players, this game is a lesson in dealing with the pressure of playing before large crowds in clutch situations. Melvin Mora told me that when Bobby Valentine was about to put him in a game at the end of the 1999 season, the New York Mets manager turned to veteran Venezuelan second baseman Edgardo Alfonzo and asked whether the rookie Mora could handle the pressure. Alfonzo didn't hesitate, "If he can play in a Caracas-Magallanes game, he can play anywhere."

But you don't need to be at the stadium to follow the progress of the game: it is televised and broadcast on several radio stations reaching even the most remote corner of country. I remember driving from Caracas to Valencia one evening during a Caracas-Magallanes game and stopped to pay a toll. "Caracas is leading 2–1 in the seventh," the tollbooth attendant shouted out as he returned a receipt.

At the next toll both, that attendant also gave an unsolicited update on the game. Neither needed to ask if I was interested: almost everyone in Venezuela cares about the outcome of a Caracas-Magallanes game. "It is doubtful that there is a single person in our country who has not heard of Magallanes," writes historian González. This may sound like an outlandish statement, but there's little doubt that it's accurate.

"Some intellectuals here don't see it that way, but baseball is part of the national identity of Venezuela," González told me. "You really need to understand baseball to understand the cultural history of Venezuela." He believes that most of his countrymen feel closer to and know more about Bob Abreu, Chico Carrasquel, and Luis Aparicio, than any historical figure, apart from Simón Bolívar.

"Beginning in October when the winter league starts, everybody talks baseball. And the love of baseball becomes even greater with the increasing number of players getting to the big leagues," explained Venezuelan sports journalist Giner García. García is the former editor of *Béisbol a Fondo*, a baseball weekly that circulated for a couple of years in the mid-1990s. He has written about the Liga Venezolana de Béisbol Profesional for *Baseball America*, produced state-of-the art media guides for three professional teams, including Magallanes, and currently is the executive director of the Salón de la Fama in Valencia.

Venezuelans love of baseball is deep—similar to the passion fans in the United States in the 1950s had when the game dominated the sports pages and kids still played in the streets. With apologies to those ardent supporters of the St. Louis Cardinals or the Boston Red Sox, Venezuelans may be the most knowledgeable fans in baseball. While they can quote the current batting average of Barry Bonds or the ERA of Randy Johnson, they are especially interested in the pursuits of the *peloteros criollos* (Venezuelan-born players) in the United States, including Abreu, Magglio Ordóñez, and Johán Santana. Box scores of all major league games and up-to-date batting averages and pitching records of the more than forty Venezuelans in the big leagues are reported in half a dozen Caracas dailies. Once a week they also list the stats of every *criollo* in the minor leagues.

Not only can fans scour the sports pages, but they also have access to a large body of written material. There are books on statistics and history and even a dictionary of baseball terms used in Venezuela. García was involved in producing an outstanding volume, *Venezolanos en las grandes ligas,* which contains detailed biographical sketches and interviews with each of the seventy Venezuelans who had made it to the big leagues when the second edition was published in 1994. Venezuelans can also watch or listen to MLB games and follow their favorite teams or players via the Internet.

"Baseball is in our blood," says Iván Medina. Anyone who wants to know the status of any Venezuelan playing professional baseball should contact Medina. He maintains a list with the current statistics of 1,250 Venezuelans playing in the United States, Dominican Republic, Mexico, Taiwan, Italy, and Venezuela. An architect by training, a baseball junkie by desire, Medina has worked as a baseball announcer and commentator for radio and television for the past fifteen years. Currently, he is an advisor on player development to the general manager of the Caracas team and works on the radio broadcasts of Caracas games. But Medina's first love is statistics. He founded a company in the early 1990s, Quality Sports Production, that is the official compiler of data for the Liga Profesional de Béisbol Venezolano. He is also the author of the *Registro del béisbol venezolano 1946–1995,* the most authoritative statistical book on Venezuelan professional baseball.

"Baseball is the best it has ever been in Venezuela, and it is getting better," said Medina. "Much of the surge in baseball is due to Andrés [Reiner]. He was the person who opened the door wide to major league baseball in Venezuela."

Javier González agrees. "People in Venezuela know about players, but they don't know much about scouts. They need to know more, especially about Andrés. The players have the opportunity to be successful because of the scouts," explained González. "Andrés was one of the first to scout systematically and is the father of the academies, which led to the increased pool of Venezuelan baseball players."

While the number of Venezuelans reaching the big leagues increased dramatically during the 1990s, the first *criollo* to play in the major leagues, Alejandro Carrasquel, made his debut in 1939. Carrasquel was pitching in the Cuban league in 1939 when legendary scout Joe Cambria signed him to a contract with the old Washington Senators. A few months later on April 23, Carrasquel made a relief appearance to pitch to Joe DiMaggio. The Yankee Clipper, who led the American League in hitting that year with a .381 average, hit a comebacker to the pitcher for an easy out. In the sixty-seven years since Carrasquel arrived in the big leagues, 213 Venezuelans have followed in his footsteps. Venezuelans are proud of all the players who have reached the major leagues, but who is the all-time fan favorite?

Some would argue that Andrés Galarraga merits this distinction not only for achievements on the field—eighteen years in the major leagues and 399 home runs—but also for the courage he demonstrated in his two successful battles against cancer. Galarraga, who retired just before the start of the 2005 season, is enormously popular in his home country. As in Mexico in the early 1980s, when the success of Los Angeles Dodgers pitcher Fernando Valenzuela created "Fernandomania," the exploits of Andrés Galarraga produced "Galarragamania" in Venezuela.[18]

While Andrés has great admiration for his *tocayo* (namesake), Andrés Galarraga, his very favorite player is Alfonso "Chico" Carrasquel.

"He was my idol when I was fifteen or sixteen in 1951 and 1952," said Andrés. "He was the king of the jungle. He always played hard, was low-key and had a great personality. He is still my idol today."

"Chico" Carrasquel was one of those fans that came out to welcome home the Venezuelan team in October 1941.

"I was barely thirteen when the national team won in Havana," recalled Carrasquel almost sixty years later. "I remember walking all the way to La Guaira to greet the champions. All the kids of that time wanted to be like the heroes of Havana." But he also had another inspiration, his uncle, Alejandro Carrasquel.

Ten years after Chico Carrasquel made his pilgrimage to La Guaira, he was selected to the 1951 American League All-Star Team, becoming the first player from Latin America to achieve that honor. He established the record for double plays (113) by a rookie shortstop in 1950. Carrasquel also led the American League in fielding percentage in 1951, 1953, and 1954. Carrasquel always returned home to Venezuela, playing in twenty-one consecutive winter league seasons—mostly with Caracas—between 1946 and 1967. He hit the first home run in Venezuelan professional baseball. His commitment to playing in Venezuela—even when his combined summer and winter total of more than 200 games a year probably shortened his big league career—and his enthusiasm for the game made him one of the most popular players of all time in Venezuela.

After trading Chico Carrasquel to Cleveland in 1955, the Chicago White Sox opened the 1956 season with another Venezuelan, Luis Aparicio, at shortstop. Aparicio was selected as the American League Rookie of the Year, becoming the first player from Latin America to win the award. He holds the major league record for the most assists by a shortstop (8,016), and led the major leagues in stolen bases for nine consecutive years between 1956 and 1964.

The Dickson Baseball Dictionary has an entry for an "Aparicio double," defined as "a walk and a stolen base."[19] Aparicio was also durable, playing 2,581 games at shortstop, more than any player in the history of baseball. When he was inducted into the National Baseball Hall of Fame at Cooperstown on August 12, 1984, it was a national day of celebration in Venezuela.

On April 13, 2004, Venezuelans again were filled with pride when Ozzie Guillén took the field for the Chicago White Sox home opener as the team's manager, the first Venezuelan to lead a major league team. Chico Carrasquel and Luis Aparicio joined Guillén on the field for the pregame ceremonies. And the trio was very familiar to the fans: for twenty-eight of the forty-eight seasons between 1950 and 1997, one of the three was the White Sox's starting shortstop.

The Museo de Béisbol does not yet have a statue of Johán Santana, but I'm sure plans are being made for a special tribute for the 2004 and 2006 America League Cy Young Award winner. Winning the award in 2004 was indeed an exciting moment for him, for the Minnesota Twins, for Venezuela, and for the staff of the Astros' academy who developed Santana. Clearly this was the most important event in Venezuelan baseball since Aparicio was enshrined in Cooperstown.

"You can't imagine how big this is," Andrés told *USA Today Sports Weekly*. "It's a big thing in this country [the United States], right? So just imagine how big it is in a much smaller country that loves baseball."

Two days after Santana won the award, he was declared a national hero by President Hugo Chávez and honored at a reception at the president's residence. Three of the five surviving members of the legendary 1941 team were in attendance as were former major leaguers Luis Aparicio, Chico Carrasquel, and Pompeyo and Víctor Davalillo. All radio and television stations in the country were required to broadcast the speech and ceremony at which Santana was given one of the highest honors the Venezuelan government grants—the Orden del Libertador en su Tercera Clase, Grado de Comendador.

In his acceptance speech Santana thanked his family and friends and President Chávez, and he made it clear that he did not consider the awards he had received as his alone, but belonging to all Venezuelans.

"I'm pleased to be Venezuelan, to represent my country and to hold our flag high, and to have such pride and deep feelings as a Venezuelan," said Santana. Chávez congratulated Santana, called him a national hero, and evoked the great moments of Venezuelan baseball history. While Chávez was speaking, Pompeyo Davalillo approached the podium unexpectedly and handed the president the trophy the *los héroes del 41* had won in Havana. Baseball as a source of Venezuelan national pride, now represented by Johán Santana—the hero of 2004—had come full circle.

3

The Astros Go South

Scouting in Latin America

The Astros' Venezuelan scouting venture in the late 1980s did not occur in a vacuum. Major league organizations have long searched for players in the Caribbean region, and the Houston franchise was one of the pioneers in the market. There is little continuity, however, in any organization's scouting efforts in Latin America. The level of involvement depends on the philosophy of the owner, the general manager, and the scouting director, and over the years there has been and will continue to be a great deal of turnover in these positions. Houston is no exception, but the franchise is unique in that current Astros president of baseball operations, Tal Smith, was there in the beginning. No one knows more about the history of the Houston organization than Smith, who started his baseball career with the Cincinnati Reds in 1958 and went to Houston when Reds GM Gabe Paul was selected to put together the Colt .45s expansion team.

On November 1, 1960, before John F. Kennedy was elected president of the United States, Smith began his job as assistant to the general manager of the new National League franchise that would not play its first game until April 1962. But after less than six months, the general manager he was assisting, Gabe Paul, left the Colt .45s in a dispute with Houston owner Judge Roy Hofheinz. In April 1961 then under new general manager Paul Richards, Smith was placed in charge of the Colt .45s minor league system. By 1965 Smith had become the Astros' vice president and director of player personnel. At the end of 1973 he left the Houston organization and was named executive vice president of the New York Yankees.

Smith returned to Houston in August 1975 as the Astros' general manager and became club president in 1976. In 1980 he was named by the *Sporting News* as the Major League Executive of the Year but was fired shortly thereafter and opened a consulting firm, which the Astros media guide describes as performing "specialized functions for baseball clubs and other sports interests."

In November 1994 Smith began his third tour with the Houston organization when he was named president of the club, a position he still holds today. Basically he acts as an advisor to owner Drayton McLane and as an intermediary between McLane and the GM.

Smith is always courteous and thoughtful, qualities that made him one of the people Andrés respected most in the Astros' organization. I visited with Smith on numerous occasions over a ten-year period. His detailed responses to my questions reflect his almost fifty years of experience in the game. He explained that the initial interest of the Houston franchise in scouting Latin America was the outgrowth of his work as an administrative assistant for scouting and player development with Cincinnati between 1958 and 1960.

"In those days the Reds had a working agreement with the Cuban Sugar Kings and there was a very strong relationship between the Reds general manager Gabe Paul and Bobby Maduro, the owner of the Havana club. I was familiar with that arrangement, and we had an awful lot of Cuban players in the Cincinnati system—Miguel Cuellar, Orlando Peña, Tony González, Tony Taylor—as a result of that. Tony Pacheco, who lived in Cuba, was a scout for the Cincinnati organization, and I had come to know Tony quite well," said Smith. "I came to Houston during the crisis of Castro in Cuba and I heard Tony Pacheco on several occasions say he was concerned about getting his family out of Cuba," said Smith. "We hired Tony to come to work for the Houston Colt .45s. I recall meeting Tony and his wife and three children at the Houston airport in May 1961, and all they had with them was what they had on their backs and a little carry-on bag. Tony went on to work with the Houston organization for a great many years, and he obviously had roots throughout the Caribbean and was a big proponent of the Latin players, and between the two of us we started to foster a program that emphasized scouting in the Latin countries."

I asked Smith who was the first player the Colt .45s signed out of Latin America.

"Remember José Arcia—the pitcher and shortstop who played a little bit with the Cubs and Cardinals?" asked Smith. "That's an interesting story. He was the last player to get out of Cuba. Pacheco had arranged to sign him for us, or had reached an agreement with him, before Pacheco left Cuba. But then Arcia couldn't get out."

In fact, Arcia had been signed to a contract with Houston in March 1961, only a month before the Bay of Pigs invasion and increased tensions between the United States and Cuba. He had been assigned to the Salisbury club in the Western Carolina League but was unable to leave Cuba until November.

"We were at Colt Stadium in December 1961 or January 1962 getting ready for the 1962 season when somebody on our staff gets a call from the Houston police department that they had a young Cuban player. It turned out to be José Arcia. At that time José had to be seventeen, maybe eighteen, spoke virtually no English, and somehow had gotten out of Cuba. He made his way to Houston and then didn't know what to do, and the police found him wandering around looking for help. When we discovered that he was here, we had to find something for him to do until spring training started," said Smith.

"We were in the finishing stages of constructing Colt Stadium, a temporary facility, and we used folding chairs instead of permanently installed seats. So José was asked to work for Dick McDowell, who was my assistant, and who was in charge of getting the seats in place. Dick hadn't met José and didn't know anything about him and hollered at José in English to move the chairs here and there—without realizing, of course, that at the time José's English was still in the working stage. But we worked through all that and José spent several days helping around the ballpark," said Smith.

"He got paid and we provided lodging and meals until spring training started. As I recall, it wasn't a long period of time. Arcia went to minor league camp and eventually went on to play in the big leagues. Anyway, he has some major league time and it's an interesting story," said Smith.

After I turned off the tape recorder, Smith added, "I hope we paid him."

Arcia's career with the Houston organization was short-lived; Cleveland acquired him in 1962, and in 1964 he was traded to St. Louis. After three years of pitching in the minor leagues and compiling a 21-17 record, Branch Rickey himself converted Arcia to shortstop. In 1964 Rickey then in his eighties, was serving in an advisory capacity with the Cardinals in the fall instructional league. "He came to me after one of our practices and told me he'd like to see me work out in the infield for a few days," Arcia recalled. A couple of days later, his pitching career was over, and he became a middle infielder.

In 1967 Arcia was acquired by Chicago and made his major league debut with the Cubs in April 1968. After the season, he was selected by San Diego in the expansion draft and played second base and shortstop on a regular basis with the Padres in 1969 and 1970.

While Arcia was the first player from Latin America acquired by Houston, the distinction of being the first to play in a major league game for the franchise goes to Román Mejías. Pittsburgh Pirates scout Howie Haak (Haak would become one of Andrés's mentors) signed Mejías out of the Dominican Republic in the early 1950s, and Houston selected him in the expansion draft in 1961. In the Colt .45s inaugural game in 1962, Mejías hit two home runs and had six RBI and went on to have a .286 batting average and 24 home runs for the year, but at thirty-two he was nearing the end of his career. After the season, he was traded to the Boston Red Sox where he played for two more years.

"Pat Gillick came on board the organization in 1963," said Smith. "He had been a pitcher in the Baltimore organization, and this was his first role in the front office. Pat and I worked together with Pacheco, and Pat became a big proponent of the Latin market and Latin players. Between him and Pacheco, they built up our system, and we were very active in the Dominican and Venezuela. And so that was sort of the origin, that's how it started."

Gillick was originally hired as the Colt .45s assistant farm director and eventually became director of scouting during his ten years with the organization. In 1973 Gillick went with Smith to the New York Yankees where he was the coordinator of player development for a couple of years before moving to the new Toronto franchise in 1976. During his seventeen years with the Toronto organization—most of the time as executive vice president for baseball—the Blue Jays won World Series titles in 1992 and 1993. Gillick was then GM of the Baltimore Orioles for three years and Seattle's GM for two years before taking the GM job with Philadelphia in 2005.

Gillick hired scout Epifanio "Epy" Guerrero to work for him in the Dominican Republic and established a working agreement between the Astros and the San Pedro de Macorís team in the Dominican winter league.

The first player discovered by Guerrero and Gillick was César Cedeño. Signed by Houston in 1967 when he was sixteen years old, the five-tool prospect was patrolling center field in the Astrodome by the time he was nineteen. In the next three seasons, Cedeño became one of the top players in baseball and was being compared to Willie Mays, Hank Aaron, and Roberto Clemente. In 1972 Cedeño hit for a .320 average, with 22 home runs and 55 stolen bases, won a Gold Glove, and was selected the Astros' MVP. Cedeño hit for average, had power, stole bases, and won five consecutive Gold Gloves. He played twelve seasons for the Astros between 1970 and 1981 and ranks in the top five all-time Houston players in ten career categories: stolen bases (1), runs scored (3), extra base hits (3), doubles (3), at bats (4), hits (4), games played (5), home runs (5), RBI (5), and batting average (5). The 2002 Astros media guide describes Cedeño as "one of the greatest players in the history of the Houston franchise." Some wonder then why Cedeño's number (28) has not been retired and hanging from the rafters at Minute Maid Park. Others want to know why he did not spend more time in jail for his off-the-field behavior. And one particular incident in the Dominican Republic in 1973 has haunted Cedeño ever since.

On December 11, 1973, a nineteen-year-old woman, whom Cedeño had taken to a Santo Domingo motel, was shot to death. Cedeño fled, but several hours later turned himself into the police. He was initially charged with voluntary manslaughter and jailed. Tests later showed that Cedeño had not fired the weapon. Astros GM Spec Richardson along with Gillick and Guerrero went to the Dominican Republic and met with Cedeño and Federico Antún, one of the owners of the San Pedro de Macorís club. Antún was also the Dominican ambassador to the United States. After much legal maneuvering, Cedeño was found guilty of involuntary homicide, fined $100 dollars and allowed to return to the United States.

In 1990, three years after he ended his seventeen-year major league career, Cedeño began to work as a coach for the Astros' rookie team in the Gulf Coast League. After three years he moved to the Astros' Quad City team in the Midwest League for the 1993 and 1994 seasons. Cedeño moved to Venezuela in 1994 and began coaching with Magallanes, a team he has worked for off and on ever since. In 1999 Andrés brought Cedeño—most often referred to as CC—onto the staff of the Astros' Venezuelan academy where he taught fielding, running, base stealing, and hitting to the young prospects. Andrés considered Cedeño to be an excellent instructor, but when CC came to work late too often in 2002, he decided to let him go. His reasoning was basic: how could you expect the young players to be punctual if their coach is not on time?

Apart from Cedeño, five other players from the Dominican Republic signed by Gillick and Guerrero reached the big leagues with Houston, the most successful of these was catcher Luis Pujols. Of the first forty Dominicans to play in the major leagues, five were signed, developed, and made their debut with the Houston Astros.

The Astros' Latin American scouting focus lapsed when Smith and Gillick left in 1973. Smith returned to the Astros in 1975 but without Gillick. Tony Pacheco—who had also left with Smith in 1973—rejoined the organization in 1975 and remained with Houston until his death in the mid-1980s.

In the 1960s and early 1970s, the major competition in Latin American scouting for the Astros came from the Pittsburgh Pirates and Howie Haak; the San Francisco Giants, who had signed Juan Marichal and the Alou brothers in the 1950s; the Los Angeles Dodgers; and the St. Louis Cardinals. In this early period of scouting in Latin America, organizations were still adjusting to the shift toward the Dominican Republic from Cuba, which had been the major supplier of players until the Cuban government abolished professional baseball in 1962.

"Speaking of Cuba, after I came back to Houston [in 1975]," said Smith, "we took a trip to Cuba. We took our manager Bill Virdon and all of our coaching staff except Tony Pacheco—for obvious reasons—myself, three players, Bob Watson, Ken Forsch and Enos Cabell, and their wives. I think there were eighteen or nineteen people in our traveling party."[1]

This was 1977 and no major league team had been to Cuba since 1959. Smith recalls being in the office of a Cuban sports official who asked, "Do you want to say hello to Fidel? The official handed the phone to Smith, who was greeted by the Cuban leader. Castro expressed hope that the trip was going well and apologized for not meeting with the Astros' delegation, but assured Smith that he would see that all their needs were met.

"You know it was an exciting thing to do, and we thought it might give us an advantage," explained Smith. "Basically we conducted clinics. Bill Virdon and the coaches and players worked with the Cuban national team. From a baseball standpoint, I thought there was a common bond," said Smith. "Our interest was, of course, in getting a firsthand look at the Cuban talent, trying to establish a relationship, and to foster that relationship in the event that the situation would open up in the future."

After the Astros' 1977 visit, no major league team returned to Cuba until the Baltimore Orioles played an exhibition game against a Cuban team in Havana in March 1999. Because Major League Baseball had arranged the event, each organization was asked by Commissioner Bud Selig to send a representative, and Andrés Reiner was given the assignment. He did not want to go, but dutifully complied with Astros' GM Gerry Hunsicker's request. For Andrés, it's not much fun to see players you have little chance of signing.

The night before the game, I caught up with Andrés at a reception on the patio of the classic old Hotel Nacional. There were several hundred people in attendance including some of the Baltimore players, Orioles owner Peter Angelos, television and film producer Barry

Levinson, Vermont senator Patrick Leahy, and most of the Cuban sports hierarchy.

Andrés bumped into Rodolfo González from the Cubans sports ministry. González had spent two years with the Cuban embassy in Venezuela and had worked with Andrés to bring the Cuban National Team to Venezuela to play exhibition games with Magallanes and Caracas in 1996. González offered Andrés an opportunity to see some of Cuba's best baseball players work out. That was not only against the rules of Major League Baseball but, because of the U.S. embargo against Cuba, against U.S. law as well. Instead of politely saying "Thanks, but no thanks," Andrés had the following response:

"When I was young I didn't care about seeing naked women in photos if I couldn't have the real thing. It's the same with baseball. Why do I want to watch any of these players if I can't sign them?"

After the game Fidel Castro hosted a reception for the visitors from the United States, and greeted each guest upon their arrival.

"I don't need a translator," said Andrés in Spanish as he approached the Cuban leader.

"And where did you learn Spanish?" asked Fidel.

Andrés explained that he was Venezuelan.

"*¿Con esa cara?* (With that face?)" inquired Fidel.

Andrés replied that he was born in Hungry.

"Why didn't the Astros come to play against us?" asked Fidel.

"You didn't invite us," responded Andrés.

"Why don't you talk to Major League Baseball and the Astros about our team playing some games in Houston?" queried Fidel, adding "And then the Astros can come to play against us in Cuba."

"Sure," Andrés said, and that was the end of the encounter. Fidel went back to glad-handing, and Andrés got ready to board the charter back to Florida and spring training.

Although the Astros are aware of Cuban talent when and if it becomes available, no Cuban player has been signed and developed by the Houston organization since José Arcia in 1961. Pacheco still scouted and signed players in Venezuela, but when he became ill in the early 1980s, the Astros focused their Latin American recruiting almost exclusively on the Dominican Republic.

Julio "Sijo" Linares, Special Assistant to the GM/Dominican Republic Operations, has been the face of the Astros in the Dominican Republic for thirty-five years. Linares joined the organization in 1973 after finishing a fifteen-year playing career in the minor league system of the San Francisco Giants. With the Astros, Linares has supervised scouting in the Dominican Republic, and for a time all of Latin America, as well as serving as director of the club's academy located near his hometown of San Pedro de Macorís. He has also been a manager and coach at the minor league level and spent three years as a coach with the Astros major league team from 1994 to 1996. While he did not occupy all of these positions simultaneously, he was often asked to play too many roles in the organization. It was difficult for him to oversee scouting while he was also serving as manager in the Florida State League or being a big league bench coach in Houston.

But multitasking was not the only the obstacle he faced. In scouting the Dominican Republic, Linares has had to compete with big-market teams that were dishing out huge bonuses while he was limited to offering more modest sums. He had to do battle against organizations such as the Los Angeles Dodgers and Toronto Blue Jays (whose scouting efforts between the late 1970s and early 1990s were led by Pat Gillick and Epy Guerrero) that were constructing large complexes, while the Astros maintained a very modest facility. And Linares has also had to compete with scouts willing to bend, if not break, any rules laid out by the Dominican government or Major League Baseball. As a result, Linares has not always been able to deliver top prospects to Houston. Despite those obstacles, he did sign seven players who went on to play in the major leagues with the Astros. The most successful of whom were catcher Raúl "Tony" Eusebio and shortstop Andujar Cedeño.

Signed in 1985, Eusebio played parts of nine seasons with the Astros between 1991 and 2001, had a career batting average of .275, and was the most underrated player on the Houston big league club during the 1990s.

Although related to neither César Cedeño nor Joaquín Andujar, because of his name Andujar Cedeño attracted a great deal of attention when Houston signed him in 1986. The very talented Cedeño became one of the Astros' top minor league prospects but had a disappointing, and short, major league career. He made his debut in 1990 and played for five seasons with the Astros, his best being the 1993 campaign when he hit .283 with 11 home runs and 56 RBI as the starting shortstop. After being traded to San Diego in 1994, Cedeño returned to the Astros to play in three games in 1996—his last in the big leagues. In the winter of 2000, he died in an automobile accident in the Dominican Republic. He was only thirty-one years old.

One the most successful products of the Astros' scouting ventures in the Dominican Republic, Manny Acta, a middle infielder, was signed by Linares in 1986 and played for six years in the Astros' minor league system. However, he never played in the major leagues. In the early 1990s, after being sent to scouting school by Linares, Acta did a self-evaluation: "I ended up with a number that showed that I was not going to be a big league player," Acta told me. He began his coaching career with the Astros' team in Asheville, North Carolina, in 1992. Between 1993 and 2000 Acta managed three different A-ball teams for the Astros, worked as a coach with the organization's Triple-A New Orleans affiliate in 2001, and between 2002 and 2006 was the third base coach for the Montreal Expos and New York Mets. He has managed winter league teams in both the Dominican Republic and Venezuela and was the manager of the Dominican entry in the World Baseball Classic in 2005. In November 2006 the thirty-seven-year-old Acta was named to lead the Washington Nationals, becoming the youngest major league manager.

But during the late 1980s, the Astros' Dominican pipeline almost completely dried up. No player signed by the Astros out of the Dominican Republic between 1987 and 1995 advanced beyond A-ball. It was precisely because of this drought that Bill Wood was so interested in Andres's scouting proposal for Venezuela.

Before the Houston organization began to look for players in the Dominican Republic in the mid-1960s, they were already involved in scouting in Venezuela, although few *criollo* players were signed. In 1963, Gillick and Pacheco discovered outfielder José Herrera who made his big league debut with the Astros in 1967, becoming Venezuela's fourteenth major leaguer. Herrera was the only Venezuelan native to play for the Astros until the products of the academy began to arrive in the mid-1990s.

"José Herrera was supposed to be one of the best hitters in the game," remembered Andrés. "They took photos and films of his hitting because they said he had the most perfect hitting mechanics they had ever seen." The films made by Gillick and Pacheco were used to instruct young players in the Astros' organization. "But he had no position, plus not much desire to be a star in baseball," said Andrés, which helps explain why, even with "the perfect swing," Herrera's major league career was short-lived. The Astros called up Herrera, an infielder/outfielder, in June 1967, and he got one hit in his four big league at bats that season. With Houston in 1968, he hit .240 in a hundred trips to the plate. Selected by Montreal in the expansion draft, Herrera played a few games with the Expos in 1969 and 1970.

Pacheco signed brothers Alvaro and Roberto Espinoza in 1978. Alvaro remembers playing with the Astros' teams (they had two—orange and blue) in Sarasota in the Gulf Coast League in 1979 and 1980 and then being released after the 1980 season. He was signed by Minnesota in 1982, and after three impressive minor league seasons, was brought up by the Twins. He played in the major leagues for twelve seasons and is currently an infield instructor with Pittsburgh. Roberto never made it the big leagues. Until I told Alvaro Espinosa in 2003, he was not aware that he had been the last player signed by the Astros in Venezuela until his nephew—Astros catcher Raul Chávez—joined the organization in 1990.

"When I first came to Houston, we had a couple of Venezuelan players under contract, Alvaro and Roberto Espinoza," recalled Wood, who started working for the Astros in 1976. "After those brothers left the organization, we really slacked off in our Venezuelan efforts altogether."

"I asked Lynwood Stallings, who was the farm and scouting director then, why we didn't have a bigger presence in Venezuela in the late 1970s, and he said the players had not proven to be as hungry, they didn't work as hard, they were not as driven, and we didn't feel like the program had merit at that point," explained Wood. Stallings was comparing the Venezuelans to players from the Dominican Republic.

In 1984 when Andrés explained that the situation had changed in Venezuela and that young men were now interested in careers in professional baseball, Wood listened attentively. When he took over as the Astros' general manager in 1988, he jumped at the opportunity to reenter the Venezuela market.

Not only did the new Houston franchise attempt to acquire players from Latin America, it also tried to establish a fan base in South Texas and Mexico by broadcasting games in Spanish. In addition to KLVI in Houston, there were six other radio stations in Texas that carried all of the Colt .45s games beginning with the 1962 season. In the late 1960s, when franchise owner Judge Roy Hofheinz wanted to introduce the new Astrodome to Latin America, the network expanded on Sundays for *The Astros Game of the Week* which was sent by short-wave free to sixty radio stations in Central and South America and the Caribbean, with the feed to Mexico retransmitted to eighty other stations.

The leading figure in that effort was René Cárdenas, the play-by-play announcer on the Spanish-language broadcasts of Colt .45s and Astros games from 1962 to 1975. Cárdenas, a pioneer in Spanish-language baseball broadcasting, worked for the Los Angeles Dodgers between 1958 and 1961, for the Texas Rangers in 1982, and again with the Dodgers from 1982 to 1988, before retiring. For a few years in the late 1970s, Cárdenas went home to his native Nicaragua where he was bird dog scout for the Astros. Currently, he lives in Houston and writes a column for the Astros' Spanish-language website and for *La Prensa*, a Nicaraguan newspaper.

"Judge Hofheinz asked me come to Houston because he wanted to offer me a job as a broadcaster," explained Cárdenas. "So I came over and discussed the deal, and I accepted. After we signed, he said. 'OK, now you have a job. I don't have time to be looking for the person who will be helping you with the broadcast. So please feel free to do whatever you want and just let me know.'"

"So I decided to go after Orlando Sánchez Diago, whom I had met a few years earlier during winter baseball in Nicaragua. I knew that he had gone back to Cuba and after he got there, Castro took over, and he ended up in Venezuela as a refugee," said Cárdenas. "I called him and said 'Orlando, I would like for you to come here as my *compadre* to do the broadcast of the Houston games. Are you interested?' He said, 'Yes, I'd like to work with you, but I have an old Cuban passport that is not good anymore, and my U.S. work visa is also expired.'"

"So I went back to Judge Hofheinz and told him, 'My friend from Venezuela doesn't have his papers. Do you know anybody in Washington who can help us?'"

"Yes, I know somebody—Lyndon B. Johnson," replied Hofheinz. "I'll just call Lyndon and tell him to call the American Embassy and order them to give Orlando a visa so he can come over and work for us."

"Judge Hofheinz picked up the phone and called Blair House, where the vice president was living and started talking to Lyndon about cattle and politics and joking around, and then he said. 'Let me tell you what I called you for. I need this man over here. Can you do something about it?'" remembered Cárdenas.

Johnson asked for the person's name, and then directed Hofheinz to inform Sánchez Diago to be at the United States Embassy in Caracas the next day at 10:00 a.m.

"Orlando was here in Houston two days later," said Cárdenas.

Sánchez Diago broadcast Astros games with Cardenas until 1975 and then returned to the air for a second stint from 1987 to 1992.

Cárdenas explained that in the early years he and Sánchez would transmit home games live, but when the Colt .45s were on the road, the two would listen to the English broadcasts and translate. They had no problem with the narration of Gene Elston or Al Helfer, but some of the comments and the heavy southern accent of color man Loel Passe proved difficult.

"It was a nightmare trying to understand Loel Passe because of his accent and his unusual phrases," remembered Cárdenas. "I could not possibly translate some of those words into Spanish and so I just remained silent."

I grew up in Houston listening to Passe broadcast the Double-A Houston Buffs games during the 1950s and can understand Cárdenas's point. After all, how would you translate "Hot ziggity dog and sassafras tea?"

4

From Zero to Prospect

The Astros' Academy

With the Astros on-board, Andrés was ready to put his vision into action. Given his commitment to Valencia, when he thought of opening a facility to prepare players, it was a no-brainer to locate there. He used his connections with the Magallanes baseball team, the University of Carabobo, and the business sector to open the academy in August 1989.

"We started first with an agreement with Magallanes and used the facilities at the stadium where Magallanes plays, including the clubhouse," Andrés told me. "After two months of working there, I felt it was not a good place for young players. We were too exposed: everybody could see us work and talk to the kids."

The first instructor hired was Jesús Aristimuño, now in his late fifties, who has been with the academy since the beginning and has seen every player who has passed through the gates. At the time Aristimuño was also employed as a coach by Magallanes and worked as an instructor for the youth league teams of Industrias Venoco (the Venezuela-Orinoco Company) in Guacara, a small town about ten miles east of Valencia. Although Aristimuño played in the minor leagues in the United States for ten years, he is better known in Venezuela for his fourteen seasons as a middle infielder with Magallanes between 1965 and 1978.

In October the Astros began to use a playing field and small clubhouse inside the grounds of Industrias Venoco. The Academia de Béisbol de los Astros de Houston was located in the sports complex the Industrias Venoco provides for its employees. Although Andrés was acquainted with some of the Venoco executives, it was Aristimuño's relationship with Venoco that resulted in the Astros locating their facility there. For the Astros, the Venoco site offered a secure situation on private property and was thus off-limits to scouts from competing major league organizations. For Venoco, working with a big league club was a source of pride; in addition, they would receive both technical assistance on maintaining their field and instruction for their youth league teams.

In the early days of the academy, Andrés was under the supervision of Julio Linares, the Astros' Latin America scouting director, who lived in the Dominican Republic. Linares was delighted by the prospect of working with Aristimuño, whom he had first met in spring training in Arizona in 1966 when they both played in the San Francisco Giants' minor league system.

In early 1990 the Astros formalized their agreement with Industrias Venoco to lease a baseball diamond, office, and locker rooms from the company. "At first there was only a gentlemen's agreement to use the facility," explained Andrés. "But then when we got Julio here, he really liked the complex and the program."

"Venoco buys some its primary material from Houston companies, and the Astros look for some of theirs here in Venezuela," Miguel Romero, an engineer trained at Georgia Tech and at the time vice president of the Club Venoco, the sports and social arm of the company, told me in 1990. He described the agreement with the Astros as a joint venture. "The Astros get a facility, and we have our field improved. We are also getting a lot of baseball know-how from the Astros."

In 1990 the Astros also signed a formal written agreement with the Magallanes ball club. Under the arrangement, Houston would send five players, a manager, a pitching coach, and a trainer to Magallanes. In addition Houston would have the first option of signing Venezuelan players under contract to Magallanes.

Now it would be up to the scouts to bring in the players to be developed.

"Scout is familiar as a military term, but its roots refer more generally to a searcher, a sensitive recorder of information, carefully sifting out significant details," writes Kevin Kerrane in his classic work on the subject, *Dollar Sign on the Muscle*.[1] He notes that the word is related to the French *écouter*—to listen.

As Ralph Avila, a veteran scout and founder of the Los Angeles Dodgers academy in the Dominican Republic pointed out to me, the word "scout"—even in the baseball context—has many meanings. There are advance scouts who file reports on the major league team their organization will next play. There are scouts who keep tabs on minor league players who they might want to acquire in a trade or in the annual Rule 5 draft. There are also professional scouts that rank university and high-school players for the free-agent draft in June. Finally, there are scouts like Avila and Andrés, who are the gatekeepers of the major league dream in Latin America.

Scouts often describe working in Latin America in nostalgic terms, "the way it was in the United States before the draft." Players are sought, courted, sometimes hidden from other scouts, and, hopefully, signed. Projecting the future size and potential of a skinny fifteen-year-old is more difficult than looking at a high-school senior in the United States. And a scout's instinct is crucial; occasionally a player must be signed on the spot before a scout from another organization shows up.

In Venezuela the key to scouting is exploration. While traveling around Venezuela with Andrés, one sees the respect he has for the players. His reserved, conservative style also wins the parents' trust. These qualities coupled with his knowledge of baseball and his ability to switch between two languages and cultures made him an important point man for the Astros in Venezuela. When Andrés wore his Astros cap in Venezuela, he was cognizant that he represented an organization trying to get a foothold in the country. In the end it is the person representing the club, and his skill at selecting talent, that is the bottom line.

In addition to seeing Venezuela as another outpost on the frontier of scouting, Andrés viewed it as a laboratory to test his ideas for more efficient production of talent for major league baseball. For the vast majority of those working in baseball, scouting and development are separate functions not to be combined. For Andrés the two are integrally linked. He argued that baseball was experiencing a crisis related to scouting and development. The industry needed to obtain high-quality raw material in a sufficient quantity at a fair cost and then transform it quickly and efficiently into the final product: major league players. Andrés wrote a memo addressed to Tal Smith summarizing his ideas on the subject and gave it to Smith when he returned to the Astros' organization in 1994.

For Andrés the baseball industry had made two fundamental modifications in the previous one hundred years. The first was Branch Rickey creating the minor leagues with the purchase of the first farm club in the early 1920s and then hiring scouts to sign players to fill out the rosters of those teams.

"Mr. Rickey's theory was to obtain quality from quantity; however, I don't think that this theory is applicable today," wrote Andrés. He believed it was actually the reverse: "We should produce more efficiently." The goal should be to generate more major leaguers from fewer players signed.

The second fundamental change in baseball was free agency in 1973. Although this was logical and predictable, Andrés thought MLB teams approached it in a misguided way. The indiscriminate signing of free agents in an attempt to produce winning teams was wrong. "Finished products cannot be bought at a high market price for a profit."

The most notable weakness of the current system was that organizations were not producing a sufficient quantity of major league players and thus had to rely on free agency to fill in. The industry was converting less than 7 percent of its raw material. Andrés believed that with more emphasis on scouting and development, this could be improved to 12 or 15 percent. It would also be possible to cut the average time for reaching the major leagues from six years to four years. He felt that it was a mistake to believe "that money spent on scouting and development is an expense, when in reality it is the best capital investment possible in the baseball industry."

To accomplish these objectives he proposed that:

- "Scouting and development should be unified into one totally monolithic department." This is the only way to have good communication between all members of these departments.
- Managers, coaches, and instructors should work with scouts during the off-season to decide which kind of players should be selected in the June free-agent draft. In April and May, the technical development people should play a role in evaluating who will be drafted.
- "Our scouting should put more effort in finding young *athletes* to be developed rather than those college players of great performance."

These were obviously objectives that would have to be applied throughout the Astros' minor league system and not just in Venezuela. Andrés understood that while he might have had little influence within the Astros' organization outside of Venezuela, he could implement some of these changes at the academy.

When I re-read Andrés's memo while researching the book, I realized that the ideal player he was proposing to recruit was nearly the opposite of what was proposed in *Moneyball*, Michael Lewis's best-selling account of the Billy Beane regime in Oakland. For Beane and Lewis, there is only one way to find baseball players and that is by looking at statistics, preferably those of young men who have played at the collegiate level. Lewis ridicules old-fashioned scouts who comb the countryside looking for players with "good" bodies and physical tools. Whatever validity the Beane approach has—and there is some doubt whether the Oakland GM has discovered "the secret of success in baseball"—is beside the point. The ideas presented by Lewis cannot be applied in Venezuela (or anywhere else in Latin America for that matter) where the vast majority of players are not going to college and where there are no statistics available. And statistics, although a valuable tool in evaluations, tell us very little about the intangibles that are possessed by a potential major league player.

"Scouts see a small sample of a player's performance and thus can't pick up long-term trends that show up in certain statistics. But no computer printout can measure heart, hustle, intelligence and physical attributes," wrote Paul White in *USA Today Sports Weekly*.[2]

The academy setting, in which a player might stay for a year, establishes a track record. The staff can get a read on the intangibles and is better able to evaluate the player, and only then will he be signed. Andrés, like Rickey, saw the need to project players further into the future. The way Andrés saw it, players are not born, but developed. Athletes are born and it's up to the organization to develop them.

While Andrés is quick to point out that his idea for laying out a combined scouting and development plan is not original, it is certainly unique in the Venezuelan context. He explained that he had learned a great deal about baseball during the early 1980s, especially scouting, from four members of the Pittsburgh organization: the legendary Howie Haak; Texas League president Tom Kayser; Murray Cook, now with the Office of the Commissioner of Baseball; and Branch Rickey III, current president of the Pacific Coast League.

At the end of the 2004 season, both Kayser and Rickey were in Round Rock, Texas, to mark the transition of the Round Rock Express from Double-A to Triple-A status. I asked Kayser, who in the early '80s was the assistant minor league director for the Pirates, how he thought he'd influenced Andrés.

"It may have been some of the aspects of treating players humanely. With Pittsburgh, at Bradenton, we would bring in people who would help with acculturation aspects—finances, English lessons, nutrition," explained Kayser. "Back in the early and mid-80s, those things weren't being done yet. Complexes were not as prolific as they are now."

I asked Branch Rickey III, the grandson of Branch Rickey, why he believed he had made such a lasting impression on Andrés.

"There was a relationship between the Pirates, for whom I was working in player development and the Magallanes ball club. Andrés was representing Magallanes and from the very first handshake there was a very, very unusual sense of comfort and confidence," recalled Rickey. "For me, his character shines through with his handshake."

"Our friendship sparked Andrés into wanting to have more of an external relationship and have some on-going major league contact. He considered himself kind of an outsider to the established baseball community [in the United States]. By maintaining the relationship with the Pirates, coming to spring training, and meeting and traveling with Howie Haak, I think he gained confidence that he was not an anomaly, not just somebody who couldn't break in. He had a vision, and he found an awful lot of people with the Pittsburgh organization that treated him as a counterpart," said Rickey.

I asked Rickey if Andrés had offered the Pirates the opportunity to get involved in the academy project that the Astros eventually put into operation.

"It was very, very obvious to me that we had a chance to get in on the ground floor and kind of corner the market in Venezuela by setting up an academy."

"But you didn't do it," I pointed out.

"Oh, it was a time in which Pittsburgh was having so much success in the Dominican Republic, in Puerto Rico, through the influence of Howie Haak's supervision—the shame was that we weren't needy enough, we weren't desperate enough. We were winning division titles and not making money. I don't think that our leadership saw the peculiar advantage of spending more money in Venezuela to potentially make a breakthrough there. There was no track record of Venezuelan production. And Andrés Reiner was not particularly a name that you just dropped on baseball people," said Rickey.

While his friendship with Kayser and the younger Rickey boosted Andrés's confidence, it was his travels with Howie Haak in Venezuela that convinced him he could be a scout.

"He is my mentor," said Andrés. "He taught me not to be a fan, but a professional." Although Haak was Andrés's mentor, he was not his role model: Andrés does not smoke, chew tobacco, nor use the wide array of four-letter words that Haak did.

"Among his colleagues, men who themselves see life as one long road trip, Haak was honored for this durability . . . But he was most famous for his work in Latin America, where he had opened up whole countries for major-league scouting," writes Kerrane in *Dollar Sign on the Muscle,* which includes a detailed account of Haak's career.[3]

Haak, who began his scouting career with the Brooklyn Dodgers in 1947, went to Pittsburgh in 1951 with his mentor Branch Rickey and spent more than thirty years with the Pirates organization combing Latin America for prospects. His success stories include Tony Peña, Tony Armas, Omar Moreno, Manny Sanguillen, and Julián Javier.

In the early 1990s, Haak worked for the Astros for a couple of seasons as a special assignment scout covering the major leagues and did not travel outside of the United States.

"I don't know if I have told you this before, but it is a wonderful story about Howie," said Andrés. "He was working with the Astros and Bill Wood told him it was going to be his last year. The only thing Howie asked for was an opportunity to go to Venezuela for the last time. Bill called me and said 'Andrés, Howie is going to Venezuela and I know you have a good relationship with him, but he can't go to the academy. That is an order. Take him to the games, take him where you want, but he can't go to the academy.'" Wood feared Haak would be a negative influence on the young players.

"I said to Bill, 'I don't think I can handle that.' He said 'It's an order, you have to.' So I went to pick Howie up at the Caracas airport and it was like 2:00 a.m. when we arrived in Valencia. The first thing he asked me was 'Andrés what time does the academy open? When do I have to be ready?'"

"I told him to rest in the morning and I would pick him up at noon. The next day I called Bill and said, 'I'm sorry, I don't care if I lose my job, I just can't do this to this old man. He has been so good to me. I know how to handle Howie, please let him come to the academy. Finally, Bill said 'OK, but if we lose any players, it will be your fault.'"

"Howie sat down on a chair behind home plate and he spent the whole morning there. That was the group of Petagine, Abreu, and Centeno. There were like fifteen players. When it ended, he said 'Andrés, this pitcher [Luis Sojo—one of the first Venezuelan players released by the Astros], will never play in the big leagues. But, let me tell you, I have been in Latin America for more than twenty years, and I have never seen as many prospects on one field as I see here.'"

"Coming from him it meant a lot to me," said Andrés.

While Andrés was securing the agreements with the Magallanes club and Industrias Venoco, he was simultaneously involved in the difficult task of selecting the scouts, coaches, and instructors who would find and develop the players. It would be a slow and deliberate process. Once Aristimuño was on-board, Andrés brought in Rubén Cabrera as the pitching coach and scout. He also hired a part-time trainer, and arranged for an instructor at the University of Carabobo, Dr. Lester Storey, to work with the prospects on physical conditioning and the art of running. Finally, he employed Luis Carmona to teach English classes three days a week.

In the first few years, Andrés could sign players only with the approval of Latin America scouting supervisor Linares or scouting director Dan O'Brien. If Andrés, Aristimuño, and Cabrera liked a prospect, they would notify Linares or O'Brien. And if the signing money was significant—and in the early days this was probably anything over $25,000—Astros assistant general manager Bob Watson and GM Bill Wood would be involved.

In early 1990 before the first player was signed out of the academy, O'Brien and Watson traveled to Venezuela to check out the facility at Venoco. O'Brien was not totally convinced that Venezuela was going to be a fountain of talent and upon his return urged me not to expect too much too soon from the academy. "When you are starting from scratch like this, you have to be patient. We would like to build up a steady stream of Venezuelan players coming into our system," said O'Brien. "Ultimately you would like a Venezuelan big leaguer to show for your efforts, and far down the road that will be a way to measure how we have succeeded. But I don't think we can put a timetable on that."

Watson, who in his seven years working with the Astros made seven visits to the Venezuelan academy, was more upbeat than O'Brien in his assessment in 1990. "I feel that the next real hotbed of talent is Venezuela. It is an untapped source of talent for major league baseball."

But except for a few possible prospects, there was little to excite Watson and O'Brien on their first visit to the academy. The facility consisted of two baseball fields and little else. The would-be Astros were on the field from 8:00 a.m. until noon Monday through Friday, with most of their time spent on hitting, fielding, and pitching drills. Players worked out at a gym that was open to the public, had their English classes three afternoons a week at a Venoco company building, and once or twice a week had cultural orientation sessions. There were no dormitory facilities at the academy: the players were housed and fed at the Hotel Nacional in downtown Valencia. The complex remained unassuming until early 2003.

"I guess the word academy made me think of the Air Force Academy, or the Naval Academy or something with more structures and fields," remarked then Astros manager Larry Dierker after taking a look at the playing field and the modest clubhouse and offices at the Astros' training facility. Dierker and GM Gerry Hunsicker visited the academy in March 2001, when Houston played Cleveland in a two-game exhibition series in Valencia. "I'd heard so much about it, I was a little surprised that it was not as much of a baseball complex as I anticipated," said Dierker. But as he watched the players go through their workouts, he became more impressed. "It was obvious that the players had been drilled because every infielder was picking up ground balls exactly the same way, and taking the exact same cut and steps before throwing the ball."

Hunsicker, a frequent visitor to the academy, was accustomed to the modest complex. "You don't need mahogany lockers and carpets on the floor," he told me. "You just need a nice, comfortable environment to allow your kids to play and develop." And that, he concluded, was precisely what the Astros had in Venezuela.

Academy, school, complex, facility—call it what you like, but a popular dictionary's definition of an academy as "a school offering instruction in a special field," seems to fit the best.

"I use the word academy because it reflects the learning that takes place here," Andrés told me on my first visit in May 1990. For him the young baseball players working out were like fledgling concert pianists or ballet dancers: they had to possess certain physical skills, required instruction and training, and needed to be nurtured and helped to gain self-confidence.

"At the academy, Andrés gets to know a player's makeup. Some kids do not have the makeup to go out and let them have a chance to be successful," explained David Rawnsley. Rawnsley was the Astros' assistant scouting director and the director of international development during the academy's early years. "The academy weeds out players. The important part of the selection process is not so much the player you bring into the academy, but the player who graduates," said Rawnsley.

"The academy is where a player goes from zero to almost being a prospect," Andrés told me. "Most scouts only want to see what they can get today. I'm the opposite. I want to see today what I can get tomorrow. If I can watch fourteen- and fifteen-year-olds for a year and a half, see how they improve, and get to know their parents, I have a better chance to sign them. If I see a seventeen-year-old kid today, there will be four or five organizations pursuing him and it will be a lot more difficult, and expensive, to sign him."

When I visited the academy in May 1990 the Astros had only three Venezuelan players under contract. Raúl Chávez, then a shortstop and the first player signed by Andrés, and first baseman Roberto Petagine—both of whom were playing with the Astros' rookie team in Florida—and Henri Centeno, a middle infielder signed a few weeks earlier and working out at the academy preparing to play in the Dominican Summer League.

"Raúl Chávez came the first day we opened the doors, introduced himself and said, 'I want to come to the academy and I want to improve.' He stayed for six months, did improve, and was signed," explained Andrés. Chávez, then sixteen years old, grew up nearby in Guacara in a baseball family. His uncle, pitching coach Rubén Cabrera, brought him in. Another uncle is former major league player Alvaro Espinoza.

Andrés discovered Roberto Petagine, eighteen, a power-hitting first baseman while he was playing in a Criollitos (youth league) tournament on the tourist island of Margarita. Petagine spent three months at the academy before being signed. "He's a great kid, capable of working alone for hours with no supervision," explained Andrés. "He wanted to be a baseball player, and he will be a good one."

Henri Centeno, twenty, was a middle infielder with soft hands who

Andrés envisioned as a "Ricky Henderson clone" who would drive opposing pitchers crazy at the Astrodome. Centeno, from Casanay in eastern Venezuela, also the hometown of Jesús Aristimuño, the scout who recommended him, was signed in early May 1990.

There were also three unsigned players being evaluated by the Astros' staff, but only one caught my eye. He was skinny kid—about 6-0, 145 pounds—with a great smile and had just turned sixteen. He was working out at shortstop, although he would probably find another position. And one thing the staff was sure of: this left-handed kid was a natural hitter. I had a photographer take his photo along with the other unsigned players but had assured Andrés I would not use them, nor mention the players in a series of articles I was writing for the *Houston Post*, until they were signed. But Bob Kelly Abreu wanted to know if I would send him a copy of his photo—and not just a snapshot—but a giant print. As soon as the photos were developed, I had a poster-size image sent off to Abreu. Three months later, Abreu became the fourth player signed by Andrés.

Obviously not all players evaluated by the Astros' staff at the academy were signed. One prospect who left without signing was Omar Daal. In 1989 Daal, then seventeen, had just returned home to Venezuela from Canada where he pitched for the national junior team. Filled with the excitement of representing his country abroad and the knowledge that major league scouts had been watching him, he was ready to begin his professional career. Rubén Cabrera brought Daal to the academy, and he worked out with the Astros' staff for a couple of weeks. They really liked his curve ball, but Daal was not interested in making suggested changes to his pitching mechanics. And more important, there was an issue of money and the fact that the Astros had not yet signed their first prospect.

"I got to the point where I thought I could not sign him, because at that time any bonus over $3,500 was impossible. The front office in Houston was not going to approve it. And I believe Daal was thinking more in terms of $25,000. I told him it would be best for him to go home," recalls Andrés. A year later, Daal was signed by the Los Angeles Dodgers and played for eleven seasons in the big leagues.

"I made a mistake, I should have signed him," Andrés told me after Daal had become an established major league player. But not many mistakes were made. Andrés and his staff saw hundreds of players at tryouts, tournaments, and at the academy during the first two years, and the success rate is proof of how selective they were. Of the five players signed in 1990, three—Abreu, Chávez, and Petagine—went on to play in the major leagues. In 1991 nine players were signed, and five of them—outfielders Melvin Mora and Richard Hidalgo, pitchers Oscar Henríquez and Edgar Ramos, and infielder Alejandro Freire—made it to the big leagues. Of the first fourteen players signed by the Astros out of the academy, eight reached the major leagues.

5

From Tunapuy to Guacara

The Search for the New El Dorado

Scouting in Venezuela is not easy. The country is slightly larger than Texas with a population of twenty-five million, and the distances between cities are long: a bus ride from Maracaibo to Maturín is more than eighteen hours. Prospects are scattered throughout the country, and finding them requires a great deal of planning and hard work. Although Aristimuño and Cabrera would be able to scout areas near Valencia as well as serving as instructors at the academy, and Andrés himself would be searching for players, it was necessary to hire at least two other scouts: one to cover eastern Venezuela and the other to cover the Caracas metropolitan area. Those scouts, Andrés expected, would give him weekly or monthly reports before he would then make a trip to check out the prospects.

His first choice to cover the vast eastern section of Venezuela was Rafael Cariel.

"I first met Cariel when he was signed for professional baseball at the age of seventeen in the early seventies," explained Andrés. "I was close to him during his career as a player with Magallanes. He took his profession very seriously, and he is extremely intelligent. He injured his arm, didn't get to the big leagues, and retired when he was quite young, just twenty-nine, but he was the best defensive catcher that Venezuela had at the time."

When Cariel, who reached Double-A in the Pirates organization, retired from professional baseball in the late 1970s, he went to work at the University of the Oriente in Cumaná—several hundred miles east of Valencia.

"I spent half of 1989 trying to find Cariel, but no one could tell me where he was," said Andrés. "My boss was asking when I would sign a scout for the eastern part of the country, and I said, 'When I find Rafael Cariel.' I was almost desperate. So one afternoon in early October, I went to a practice with the Magallanes team, and the first guy I see on the field was Cariel, and a couple of days later I signed him."

In late 1989 Cariel arranged a tryout in Tunapuy, a small town on the Paria Peninsula, much closer to the island of Trinidad than to Caracas. Cariel put the word out that there would be a tryout, expecting that a handful of hopefuls would show up. He and Andrés arrived at the ballpark and were shocked to discover between forty and fifty players ranging in ages from fourteen-year-old boys to grown men. Not only were there more players than they expected, there were no prospects—not even one that they thought worth taking back to the academy. But Andrés and Cariel were not disappointed; the worst thing is to have a tryout and have no one show up. Andrés still reflects back on the Tunapuy adventure as an example of the difficult start to what has become a very refined operation. And while he might argue that he was not applying Branch Rickey's "quality out of quantity" principle, the tryout camps the Astros held throughout Venezuela acted as the first filter for prospects in an ocean of young men with major league dreams.

Andrés himself had many contacts in Venezuelan baseball, ranging from youth leagues through the professional ranks, and most of the academy staff was drawn from players he'd met during his affiliation with Magallanes. Each of these scouts and instructors in turn had their own network of contacts in baseball. And when the scouting project got off the ground, more contacts were generated, and the network expanded like a giant web that covered the length and breadth of Venezuela. No matter how optimistic Andrés was about establishing a scouting presence, it is unlikely that he anticipated the formation of the extensive network of contacts that was built throughout the country over sixteen years.

The case of Cariel is a good example. When he began working as a scout in 1989, he had only a few contacts, mainly in Cumaná. Systematically, he began to travel throughout eastern Venezuela, going to tournaments and youth league competitions, conducting tryouts, and visiting with friends. Coaches began to call and inform him of a game, friends would tell him about a possible prospect, or parents would call and ask him to take a look at their son. He soon knew the region like the back of his hand; it is unlikely that there is a single small town in eastern Venezuela where Cariel has not been and does not have a connection.

While traveling in rural Venezuela can be exhausting, it is seldom dangerous. But venture into the country's large urban areas and all bets are off.

"Sometimes I'm afraid to go to some of the areas where players come from, but you have to go," Cariel told me. He was referring to the endemic social violence in Venezuela's urban housing projects, such as those in Guarenas, a city a few miles east of Caracas. "A friend called and said come over to Guarenas and see one of our players, so I went over to take a look," recalled Cariel.

The player he went to see was Richard Hidalgo, who immediately went to the academy and was signed by the Astros in July 1991. Although Hidalgo showed tremendous potential, he was too young to sign when Cariel first saw him, and he needed to be developed. When Hidalgo entered the academy in November 1990, he had only a very slow 7.1 second time in the sixty-yard dash. Andrés put him under the tutelage of Dr. Lester Storey. "When Richard Hidalgo first came here and we told him to run sixty yards, I thought he was going to fall down before he finished. He just didn't know how to run," recalled Dr. Storey. "Now he does. I tell the young men, 'You don't have to be the fastest runner, but we want you to run *con elegancia* (with elegance),'" said Dr. Storey.

Dr. Storey—no one calls him by his first name—now in his mid-fifties, was a track and field star representing Venezuela in international competitions. After his running career was over, Storey went to Italy and received a degree in sports medicine and was hired by the Universidad de Carabobo located in Valencia—a position he still holds. Andrés was interested in teaching the young players about physical fitness, conditioning, and the art of running and hired Dr.

Storey as a part-time consultant. In 1990 I saw Dr. Storey, then thirty-eight, running with a group of young players who seemed to have a difficult time keeping up with him. "When Dr. Storey runs and does exercises with teenage players, he sets a good example of what we are trying to do," Andrés commented. "You not only have to tell the players what to do, you have to show them how to do it."

On a January 1991 visit to the academy, Bob Watson, Dan O'Brien, and minor league director Fred Nelson watched all prospects run sixty yards. When Hidalgo ran it in 6.6 seconds, everyone was shocked. "I thought my stopwatch was not working correctly," said Andrés. "This was the beginning of the development of Richard. It will be a great moment for the entire staff of the academy when Richard gets to the major leagues."

At the end of 1990, Andrés opened a satellite facility near El Hatillo, a beautiful small town in the hills above and thirty minutes away from the noisy traffic of Caracas. El Hogar de los Astros de Houston (The Home of the Houston Astros) offered the opportunity to bring in players from the metropolitan Caracas area, and if a prospect was discovered, send him to the academy at Guacara. "It acts as a filter for our main academy," Andrés told me when I visited there in late 1991. It also allowed the young players to continue their education while working out in the afternoon. The complex was very small—only one diamond and an additional pitching mound.

El Hatillo was also the facility where current Astros scout and instructor Wolfgang Ramos got his start in the organization in 1991. Ramos, the person responsible for running the day-to-day operations at El Hatillo, is very outgoing, upbeat, and jovial. He was a third baseman in the Boston Red Sox minor league system for eight seasons between 1977 and 1987 and played ten seasons in winter ball including five with Magallanes between 1983 and 1989. Ramos also played professional baseball in Holland, Mexico, and Italy. When he returned to Venezuela from Italy in 1990, there was a message for him to call Andrés.

"He wanted me to work at El Hatillo," recalled Ramos, adding, "at a very low salary." Ramos accepted the offer. At El Hatillo, Ramos would evaluate one or two players daily and decide who would stay longer. Andrés would make the four-hour round trip from Guacara each Tuesday to check on players. In the beginning, there was not much for Andrés to look at.

"Then 'Manacho' [Oscar Henríquez] showed up, and in the next year and a half he was followed by Alejandro Freire, Alberto Blanco, Oscar Padrón, Niuman Loiz, Carlitos Hernández [a second baseman not to be confused with the left-handed pitcher by the same name also signed by the Astros nor with the former Los Angeles Dodgers catcher, Carlos Hernández], and Freddy García," said Ramos. Freire, García, Henríquez, and Hernández developed into major league players.

In 1994 after four years of operation, the facility at El Hatillo was closed due to the labor stoppage in Major League Baseball and subsequent budget cutbacks. Ramos spent a year as an unpaid associate scout for the Astros, before being hired back in 1995. In addition to being an instructor at the academy and scouting in the Valencia area, Ramos began to work in the afternoons at Venoco in their sports programs, a job he still holds. Ramos is also employed as a coach by the Caracas team in the Venezuelan winter league. This multiple job pattern was something most Astros scouts and instructors would adhere to. In this way Andrés was able to maintain a top-flight staff without having to use his entire budget from the Astros to meet all of their salary needs.

"My greatest satisfaction in life is working here with the Astros," Ramos, now in his early fifties, told me. "They treat people like people. I'd put my hands in fire to defend Andrés." If I had made only one visit to the academy and heard this kind of testimonial, I would have been very skeptical. But after sixteen years of observation and conversations with other instructors and scouts working for the Astros who have made similar glowing remarks, it became clear that the staff truly understood they worked in a very special atmosphere.

I met with Andrés often during the early 1990s for his assessment of players he'd signed who were making their way through the Astros' minor league system. "You won't believe how good this kid is," or "If he doesn't get injured, he'll be a major league player," he'd tell me. While he was not always correct, Andrés did have a good sense of which prospects possessed the right combination of skill, ability to work hard, motivation, personality, and luck that would take them to the major leagues. I also began to understand the language scouts use—terms that make author Michael Lewis shudder—when writing their reports: "Gorgeous pitcher's body. Tall, slender, flexible, broad shoulders, long arms, big hands, big frame that will fill out," described one prospect. And I learned that "soft hands" and "great range" were important attributes for shortstops.

Here are a couple of examples.

"Richard Hidalgo is the perfect combination in some ways. He has speed. He is a 6.6 runner. He will possibly lose some of this because he will become heavier and bigger with age. He will be a good average hitter, and he will have power. He will be an outfielder, and I would say in our organization he would be for sure a right fielder. I know that he would be able to play center field in almost any other organization (perhaps not in St. Louis) with his speed, and defensively he is excellent. He has a great arm, and it will get even better," Andrés told me in June 1993. At the time, the seventeen-year-old Hidalgo was evoking comparisons to former Astros star César Cedeño. Of all the players signed by Andrés, none had a higher ceiling than Hidalgo.

But he was also very impressed by a young man he and Aristimuño had signed nine months earlier.

"Carlos Guillén is something special. He has the kind of personality that you are always looking for," said Andrés. "He is an aggressive player on the field, but he is the nicest person that you can find. He finished high school and is a very intelligent kid. He knows how to play baseball because he started to play when he was five years old. He's a switch hitter—a real switch hitter. I mean he can hit from both sides of the plate, not that he learned how to hit from both sides. He has some power. In projection, I would compare him with Ken Caminiti. He might be a higher average hitter than Caminiti. Because he has a great arm, we switched him from outfield to third base. And I wouldn't be surprised if he could make the change from third to shortstop. He has very soft hands and excellent coordination."

In 1993 there were probably only one or two people in the front office in Houston who would have recognized Guillén's name. Two years later, when Guillén was on the list of players to receive visas for the United States, someone in the Houston Astros' scouting department called Andrés and asked, "Who is this guy?"

"You know what a five-tool player is?" Andrés asked rhetorically, "Well, Carlos Guillén is a six-tool player. The sixth is a combination of his personality and his intelligence."

The 6-1, 180-pound Guillén, a native of Maracay, about sixty miles west of Caracas, played on the same youth league team with Bob Abreu and had long dreamed of reaching the big leagues.

"I was watching a major league game on television with my father when I was ten years old, and he asked if I would like to play in the U.S. I said 'Sure,'" explained Guillén. "Obviously I wanted to play in the U.S.; I just didn't have any idea of how I would get there. But as I got older, I began to understand how it worked; if you were dedicated, going to the U.S. was a real possibility."

By the time he was fifteen, Guillén was a hard-throwing pitcher sought after by several major league organizations. "I thought I was going to sign with the Dodgers, but Bob Abreu told me to check out the Astros," said Guillén. "I decided I would go to the academy and see for myself. I knew it was a good organization, and it was the most well known in Venezuela."

After a couple of weeks at the academy, Andrés wanted to sign Guillén as an outfielder and went to his home to make an offer. He remembers Guillén's father telling his son that it was his decision to make, but not to forget that the Dodgers were offering him twice the amount of money. The Astros signed the sixteen-year-old Guillén on September 19, 1992.

Guillén played in only 18 games in the Dominican Summer League in 1993 because of a shoulder injury and missed the entire 1994 season recovering. In 1995 an elbow problem limited him to only 30 games in the rookie Gulf Coast League. In 1996 Guillén hit .330 at Single-A Quad City and was selected to the Midwest League All-Star team, but his season ended after only 29 games after dislocating his shoulder. After four years, Guillén had played in only 77 games and still landed on the list of the top ten prospects in the organization. He was added to the Astros' 40-man roster. Andrés believed that Guillén was destined to be a shortstop, but he was the only person in the Houston organization who envisioned Guillén playing the position at the major league level. Although Andrés raved about most of the young men he signed, it was clear that Guillén was at the top of the list of his favorite players.

By 1993 I began to see the fruits of the academy when the Astros' Double-A affiliate Jackson, played in San Antonio only a short drive from my home. That year, first baseman Roberto Petagine was clearly the dominant player in the Texas League. He led the circuit in four offensive categories—batting average (.324), doubles (36), on-base percentage (.442), and walks (84)—and was named league MVP.

Also in 1993 Bob Abreu had an outstanding year at Osceola in the Florida State League, hitting .283 with a league leading 17 triples, and Hidalgo and Melvin Mora were selected to the South Atlantic League All-Star team. I looked forward to the possibility of seeing one of Andrés's prospects in a nearby ballpark on a regular basis.

In 1994 I accompanied Andrés to San Antonio to see the Jackson team and visit with Raúl Chávez and Bob Abreu. We met the two players at the team motel, and after a bit of small talk, Andrés got down to business. He asked Chávez about his transition to catcher, then turned to Abreu and inquired about his efforts to improve his outfield defense. Both young men were really interested and seemed to enjoy Andrés's company. They knew that he had always given them sound advice. Over the next few years I would often witness Andrés teaching and counseling young players, not in a heavy-handed or preachy style, but in a manner they found helpful. He asked both players what they were going to send their moms for Mother's Day only a few days ahead. Neither had anything in mind but promised to have something for Andrés to take back to Venezuela. The next day Chávez had written a note to his mother on one of his baseball caps and included a $5 check he got from a fan for hitting a home run (the only home run he hit in the 1994 season). Abreu still had nothing and Andrés suggested he send a photo. "Of me?" asked Abreu. "Not of me," responded Andrés.

"I hope the Astros don't expect all the Venezuelan players to be as good as the first group," Andrés told me. While the front office certainly did not expect a future major leaguer with every signing, they did come to rely on a regular supply of quality prospects from the Venezuelan pipeline. But Andrés believed that the Astros needed to invest more money into the Venezuelan program or risk losing their edge. "They will realize what a gold mine they have here when guys start getting to the major leagues," said Andrés, "but by then it may be too late."

On April 4, 1994, Petagine became the first academy alumni to reach the big leagues when he appeared in a game with the Astros. But it would be just one of eight games he ever played for the club, and he never even got a base hit with the Astros. After the 1994 season, Petagine was traded to the San Diego Padres in a twelve-player deal. My excitement of only the year before turned to disappointment. I had naively believed that I was going to see all of the players developed at the academy spend most of their careers with the Astros.

By 1995 Venezuela had become the new El Dorado in the search for baseball players, and the Astros were clearly in the forefront. Between 1989 and 1995 several hundred players were evaluated at the academy. Some spent over a year at Guacara, while others would show up for a tryout, demonstrate very few skills, and not be invited to return. Forty-three prospects were signed by Houston during those first six and one-half years, and sixteen eventually made it to the major leagues—an amazing 37 percent success rate. Nothing approaching that figure had ever been accomplished in baseball. Clearly the Astros' timing in entering the Venezuelan market in an organized, well-thought-out way could not have been better. During those early years with little competition, the Astros basically had the key to the candy store, and they signed most of the country's best players. Other major league organizations, however, in great part spurred on by the success of the Astros, began to increase the number of scouts they employed in Venezuela and to establish more academies. They also were handing out exorbitant bonuses. In 1994 the New York Yankees gave pitcher Tony Armas Jr. $125,000 to sign—three times the highest amount ever given in Venezuela. In 1996 the Yankees raised the bar by fifteen times when they gave a $1.6 million bonus to infielder Jackson Melián. Houston was now being challenged for supremacy in the market.

"Andrés Reiner and his staff have done such a tremendous job for us that they have put Venezuela at the top of many organizations' lists of where next to look for talent to play in the big leagues," Bob Watson, then Astros GM, told me in 1995. "The first three or four years we were out front by ourselves. Now the competition is really starting to pick up, but we are staying a couple of steps ahead of them because of planning."

But the Astros cut the budget of the Venezuelan program beginning in 1994, and Andrés believes the reductions set the academy program back at least two years and reduced his ability to recruit and train players. Not only was the facility at El Hatillo closed, but the staff at the academy had their salaries cut in half, the English classes were curtailed for two years, and Andrés even had to borrow money from Watson to make a crucial scouting trip to see Johán Santana.

But despite the increased competition and budget cutbacks, Andrés was able to sign four players over the next two years who made it to the major leagues, Santana, Félix Escalona, Donaldo Méndez and Wilfredo Rodríguez. Three of them, however, were taken in the Rule 5 draft and made their debuts with other teams; only Rodríguez played for the Astros. Clearly, as Watson had noted, other major league organizations were keeping an eye on the Astros.

Two more academy players reached the big leagues in 1996. On August 30, catcher Raúl Chávez made his major league debut with Montreal. After playing for six seasons in the Astros' minor league system, Chávez had been traded in late 1995 to the Expos. Two days later, on September 1, outfielder Bob Abreu appeared in his first major league game with Houston as a September call-up.

During 1997 four more academy alumni made their major league debuts. On May 21 right-handed Edgar Ramos, selected by Philadelphia in the Rule 5 draft in December 1996, pitched for the Phillies. Ramos appeared in four games, posted a 0-2 record and never played again in the big leagues. On September 1, Richard Hidalgo made his debut with the Astros. He was followed on September 7 by right-handed pitcher Oscar Henríquez and on September 16 by another academy product, Panamanian-born right-handed pitcher Manuel Barrios. That September experience was all either Henríquez or Barrios had with Houston: in December, both pitchers along with a player-to-be-named-later were traded to the Florida Marlins for outfielder Moisés Alou. Andrés was pleased that Houston was able acquire a high-value player for what would turn out to be two marginal pitchers.

On July 17, 1997, Andrés began a new role with the Astros when he was named special assistant to General Manager Gerry Hunsicker. While he would still be in charge of the academy, Andrés would also visit all of the Astros' minor league affiliates and evaluate players—not just those from Latin America—and report directly to the general manager. Because Andrés was going to be out of Venezuela for extended periods of time, he needed to find a capable person, someone who shared his vision and in whom he had complete trust, to run the day-to-day activities at the academy. He chose Pablo Torrealba.

"I saw Pablo working with an organization for young players when I went for a tryout in Barquisimeto. I knew by the way he was handling those kids that he has an enormous ability to teach. He is an extremely bright and intelligent man on and off the field," explained Andrés. He became more familiar with Torrealba when the former major league pitcher was the manager of the Magallanes team, loaded with Astros prospects, in the Liga de los Andes—the rookie or development league of Venezuelan professional baseball.

Torrealba, now in his early sixties, was signed by Atlanta in 1966 and after nine years in the minor leagues, made his big league debut with the Braves in 1975. He spent two seasons in Atlanta and played one year in Oakland before finishing his major league career with two seasons with the Chicago White Sox. He also played seventeen years with several teams in Venezuelan winter baseball.

He was hired as a pitching instructor for the academy in 1993 and slowly assumed more of an administrative role, which culminated in his becoming the coordinator of the facility in 1998. He is also an instructor and scouts on weekends. On my visits to the academy, Torrealba has often driven me around Valencia, and when I went to his hometown of Barquismeto, he gave me a tour of the city. In a country where almost everyone seems to have his foot stuck on the gas pedal, Torrealba drives very slowly. When I asked Rafael Cariel, a former teammate, about this, he replied half-jokingly, "That is exactly the way he pitched. Slow and deliberate and they were long games."

Torrealba is a low-key, very conscientious, no-nonsense kind of person. He does not say much, is always very pleasant, but is not afraid to be critical. He is a good administrator and clearly understands what Andrés wants to accomplish. The principle reason he enjoys working at the academy, he explained, is Andrés. Torrealba told me, "He is like my second father. He is honest and sincere, and that is difficult to find."

"People know about what we have done in Venezuela, and about the kids who have made it," explained Torrealba. "They know that we are responsible and that we are serious. And of course, that is the image we try to sell. We don't tell parents and players anything we can't do."

The fact that the Astros came into Venezuela in an organized fashion in 1989 and in just four years had several players in the pipeline to the major leagues helped to establish that image. The successful track record of the Astros' Venezuelan players advancing through the minor leagues became part of the Astros' mystique. Many organizations were signing players who had been developed at the academy but passed over by the Astros. Andrés believes this number may be as high as one hundred, and not all were solid prospects. A scout from an organization not deeply involved in Venezuela would often have an inflated impression of a player leaving the academy. "He might make a wrong projection because he thinks the kid is starting from zero," said Andrés.

The reputation of the Astros in Venezuela was also enhanced by the role the Houston prospects—among them Freddy García, Carlos Guillén, Melvin Mora, Richard Hidalgo, and Oscar Henríquez—played in the resurgence of the Magallanes team in the mid-1990s.

And it was the manner in which the Astros' front office treated Oscar Henríquez that really made the organization the talk of the baseball world in Venezuela. Henríquez, a 6-5, 220-pound right-handed pitcher, was discovered at the El Hatillo facility and signed by the Astros in May 1991. Henríquez's nickname is "Manacho," "Big Hands," which he explained came from a song popular when he was a child. Henríquez was a first baseman converted into a power pitcher at the academy. This was not an unusual occurrence. "None of my pitchers were pitchers," Andrés told me. "First you look for the size of the body, and then you see if there is an arm." Pitchers Edgar Ramos, Wilfredo Rodríguez, and Johán Santana also entered the academy as position players.

Henríquez pitched for two seasons in the Dominican Summer League and was 9-10 at the Astros' Class-A affiliate at Asheville in 1993. But at the end of the season, the Astros' staff noted a drop in his velocity from the high 90s to the low 80s, and some of the staff thought he had just lost his desire to pitch. He had not yet reached the bottom. When he could throw only in the 70s during the winter, Magallanes sent him to their team in the *liga paralela*.

In February 1994, Henríquez reported to the academy, but had nothing. He could barely touch 70 mph on the radar gun. Andrés and the staff wondered what had happened to the big strong kid they had signed.

"We thought it might be a problem with drugs or alcohol, but tests showed that wasn't the issue," Andrés explained. "We started to think it was something mental." Henríquez went to Kissimmee for spring training in March, and his physical exam turned up no problem. Yet he was exhausted by the slightest physical activity. Of even more concern was the fact that he could no longer speak clearly, and he'd lost his ability to grip a baseball, suck through a straw, or even take a bite of a sandwich. More blood tests were run, but nothing turned up. In April Henríquez collapsed and the Astros sent him to a hospital in Houston for ten days of extensive testing, and the source of his problems was discovered. Henríquez suffered from myasthenia gravis, a rare disorder that affects the nervous system and which was described to me by one doctor "like a car that has fuel injectors, and the fuel injectors are clogged." Once the condition was stabilized by medications, Henríquez underwent major surgery in July to remove his thymus gland. While doctors thought he would make a full recovery, his return to the baseball diamond was doubtful. He began a slow rehab involving a great deal of rest, exercising, and playing catch.

In February 1995 Henríquez began throwing at the academy, and within two months, his velocity was back in the high 90s. Now converted to a relief role, he posted a 3-4 record in the Florida State League. "It's a miracle that he was able to play last year," Andrés told me after the 1995 season. "He serves as an inspiration to younger players. And mentally he has changed. He's realized that this is a second chance that most people don't get."

I spoke with Henríquez by phone in late 1995 for a *USA Today Baseball Weekly* story on his miracle comeback while he was in Venezuela playing with Magallanes and getting ready for a game.[1] "I feel that I have been reborn and now I'm beginning a new life," he told me. "I want to work hard so I can get to the big leagues as quick as possible."

The tale of how the Astros gave an A-ball player the best medical care possible, while other organizations were releasing players with minor injuries was widely circulated in Venezuela and added greatly to the aura that the Astros had already begun to develop.

I wanted to understand how the Astros' scouts sold their product and to learn more about the hunt for players and the building of a network, so I arranged to accompany Rafael Cariel on one of his forays in eastern Venezuela and see for myself how scouting was done on the frontier of baseball.

6

On the Road to El Dorado

Scouting on the Frontier of Baseball

Rafael Cariel is an old-time scout, combing the countryside in search of prospects, romancing their families, and selling his team, the Houston Astros. Because he does not speak English nor travel to the United States, he is almost unknown to people in the front office in Houston. But Cariel has been crucial to the Astros' success in Venezuela. Originally hired as a scout to cover the eastern region of the country, he now supervises all scouting for the Astros in Venezuela. Cariel recently retired from his job at the university in Cumaná and moved to the academy in Guacara where he also works with catching prospects.

I arranged to go along on a scouting excursion with Cariel in eastern Venezuela in 1997 for an article for *USA Today Baseball Weekly*.[1] Cariel, now in his early fifties, is reserved, soft-spoken, and calm in his approach to his work. As I spent time with him, I came to appreciate his engaging personality, his subtle sense of humor, and his straightforward, honest manner of dealing with people. Cariel's success is due in no small part to his wonderful smile. He is also very thoughtful, treats everyone he meets with great respect, and is a very good judge of baseball talent.

"Mr. Reiner told me I could take a plane or ride on a burro, I just needed to bring him players," said Cariel when he greeted me at the airport near Puerto La Cruz. We got into his old VW Beetle, his preferred means of travel at the time. Cariel seldom flies and has never had to go by burro, although he does have to take a ferry to the tourist island of Margarita.

"*Vamos hacia el monte manaña*—We'll go to the countryside tomorrow—for a tryout. Today we'll check out some kids here in town." He cautioned me not to expect to find any ready-made players on our trip. "We are looking for rocks which may contain diamonds, other scouts look only for diamonds."

Fifteen minutes after I got off the plane, we were on our way to the ballpark to see a youth league game. We passed by the home of Jackson Melián, who in 1996 received a $1.6 million signing bonus from the New York Yankees.

"Here is Jackson Melián's house, do you want to take a picture?" asked Cariel. "I went to see him play four times. I talked to Jackson and to his parents. I went to the swimming pool where he worked out, and I even went to the beach to talk to his mom. I always had an open door with Jackson's family. I gave the information to Andrés, and I told him Jackson was going to cost a lot of money. Houston had all the information."

But clearly, Jackson Melián was already a diamond and not the kind of prospect the Astros would be signing. Melián had a showcase in Sarasota, Florida, agent Scott Boros got involved, and several organizations made offers. Cariel's scouting reports on Melián, however, were not wasted. Bob Watson, the Astros' GM in 1994 and 1995, who read Cariel's assessments of the young Venezuelan outfielder, was named GM of the Yankees in 1996.

Melián never developed his potential, and eight years after signing with the Yankees bounced between the minor league systems of several organizations and had played only a few games above the Double-A level. Tragically, both of Melián's parents died in a traffic accident in North Carolina in 1998 where they had gone to see him play. It is difficult to know what impact their deaths had on setting back his progress.

We went to see a couple of innings of a game composed of thirteen-and fourteen-year-olds at a stadium in Puerto La Cruz. There was no grass on the infield, and I was told that this was very common in this part of the country. The dirt infields and the erratic hops the ball takes off of them were given as reasons why Venezuela had produced so many outstanding shortstops—Aparicio, Carrasquel, Concepción, Guillén, Vizquel. As we watched, I was very impressed with the level of play. These kids start playing baseball—not T-ball—at age four, love the game, have a great support system in their families, and have great instincts—the result of playing year-round in less than luxurious conditions.

As Cariel watched the game, people came up and told him about players he should visit or the dates of upcoming tournaments. He jotted down the information. I was surprised that many of his contacts were women who are very involved in youth baseball throughout the country.

"I come out here and take notes, talk to the parents, give them my card, and I leave. I don't make a big show," explained Cariel as he wrote the name of a shortstop who made a great tag on a throw from the outfield. "At this age we don't even mention signing. But I continue to check them out as they get older."

I was witnessing Cariel develop and maintain his network of contacts. These were not bird dog scouts but simply coaches, or parents, or friends who kept him informed about players. This network, I would discover, was one of the pillars of Cariel's success, giving him an advantage over some of the competition.

Cariel is under no pressure to produce a large quantity of players, only to report on the prospects he sees. During his sixteen years on the job, he has sent fewer than fifty players to the academy, and one, Richard Hidalgo, evolved into a real gem. Two others, Edgar Ramos and Wilfredo Rodríguez pitched briefly in the big leagues, and a few more including Francisco Caraballo, Paul Estrada, and Levi Romero are still in the pipeline.

Extending from the border with Brazil to the Caribbean, Cariel's area encompasses almost one-third of Venezuela. It includes Angel Falls, the highest waterfall in the world, the large, modern industrial city Ciudad Guayana, the rich oil fields of the states of Anzoátegui and Monagas, and the enchanting Mochima National Park on the Caribbean coast.

"It is a beautiful area for the tourists, but I'm searching for players, not looking at the countryside," Cariel explained. "And it is not an easy area to cover."

His area also includes Margarita island, a major tourist destination and a two-hour boat ride from the mainland. On one of his trips there, Cariel was detained by the police for two hours because they were not quite sure what he planned to do with the radar gun he was carrying, his explanations about his job and the gun's purpose notwithstanding.

Passing slowly through small towns on the hour-long drive from Puerto La Cruz to Cariel's home in Cumaná, a number of drivers honked as he approached, and people on the street called out his name. Cariel responded with a nod or by yelling "¡*Epa*!" the most commonly heard greeting in Venezuela. By 1997 the competition for players was getting intense in Venezuela. Every organization had at least one full-time scout, and several had three or four. In fact some of those drivers greeting Cariel were scouts from the Dodgers and the Yankees.

"In the United States you go to colleges or high schools to look for players; here you have to go out into the countryside. You stay in lousy hotels. And you need to spend a lot of time with the families," said Cariel.

That same day, on our way into Cumaná in late afternoon, we passed by the home of Edgar Ramos. Ramos, a product of the Astros' academy and signed and developed by Houston, but selected by Philadelphia in the Rule 5 draft, had been sent back to the Astros only the day before. We pulled up to the Ramos home—a modest, small rural dwelling on the outskirts of town—and were greeted by Edgar's older sister. She said that Ramos had called and was angry about being sent down by the Phillies. I tried to explain—without much success—how the Rule 5 draft worked.

"I saw Edgar Ramos when he was thirteen. He was so skinny; he looked like a toothpick. I used to go watch him, but no other organization was interested in him," said Cariel. "I talked to him one time, and he said 'I don't want to talk to you.' I told him that I would respect his wishes, but that I was going to come out every time that he pitched, and that he had a very promising future."

"Well, Ramos was suspended from the league for the entire season for throwing his cap at his manager," said Cariel. Not able to play, Ramos went over the Astros' academy and eventually signed. As we drove away, Cariel turned to me and said, "When you see Edgar, ask him why he didn't want to talk to me."

The next morning before sunrise, Cariel put on his Astros cap and T-shirt and placed his radar gun, stopwatch, his book of contacts, and his notebook in the car. He carefully lifted and tied back the engine hood on his VW to prevent the motor from overheating. He didn't need a map. Even though we were not going very far or going to do very much, this was a very well-planned trip, and the preparation for it had begun eight years earlier. Cariel called ahead to set up a tryout and inquire about games being played. He knows he has to be flexible—someone might want to have coffee or have him over for dinner, and he usually complies, always keeping his agenda in mind. The night before he had showed me his book with his list of contacts. It contained hundreds of names of people throughout his area.

"When I started in 1989, I would go to these small towns, and I didn't know anybody. Now I have people all over who will call me when they see a kid." He reviews the information each year, adding new contacts and dropping a few names.

As we pulled onto the highway that would take us to the tryout at Caicara de Maturín, the sun was beginning to rise over Cumaná.

"People say this is where the sun is born," Cariel said. "It's not raining where we are going. When it rains up there, this river turns red with the mud." The winding road through the mountains passed by trees with seemingly endless shades of tropical green. Sugarcane fields dominated the valleys, while ripe mangos weighed down tree limbs, and harvested pineapples were piled high for sale by the roadside.

Cariel eats on the run. He alerted me that on our scouting trip we would not be dining in any restaurants. After driving for an hour and a half, we stopped in the small town of Guanaguana for beef stew and *arepa pelada*—a regional variation of Venezuela's corn-based staple that resembles a small thick tortilla—from a roadside stall, sat on some large boulders alongside the road, and had breakfast on a beautiful morning. Cariel asked me jokingly: "Do you think people from the front office in Houston would like this?" The total cost for the meal was about $1 U.S. for us both.

Later we would have coffee with a player's parents, eat mangos picked from a friend's tree, dine on *sancocho*—a tasty Venezuelan soup—at the home of another of his contacts, and end the day with clams and oysters on the half shell, fresh from the Gulf of Cariaco, again served from a roadside vendor. Cariel does have a favorite restaurant: a fast-food hamburger place in Puerto La Cruz—a holdover from his playing days in the United States.

Cariel knows his territory like the back of his hand—or the palm of his hand—the expression used in Venezuela. About an hour and a half from Cumaná, near the border of the states of Sucre and Monagas, we passed by a military base belonging to the Venezuela army special forces. "A few years ago, bandits used to block the road here and rob people," Cariel told me. Then he added that he didn't drive at night.

"You have to go to places that you think other scouts are not going to go. Some of these areas are so rugged you can't imagine anyone playing baseball, but they do. I had a tryout here one time," said Cariel pointing to small clearing, "The kid was about 6-6. When I came by I stopped and said to myself, 'I've got to check this guy out.' I did, but he didn't show me anything."

A player who did show something was Luis Yánez, and the story of his signing by the Astros has also become part of the mystique surrounding the organization in Venezuela.

"I have a friend in Puerto La Cruz who called and said, 'Rafael there is this kid you have to see. Luis Yánez.' I saw him when he was thirteen and took notes. I went to El Tigre to take a look at him. Luis played third base, but I knew that in Criollitos most kids also pitched. He did and threw 80 mph."

"When I met his family—his mom and dad, brother and sister—I never mentioned the word sign. They invited me to eat. I got along really well with them and I asked if other organizations had approached them. They said no that I was the first to come to their home. I asked if it was OK with them to keep up with Luis's progress and they said it was fine. I began to go to El Tigre a lot." How much is a lot? "I went about once a month, about thirty times in total. It is a four-hour drive from Cumaná each way."

Cariel kept sending his reports to Andrés, and Yánez began attending the Astros' academy for short periods to work on his mechanics. Eventually, Yánez was invited to the academy, and the Astros also paid his tuition so that he was able to complete high school.

"Now people were beginning to hear about Yánez. I went and spoke with the family and told Luis that we would like to sign him," Cariel told me. "I explained that with the Astros he would not only become a better ballplayer, but also a better person. His brother asked how much of a bonus the family should ask for. I told him, 'Ask what your conscience will let you, and what you think he deserves.' By this time several organizations had been to visit Yánez, including Los Angeles, Kansas City, Cleveland, Atlanta, Florida, and the Yankees. They had several other offers, all for more money than the Astros, but he signed with us," said Cariel.

Although Cariel never told me the amount the other organizations were willing to pony up, Atlanta reportedly offered $70,000 and the Astros signed Yánez for $34,000. "I think much of it was due to my relationship with the family, and the three years of driving over to El Tigre," Cariel added unpretentiously.

The tryout that Cariel arranged was in the municipal stadium in Caicara de Maturín, an agricultural town of about 18,000 people, and a three-hour drive from Cumaná. (There is another Caicara in Cariel's territory, Caicara del Orinoco, located further to the southwest on the Orinoco River.) As we approached the town, irrigated fields of tomatoes and tobacco drying sheds lined the road. We arrived at the house of Cariel's contact, John Fitzgerald Castro, an old friend from the university. Cariel visits Caicara de Maturín about three times a year, always stopping at Castro's house. Across the street lives Luis (I did not get his last name), who is the head of the local sports federation. Castro and Luis informed Cariel that he first needed to visit with a young man—one of the players going to the tryout—and his father. The dad believed his son was ready to go to the Astros' academy. We got in Luis's truck and drove to their house.

Cariel greeted the father and his son who appeared to be about fourteen-years-old. After a short discussion about the boy's education, Cariel suggested it would be a good idea to stay in school. A few chairs were set out in the street in front of the house. There was Cariel, the father, the kid, Luis, two other gentlemen, and me. They talked about the price of tomatoes and the upcoming governor's election. I listened. At first, little was said about baseball.

Cariel spoke very deliberately, having thought through exactly what he wanted to say. "I come by to look at the progress of these kids, not to sign them when they are this young," Cariel explained to the father. And then he put it in terms clearly understood by people in this rural community. "If you had a farm raising chickens, you would go by from time to time to see if they were getting bigger, right?" The father nodded in agreement. When we were ready to leave for the tryout, the father insisted we wait; they were preparing coffee for us. As Cariel had told me earlier; "You often have to stay longer than you planned."

There were about ten young men ranging in age from thirteen to seventeen milling around the field at the municipal baseball stadium for the tryout.

"I pick three or four players, and then I ask the local manager to pick another three because I like to work in groups of six or seven," said Cariel. "In addition to looking at the kids you have to work with them on instruction, as a way of giving something to the manager. I look at the velocity, arm strength, and hitting. I evaluate the kids on their skill level for their age. More than anything else I'm looking to see if he has a good body," said Cariel. He had them throw from the outfield, throw from the mound, and run. He never used his radar gun, and I don't think he ever took out his stopwatch. "I took notes," Cariel told me later. "Sometimes people think a player is a prospect because he is the best in the town. But often he is not good enough to even think about taking him to the academy."

It was clear that the tryout was not so much an event in itself but just an extension of the prior contacts Cariel had made. "Giving instruction to the players, having lunch with people who tell you about players, and talking to the families, all of this is very important. And it's all a part of the tryout."

Cariel had signed a player, Gabriel Rondón, from a tryout in Caicara two years earlier in May 1995. Less than a year after signing, Rondón had an off-the-field incident in the Dominican Republic and was released. He was then signed by the Mets and played for a couple of years in the minor leagues. I asked a couple of people how the townsfolk felt about Rondón. Were they upset with the Astros for releasing him? "No, we were angry with him because he was at fault," one man responded, and then using a very Venezuelan expression said, "*Botó la vaina*—He threw away his chance."

On the way back to Cumaná we went to San Antonio de Maturín to see a few innings of a game of thirteen-and fourteen-year-olds, and as often occurs, parents convinced that their sons were ready to sign besieged Cariel. "When I first started, some parents didn't want their boys to play professional baseball, but that has changed," Cariel explained. "Now in Venezuela, it is the deer who is hunting the tiger."

There were probably over 200 people in the covered grandstands (almost all stadiums are covered in these small towns because of the intense tropical sun). The first thing I noticed was that there were two guys in the stands with microphones doing a play-by-play of the game. They sounded really professional, but they were not. "The first pitch is a strike. Well it seems the umpire has called it a ball, but it looked like a strike to me," one of them said. They spotted Cariel and announced his presence, which caused every kid coming to bat after that to glance up at him.

Cariel noticed a couple of players—one showed good speed on a run to first, the other was big and had power. A man came by to tell him about a right-handed hitter with power, another gentleman approached and said, "I think my kid is just about ready to sign." Yet another parent told him other scouts, including those from Florida, St. Louis, the Dodgers, and Yankees, wanted to sign his kid. Cariel didn't comment. He just nodded and asked how the family was. He then turned to me and said, "When I'm ready to talk seriously about these players, I will."

We got back in the car and headed for Cumaná. The scouting trip was nearly over. No prospect had been signed and no player had been asked to come to the academy. I'm not sure precisely what I expected when I planned the trip, but what I got was an insight to scouting on the frontier of baseball. I caught a glimpse of Cariel's vast network of contacts and gained a better understanding of how he did his job. My two days with Cariel had a nostalgic quality. What we saw was reminiscent of the old-time scouting in the United States in the days before the free-agent draft. It was, in fact, more akin to recruiting top high-school football prospects in United States.

Although they are from vastly different social backgrounds, Cariel and Andrés are very similar in style. Both are honest, patient, and very good judges of talent. Cariel explained that it wasn't so much that Andrés taught him to be a good scout but that he had learned from observing the way Andrés went about his business.

"Andrés talks with the players as if they were his own kids," explained Cariel. "I love to go out scouting with him because I always learn something, and because it gives me more confidence in the work that I do. I always tell the truth. I tell the parents that their son will develop as a player in the academy and that the Astros' organization will take care of their son. And I tell them that if they decide to sign with another organization, that is their decision." I mentioned that he seemed very dedicated to the Astros. "Not the Astros," said Cariel. "It is a dedication to Andrés Reiner."

While we waited for my plane at the Cumaná airport, I glanced at my watch and realized that we had been watching or talking baseball from 5:40 a.m. until 10:45 p.m. I asked Cariel if he was tired. "No," he said. "We really didn't do very much today. If you didn't have a plane to catch, I would have checked out three more games."

I went on a scouting trip with Cariel again in the summer of 2001 in the state of Bolívar, Venezuela's richest and largest, extending from the Orinoco River south to the border with Brazil. While Venezuela's economy is based upon petroleum, the country also has extensive reserves of coal, iron ore, bauxite, diamonds, and gold, most of which are found in the state of Bolívar. The state's natural resources (excluding petroleum) are under the control of the Comisión Venezolana de Guayana (CVG), a government agency created in 1960. In addition, the CVG produces electricity and is also involved in promoting economic development and sporting events in the region.

Cariel is a frequent visitor to the major urban centers of Ciudad Bolívar (population 300,000) and Cuidad Guayana (population 1 million), where there is a great deal of baseball talent, but he seldom travels farther to the south on the highway that runs the several hundred miles through the Gran Sabana to Brazil. Here on the road to the gold mining community of El Dorado in the towns of Upata, Guasipati, and El Callao, the best athletes are drawn to soccer. Miguel Chacoa, an associate scout for the Astros, visits these towns to make sure that no talented athlete that might be converted into a baseball player escapes evaluation, and he also has established a large network of contacts and expanded Cariel's web in eastern Venezuela.

I had been to the state of Bolívar twice before. In May 1990 I went to Ciudad Guayana to write an article on catcher Carlos Hernández who played with the Los Angeles Dodgers at that time and later in the World Series with the San Diego Padres in 1998.[2]

In November 2000 I returned to Ciudad Guayana with the Magallanes ball club for a "home" game against Pastora at Estadio La Ceiba. Even though the city has no professional baseball team, the 28,000-seat facility is the largest baseball stadium in Venezuela. The view from the stadium press box is impressive. In the distance, ocean-going cargo ships can been seen on the Orinoco River, still three miles wide more than 100 miles from the Atlantic Ocean. Alongside the stadium runs another one of Venezuela's largest rivers, the Caroní.[3]

"You have Three Rivers Stadium in the United States, we call this "Two Rivers Stadium," said Damián Prat jokingly. Prat is sports editor of the region's largest newspaper, *Correo de Caroní*, and a longtime supporter of the stadium.

"In the beginning it was a much bigger project. It started in the time of Venezuela Saudita," said Prat, a reference to a period in Venezuela in the mid-1970s when there were few limits to the imagination of planners in the oil-rich country. The main source of financial support for Estadio La Ceiba came from the CVG.

"The original idea was to have a hotel, shopping center, and other sports facilities in addition to the baseball stadium," explained Prat. The project was put on hold in the mid-1980s due to the downturn in petroleum prices. When it was revived in the early 1990s, it was greatly scaled down with only the baseball stadium remaining. In 2000 the stadium had yet to be completed. There were no seats, only concrete bleachers, and the press box remained open to the extremely hot temperatures. But even as a work in progress, Estadio La Ceiba, with its carefully manicured grass and covered grandstands from foul pole to foul pole, was a beautiful park and, when seats are installed, will be the most modern baseball facility in Latin America.

Stadium promoters are hopeful that the large crowds that have turned out for regular-season Venezuelan League games—the 28,000 fans that attended the inaugural game in 1999 is still the largest crowd in league history—will make the venue attractive for an expansion team.

The Liga Venezolana de Béisbol Profesional expanded to eight teams in 1992 and was exploring the possibility of adding two more teams for the 2007–8 season. Three cities, San Cristóbal on the border with Colombia, Porlamar on Isla de Margarita, and Ciudad Guayana, were competing for the two new franchises. No one is more anxious to have a team locate in Ciudad Guayana than the fans of the region that turn out in droves to Estadio La Ceiba, especially when Magallanes is playing.

I accompanied the Magallanes ball club on a commercial flight from Valencia to Ciudad Guayana for the game against Pastora. This is one of the very few times during the year the team will travel by plane. Even though Magallanes plays thirty games of its 62-game schedule in its home stadium in Valencia, the entire season is like an extended road trip. The team usually travels in a modern Volvo luxury bus; the shortest trip is less than an hour to Maracay to face Aragua, the longest an eight-hour journey to Puerto La Cruz to play the Caribes. Although almost all of the Magallanes players have spent time in the minor leagues, few have had to travel nearly every day. And for all the hours they spend on the road, the team seldom stays in hotels, returning home after all road games except those in Puerto La Cruz, Maracaibo, and Ciudad Guayana.

At Estadio La Ceiba, my friend Giner García asked me to join the Pastora radio broadcast crew for a couple of innings to talk about Venezuelan baseball. In the booth were the announcer, a color commentator, García, who handles statistics, and a person who interjected commercials. To accommodate me, the commercial man—after explaining that my presence was made possible by Pepsi Cola and I believe an auto repair shop back in Pastora's hometown of Acarigua—handed me his headset for a couple of innings. I'm not sure how many fans were listening to our comments, but I had a great time.

In the top of the fourth inning with Pastora's Marcos Scutaro on second, slugger Alex Cabrera at the plate, and Magallanes pitcher Mark Guerra about to toe the pitching mound, the park was plunged into total darkness. There was not a single light in the stadium, not on the field, in the clubhouses, or in the press box. Almost all of the 12,000 disappointed fans, the vast majority Magallanes supporters, waited patiently for well over an hour for the game to resume before they slowly began to file out into the darkness. Two hours after the blackout began, the game was called. (The two teams returned almost a month later to complete the contest.) Players struggled to change out of their uniforms in the clubhouses where the only light was provided by the luminous glow of their wristwatches. And then the irony began to sink in: hydroelectric projects on the nearby Caroní River produce 70 percent of Venezuela's electricity.

In July 2001 at the tryout in the main baseball stadium in Ciudad Bolívar, Cariel aided by Miguel Chacoa took down the names of the five players they wanted to check out and jotted down their ages, height, weight, and position. Cariel kept a copy of the form for his records and sent one to the Astros' academy. Both scouts pulled out their stopwatches and timed the five would-be prospects running sixty yards. Then Cariel focused his attention on one of the two catchers. "Miguel says he is a good hitter but he does not have a position. We are trying to find him a position," Cariel told me. "Find him a position" was a phrase that I had heard on almost every scouting trip during the previous decade. When a scout sees a player with a skill or attribute—speed, size, power, a strong arm—but really not suited for the position he is currently playing, he envisions him at another position that closer matches his talents.

After an hour or so, the two scouts finished their observations for the day. Cariel then took the rake used to maintain the area around home plate and smoothed out the dirt disturbed by the players. He left the field as he found it so that the groundskeeper would not have any extra work. It was a touch of class by Cariel, a reflection of his working-class background, and part of the reason he has been successful.

The next day, Cariel, Chacoa, and I drove to the Guri Dam—the world's second largest at the time. The hour-long journey took us through terrain dominated by red dirt and scrub brush—what I imagined the middle of Australia to look like. Cariel wanted to see a few players who were the children of the *damnificados* (victims) of the 1999 floods that devastated Venezuela's coastal region near the international airport at Maiquetía, leaving thousands dead and tens of thousands homeless. Approximately two thousand people had been resettled in apartments located inside the grounds of the Guri Dam complex.

The tryout itself was rather perfunctory, and neither Cariel nor Chacoa saw any player they considered worth pursuing. But for both scouts, it was essential to comb these remote places. This was the first filter of the fine-tuned Astros scouting machine in Venezuela. The next day Cariel returned to Cumaná, and I headed to the Astros' academy. As we parted, he gave me a good-natured hard time about staying only for two days with him in the state of Bolívar.

"Milton, if you had more time we could go on a 'real' scouting trip over to Guasipati and El Callao." He was kidding of course, but I would still love to accompany Cariel on the road to El Dorado.

By early 1997 when Gerry Hunsicker was beginning his second year as the Astros GM, he felt the Astros were becoming the victim of their own success. With the increasing number of major league organizations operating in Venezuela, and the escalation of signing bonuses, he was not sure how long the Astros could complete. But he believed in the academy and in Andrés, and he increased the budget for the program. That same year, the Venezuelan Summer League, which Andrés had fought to establish for over five years, began to operate. And in the spring of 1997, *Baseball America* rated Richard Hidalgo, Carlos Guillén, and Bob Abreu as the top three prospects in the Astros' organization.

"We essentially get another first-round draft pick each year out of the Venezuelan program," David Rawnsley told me. And at bargain-basement prices, he might have added. The highest bonus paid by the Astros in Venezuela during the first seven years of the academy was $34,000.

While the Astros were producing quality players, they were leaving the Houston organization almost as fast as they arrived.

Bob Abreu played in only 74 games with the Astros in the 1996 and 1997 seasons before being left unprotected in the expansion draft for players for the new Arizona and Tampa Bay franchises. Abreu was selected by Tampa Bay and immediately traded to Philadelphia. On September 6, 1998, Carlos Guillén made his debut with Seattle. He, along with right-hander Freddy García (he would debut with Seattle in April 1999), had been traded to the Mariners in August 1998 for Randy Johnson in a move that help take the Astros to the post-season that year. While it was clearly pleasing to Andrés to see his players advanced, he had mixed emotions because they were not playing with Houston. When Hunsicker informed him of the Guillén and García trade, Andrés said, "You can't ask me to be happy. One of my eyes was smiling, one of my eyes was crying," as reported by Paul White in *USA Today Sports Weekly*.[4]

By late 1999 the Astros had also traded Manuel Barrios, Raúl Chávez, Oscar Henríquez, and Roberto Petagine and lost Edgar Ramos and Alejandro Freire in the Rule 5 draft and Melvin Mora to six-year free agency. All eventually played in the major leagues.

I'd been writing about the academy and the Astros' prospects for *Baseball America*, *USA Today Baseball Weekly*, and the *Astros Magazine* since 1990, and I had almost come to expect that the young men I had interviewed were developing into major league stars. But it was not until I saw the faces of Bob Abreu, Richard Hidalgo, or Freddy

García on Pepsi Cola bottles and in television commercials in Venezuela that I began to truly understand how important these players had become in their home country. Venezuelan fans were not only following the progress of the Astros' prospects in the minor leagues, they watched them play during the winter and wondered why Houston was so quick to part with *criollos*. The Venezuelan media used a word in Spanish that I was unfamiliar with to describe what had happened to the academy products, *despilfarrados* (squandered).

It was against this background that Andrés advised Gerry Hunsicker, "We can't afford to lose Richard Hidalgo. You will never be able to convince anyone in Venezuela that he should not be in the big leagues."

7

A Dream Come True

Ten Years at the Academy

With the main playing field manicured and a fresh coat of paint on the clubhouse, the Academia de Béisbol de los Astros de Houston had never looked better than it did at the end of November 1999. Several hundred invited guests, including Astros General Manager Gerry Hunsicker, Assistant GM Tim Purpura and Director of Scouting David Lakey, along with executives from the Magallanes club and Industrias Venoco, were there to celebrate the tenth anniversary of the complex, and to recognize Andrés's accomplishments that helped put Venezuelan baseball in the international spotlight. They were joined by the Astros Venezuelan staff and their families, about thirty players under contract to the Astros, six alumni who had gone on to play in the major leagues, and dozens of youngsters in full baseball uniforms.

Just before the afternoon ceremony began, a couple of academy graduates addressed small groups of Astros' prospects and youth league players sitting in the outfield. Melvin Mora was back in his home country for the first time as a major leaguer, and he was the most popular player in Venezuela that winter after his terrific postseason with the New York Mets. Mora explained how persistent he had been to get to the big leagues. He even had to go to Taiwan, he told them, to accomplish his goal.

"Discipline is the key to the game," Mora, proudly wearing his Mets cap, told the young players. "Don't think playing baseball is easy. Listen to the coaches, work hard, and be disciplined. Just as we represent Venezuela, you will also represent our country."

The "we" Mora was referring to was Richard Hidalgo. "Discipline is the most important thing. We had to work hard to get to where we are now," said Hidalgo. And not one for long-winded speeches, Hidalgo ended with, "I agree with what Melvin said."

"Who's he?" asked television announcer Joe Morgan when Melvin Mora came to bat for the New York Mets during the 1999 National League Championship Series. Over the course of the regular season, his first in the big leagues, Mora's performance was not much to write home about. He had only 5 hits—all singles—in 31 at bats for a .161 average. But in the playoffs, Mora lit it up, hitting .429 with 6 hits in 14 at bats.

"I first saw Melvin playing on the Venezuelan junior team in a tournament in Cuba in 1991," said Andrés. "When I got back from Cuba, I told Aristimuño to go find him. He told me that Melvin had been at the academy the day before wanting us to check him out." Within a week, Mora was signed by the Astros.

The very personable and outgoing Mora had been both a boxer and a professional soccer player before pursuing his baseball career. Quietly and without much fanfare, Mora managed to work his way steadily through the Astros' minor league system, although Andrés had to intercede with GM Wood to keep Mora from being released after his initial season in the Dominican Summer League in 1991. By 1993 Mora, after a bit of prodding by Andrés, began to play at second and third base as well as in the outfield. He had made himself into a multiple utility player and increased his chances of reaching the major leagues.

"Mora is essentially a center fielder, and an excellent defensive outfielder, but in our organization he will be the kind of player like César Tovar was in his time," Andrés told me in the summer of 1993. "Melvin can play all nine positions. He can play anywhere in the outfield. He is pretty good at second base and third base. He could play shortstop if you needed him to, and he would do the job. He caught for us. We even used him once as a relief pitcher in a game and he got the last two outs."

Mora began to blossom in 1993 when he hit .285 at Class-A Asheville. In 1994 he was promoted to Osceola in the Florida State League and hit .282. In 1995 he made the jump to Double-A Jackson where he hit .298 and was third in the Houston organization in doubles with 32 and tied for fourth in steals with 22. Mora split the 1996 season between Double-A and Triple-A and had a combined .284 average. In 1997 he spent the entire season at the Astros' Triple-A affiliate in New Orleans and had a .257 average.

At the end of the 1997 season, Mora became a six-year free agent and thus able to sign with any organization. Astros director of player development Jim Duquette told Andrés that the first player he would sign in the off-season would be Mora. But in October 1997 Duquette took a job with the New York Mets, and Mora did not have an Astros contract.

That's when Mora's road to the major leagues took a detour through Taiwan.

"I'm the one who encouraged him to go there," Andrés said. During the winter of 1997–98, a scout for the Mercury Tigers of the Chinese Professional Baseball League saw Andrés with a radar gun at a game in Venezuela and asked about Mora. Andrés explained that he was a very solid player and could play three infield positions in addition to the outfield. The scout's jaw almost dropped, and he offered Mora $80,000 a year to play in Taiwan. Andrés told Mora that if he went to Taiwan and played for three years, he would be financially set for life. Mora wasn't convinced. He had been offered a minor league contract with the Montreal Expos and an invitation to spring training with the major league club. Andrés knew the odds of a six-year free agent making it to the big leagues were not good and told Mora that after spring training he was likely going to be assigned to Triple-A or maybe even Double-A.

"Mr. Reiner, you gave up on me," said a disheartened Mora, explaining that while he appreciated Andrés's efforts he was of course disappointed that his dream of playing in the major leagues was probably coming to an end.

"When you are twenty-five, you can't be dreaming," Andrés told him. "You need to think about your family."

So Melvin packed his bags and headed for Taiwan. During the

first two months of the season, he had a .335 batting average with 37 stolen bases. But he didn't like the way players were treated and was especially concerned about the gambling elements attempting to fix the outcomes of games. In July 1998 Mora left Taiwan and the remainder of his $80,000 contract behind. He was still dreaming about playing in the major leagues.

He returned to Kissimmee, Florida, worked out in the afternoons with his longtime friend Manny Acta (who was at the time the manager of the Astros' Kissimmee team in the Florida State League), and tried to find an organization interested in him. But it was now July, and most teams were not looking to sign free agents. He went to the Astros, but the organization could only offer him a slot on the A-ball team. Andrés suggested Mora call Jim Duquette, then in his first year as director of player personnel with the New York Mets. Mora did, was signed by the Mets as a minor league free agent on July 25, 1998, and spent a less than a month at Class-A Port St. Lucie before being promoted to Triple-A Norfolk. In 1999 Mora started in Triple-A, was promoted to the Mets and made his major league debut starting at shortstop on May 30.

In 2000 Mora was traded to the Baltimore Orioles, where he became not only an everyday player but a star. He was selected to the American League All-Star Team in 2003 and 2005. And he was still Mr. Utility. In the 2000 season with the Orioles, Mora played exclusively at shortstop. In 2001 he spent most of his playing time in center field. By 2004 he had become the Orioles regular third baseman, earned the American League Silver Slugger Award for the top offensive player in the league at his position, and his .340 batting average was the highest in the history of the Baltimore organization. Mora's versatility, hard work, and determination had finally paid off.

"Melvin Mora," Andrés said, "should serve as an example for all Venezuelan baseball players because he has had to struggle so much."

In preparation for the November 1999 ceremony, the Astros' staff assembled a small exhibit of photos and newspaper clips of some of the alumni who had made it to the major leagues, including Bob

Abreu, Richard Hidalgo, Freddy García, Melvin Mora, and Magglio Ordóñez. Although Ordóñez never signed with the Astros, the instructors who trained him view Magglio as a product of the academy. More important, so does Ordóñez.

As a youngster, Ordóñez played in the streets and sandlots of his hometown of Coro, Venezuela, about four hours by road west of Valencia. He imagined he was Tony Armas hitting home runs and David Concepción making outstanding plays at shortstop. In the summer of 1990, Andrés and Aristimuño saw the sixteen-year-old Ordóñez playing in a tournament held in Coro and invited him to the academy.

Andrés wrote a scouting report on Ordóñez when he arrived there in August 1990 and projected him as above average—six on a scale of eight—in hitting ability, running speed, arm strength, and arm accuracy, with good work habits and dedication. And Ordóñez improved during his eight-month stay with the Astros.

Andrés really wanted to sign Ordóñez but was vetoed by his supervisor Julio Linares and scouting director Dan O'Brien. Neither saw the outfielder as a prospect. I asked O'Brien almost fifteen years later about passing on Ordóñez. "An honest response: I don't remember the details. But I assume there were unflattering or conflicting reports on him. But it could be we just made a mistake."

When Andrés realized that he was not going to be able to sign Ordóñez, he arranged for him to tryout with the New York Yankees. Unfortunately, the Yankees scout did not show up. Andrés then called the White Sox scout Alberto Rondón, who took a look at Magglio, liked what he saw and called Andrés and asked, "Why won't you sign him; is he doing drugs?" Andrés replied, "No, Magglio is not doing drugs, I just can't sign him, and this is a gift for you."

"When I was fifteen years old, Andrés Reiner . . . told me that he wanted to sign me," Ordóñez told a Caracas newspaper in 1998. "So I gave up high school and went to the academy. For some reason, they kept me in the academy for almost a year without telling me anything about my future." Or so it seemed like a year for Ordóñez. His scouting report is dated August 23, 1990, and he signed with the White Sox on May 18, 1991, about eight months in actuality.

"I was there for a year and *me hiceron pelotero* (they made me a player)," Ordóñez told me in 2001. "Mr. Reiner always treated me well. I know he didn't make the decision not to sign me. If they had me there for a year, it was for a reason," explained Ordóñez. "They knew that I had potential, but maybe the scouts who came from Houston to look at me didn't see it. But this is part of the game, part of life. Now I'm here. Maybe if I had signed with the Astros, I wouldn't have had the opportunity I've had here. You never know."

But the Astros were not the only major league organization to make a mistake about the potential of the outfielder. Twice when Ordóñez was in the minor leagues, he was left unprotected by the White Sox in the annual Rule 5 draft, but no team, including the Astros, picked him. And each time he was available, Andrés recommended that the Astros select him in the draft or acquire him in a trade.

At the late afternoon ceremony, at a podium set up on the pitcher's mound, Hunsicker was the first to speak to the guests assembled behind home plate.

"This is a very special day for a lot of people," said Hunsicker. "Ten years ago Andrés Reiner had a vision to create a baseball academy in Venezuela, and he convinced Bill Wood to take the risk. Many people working in baseball then did not think it would work. But ten years later, everyone recognizes the Astros as the leader in developing players in Venezuela. I want to thank Venoco, Andrés Reiner, and the Houston Astros front office back then for having developed a partnership that has been so successful. This program has been very important to the success of the Houston Astros, especially over the last four years. Without this program we would not have won three championships."

Then it was Andrés's turn.

"I thank God that I could realize my dream, and I want to thank all of the people who helped me," opened Andrés. He then introduced and expressed his appreciation to each member of his staff.

"More than just the Astros players, I think about all of the Venezuelan youngsters who have had a chance to be successful thanks to the accomplishments of some of the young men who have passed through the Astros' academy," said Andrés.

Then six of the ten players signed by Andrés who had reached the major leagues—Raul Chávez, Carlos Guillén, Carlos Hernández (the infielder), Richard Hidalgo, Melvin Mora, and Edgar Ramos—each spoke for a few minutes. I was impressed not only that these young men had been successful in baseball but also that they could get up in front of a microphone, clearly articulate their thoughts, and say something heartfelt.

Before the festivities began, the Astros' prospects, most of whom were playing in the *liga paralela* went through their normal morning workout. I stood behind the backstop of the main field with Hunsicker and Rafael Cariel during a drill for catchers. There were four catchers under contract to the Astros—Reinaldo Ruiz, nineteen; Germán Meléndez, eighteen; Oscar Alvarado, nineteen; and Héctor Giménez, seventeen. Another, Angel Valladares, sixteen, wore a red and white uniform, which clearly distinguished him as an unsigned player.

After ten years of signing the best athletes available, Andrés began to be much more selective about the players that he took to the academy. The Astros organization needed catchers and power pitchers, so that became the main scouting focus.

"We are very pleased with the young catching prospects down here," said Hunsicker. "I really believe that in the next four or five years, we are going to have a quality major league catcher come out of this academy."

"This kid has an outstanding arm," said Hunsicker, pointing to Valladares, who had just made a throw to second base. "The ball just exploded out of his hand. He gets your attention right away. If he were eighteen years old and eligible for the draft, you would have to consider him for the first round."

Less than a week later, Valladares was signed and given a bonus of $35,000, certainly not first-round money.

I walked over to watch the pitchers work out and ran into Miguel Chacoa, the Astros' associate scout living in Ciudad Bolívar. Sometimes called part-time scouts or bird dogs, associate scouts do not receive a salary but are paid when Houston signs a player they recommend. Chacoa introduced me to Romelio López, a player he discovered and recommended to the Astros. The 6-4, 230-pound and still growing López, a right-handed pitcher and former outfielder, had just turned sixteen and had spent more than a year at the academy.

At the time, I thought the Astros were on the verge of signing López. Cariel had visited the family in Ciudad Piar, about sixty miles south of Ciudad Bolívar. In summer of 1998, Andrés went to Ciudad Bolívar to meet the young man's parents, explain what the Astros could offer, and invite their son, who was about six months shy of his fifteenth birthday, to Guacara. After the family considered the proposal for a week, they gave their permission. For Romelio's father, an engineer on the trains taking the iron ore from the mines that dominate the area, his son was his family's ticket out of Ciudad Piar. Andrés would make several more visits during the next year and a half to speak with the family and discuss their son's future.

How good was López?

"After a year at the academy, he was throwing 92 mph. He was only sixteen years old, and there was really good projection," Andrés explained. Andrés believed López was really special and worth—by Astros standards—a large bonus. I asked if he was thinking in the $200,000 signing-bonus range? "$200,000 to $300,000 for me," said Andrés.

"Romelio went back home during the Christmas break in 1999 when the academy was closed. That's when the problem started and I really gave up," said Andrés. The problem was that an agent had entered the picture and there was talk of a $2 million bonus—ten times more than the Astros were thinking. Not only was the money astronomical and out of the question for the Astros, but Andrés was just not interested in giving such a high bonus to a sixteen-year-old who had not faced serious competition.

Steve Fainaru, writing in the *Washington Post,* claims the Astros told López that he could finish high school at Guacara by studying after the workouts. The young pitcher did not complete his studies—and he blames it on the Astros. López told the *Washington Post* that studying was almost impossible because he was so tired.[1]

Andrés had a different take on Romelio López and school.

"We were paying for his school, and he was going at night," Andrés told me. "He was not a very bright student. In fact, in two years he only completed one year, and finally he gave up. He said that he didn't want to go to class anymore."

López's parents, the *Washington Post* reported, believed the Astros were hiding their son from other teams. Hiding may not be the correct word, but the Astros certainly used the closed nature of the complex to work with players without having other teams watch, and there were no MLB regulations preventing them from having a fifteen-year-old there and keeping him for a extended period.

At the academy, López developed into a solid prospect. His father said he received calls from other teams, among them the New York Yankees, Atlanta, and Texas, wanting to hold tryouts. The *Washington Post* claimed that one was held in spring 1999, while Romelio was at home and that the tryout, "provoked Reiner to sever all ties with López." Reiner, the *Washington Post* reported, thought an agent had influenced López's parents to ask for more money, and Reiner is quoted as commenting, "So I told them, 'Fine, go find the market.'"

I have no doubt that Andrés told the López family to seek their son's value on the market, but that did not occur in the spring of 1999 but a year later in early 2000, after an agent had been involved. Andrés told me he believed it was the mother who made the decision not to stay with the Astros. "I want to get as much money as possible, and I know that is not going to come from you," she told him. In any event, by the end of 1999 the Astros were no longer in the market to sign Romelio López.

But by 2000 bonus expectations had gone through the roof in Venezuela in large part due to the presence of agents, who would now become regular fixtures. Also in 2000 Major League Baseball, in an attempt to "level the playing field" for all clubs extended the rule covering academies in the Dominican Republic to Venezuela. Baseball organizations operating in Venezuela would have an exclusive look at a player for thirty days only (the same rule had been in effect in the Dominican Republic for almost two decades), after which a player had to be signed or leave the academy. Because of this rule and the fact that a young man was required to be at least sixteen years old to sign, no longer would the academy be able to develop fourteen-and fifteen-year-old players. Thirty days is not much time to establish a track record. Or as Andrés put it, "In thirty days you can't decide to sign a player, you can only decide not to sign him." With less time to evaluate and develop a player, scouts had to begin to sign on tools alone—or long-term projection—and this allowed those with big pockets to take more chances, and the New York Yankees hardly needed a level playing field.

"The team has trained dozens of fourteen- and fifteen-year-old 'invitees' at the club's facility in Guacara—some for as long as two years. The practice allowed the Astros to circumvent rules that prohibit teams from signing players under sixteen," reported the *Washington Post*. But there was no need for the Astros to circumvent any rules or regulations, because there were none prohibiting any organization from having players younger than sixteen years old at the academy or keeping them for an extended period of time.

While many are aghast at the idea of players under sixteen years of age working out at the Astros' academy, few see anything wrong with families relocating throughout the United States to give their preteens a shot at a career in tennis or a slot on the Olympic swim team—sports that require many hours of practice each day. And if it was explained to parents in Venezuela that their son would be fed, housed, presented with an opportunity to attend school, and taught a marketable skill, most would not turn down that offer. When the MLB rules changed in 2000, Andrés and the Astros adjusted the way the academy operated to comply with the new reality.

Prior to 1985, MLB teams were in fact recruiting players in Latin America much younger than sixteen years old. In February 1984 the Toronto Blue Jays signed thirteen-year-old Jimy Kelly, making the Dominican shortstop the youngest player to ever sign with a major league organization. The Blue Jays were not anxious to give a contract to the barely teenaged Kelly—they wanted to keep him at their Dominican academy and let him mature and develop as a player. "But it got to the point where too many other clubs were trying to sign him so we had to," said then Blue Jays minor league director Gord Ash.[2]

While Kelly never made it to the major leagues, in December 1984 MLB prohibited the signing of players under age sixteen, which became known in the industry as the "Jimy Kelly Rule."[3]

"His signing will be a landmark in Latin American baseball if only for the termination of child labour," wrote Gare Joyce, in *The Only Ticket Off the Island*.[4]

I first saw Jimy Kelly in the Toronto Blue Jays major league clubhouse during spring training in 1988. The seventeen-year-old baby-faced Kelly was sitting alongside veterans George Bell, Tony Fernández, Manny Lee, and Nelson Liriano. Kelly was on the Blue Jays 40-man roster and beginning his fourth season in professional baseball, but he looked like he was in junior high school. My interview with Kelly did not reveal much, but I came away with the feeling that he would never really recover from being thrust into the professional game at such an early age. Kelly was released by the Blue Jays a couple of years later and played a year or so in Cleveland's minor league system. He was out of baseball altogether while still a teenager.

Before Jimy Kelly, the previous youngest MLB signing was fourteen-year-old Puerto Rican Jorge Lebrón in 1974. I remember Rubén Amaro telling me of his concern that Andrés had fourteen- and fifteen-year-old players at the Astros' Venezuelan academy. Because the practice was not prohibited and because Andrés was not signing the players until they turned sixteen, I told Amaro I didn't see it as a problem. But Amaro's perception was indelibly marked by his previous experience with the signing of Lebrón while he worked as a scout in the Philadelphia Phillies organization.

"If you're going to have a tryout, I'm going to call a kid that you've got to see. He is really something," Amaro was told while on a scouting trip in Puerto Rico. "It was an awesome show," said Amaro. Jorge Lebrón was a 5-10, 160-pound shortstop who hit the ball for power with seemingly no effort. The young player and his family were invited to come to Philadelphia at the Phillies' expense.

Lebrón—extremely talented, but still a child—stayed at Amaro's home in Philadelphia, while his parents were put up in a hotel. "One day Jorge was supposed to go to a workout at the ballpark, but he asked me, 'May I stay in the backyard and keep on playing with

Rubén and David [Amaro's sons that were about ten and twelve at the time]?'"[5]

"For about three or four nights, I had to shout at them because the only thing they were doing was jumping up and down on the beds—the three of them," Amaro told me. "Lebrón had no idea what the hell professional baseball was about. Then they put a Phillies uniform on the kid and he takes batting practice in Veterans Stadium." Team owner Ruly Carpenter was impressed and the Phillies signed Lebrón for a bonus of $37,500.

Even before he took the field, Lebrón had achieved celebrity status. The Phillies took him to Atlantic City to meet one of his heroes, Joe DiMaggio, who was there taping a television show. The media made a big deal of the event, and someone called Lebrón's father and told him that his son was worth more money than he had been given.

The fourteen-year-old made his debut at Auburn, New York, in the New York–Penn League in 1974 and became the youngest person to ever play professional baseball. The next spring, Amaro explained, Lebrón reported to camp overweight with an inflated ego and did not work on improving his game. Lebrón was with Phillies about two and one-half years and was only seventeen when released. Although he played one more minor league season with another organization, Lebrón was out of baseball at the age of eighteen.

The real age issue today in Latin America is that the vast majority of illegal signings are players professing to be younger than they actually are, thus making them more attractive to major league teams. Lying about ages and producing fraudulent documents is a survival strategy: scouts want to sign a player as young as possible so that he has time to develop and adjust before arriving in the major leagues. After September 11, 2001, because of terrorist attacks and subsequent increased scrutiny by U.S. immigration officials and more rigid enforcement by Major League Baseball, more than five hundred players, the vast majority from the Dominican Republic, had their ages revised upward.

Fabricated birthdates are not as much of a concern in Venezuela as they are in the Dominican Republic, but Andrés did get fooled a couple of times. One player who was deceitful about his age was outfielder Ingle Silva who was signed by the Astros on July 3, 2000, just one week before his seventeenth birthday, at least that's what Silva's papers stated. Some of the academy staff, including Mario González and Wolfgang Ramos, told Andrés that they were sure that Silva was older than seventeen. González checked Venezuelan government records and discovered that Silva had used a forged birth certificate and an altered passport as his proof of age. His birthday was in January 1979, not July 1983, and he was twenty-one, not seventeen.

Andrés, upset that he had been lied to and that Silva had received $15,000 of his $25,000 bonus, was determined not to pay the other $10,000. After a long process involving the Astros' front office in Houston, the Office of the Commissioner of MLB, threats to go to the police, and an unpleasant confrontation with the player's parents, Silva left the Astros' academy. He was not released, but his contract was voided by the commissioner's office. "If you release him, you have to pay him the other $10,000," Andrés explained.

Andrés told me that in addition to being a scout, he now had to take on some of the duties of an FBI or CIA officer to ferret out those players using altered documents.

The day after the anniversary celebration, the academy returned to its normal schedule. During the period between October and December, this included a home game in the Liga de Desarrollo, also known as the *liga paralela*—the rookie league that was formerly the Liga de los Andes, and now centered in the academies in the Valencia area. The purpose of the league is to provide playing time for the increasing number of Venezuelan prospects under contract to major league organizations. It was certainly not designed to make money; no admission is charged, and almost no fans, other than immediate family of a few of the prospects, attend the games. The starting pitcher for the Magallanes entry in the game I saw was a twenty-year-old left-hander who needed more innings than he could get with the main winter league club. That morning, I watched Johán Santana perfect his pitches in almost total obscurity. Less than a month later, he was selected by Florida in the Rule 5 draft and traded to Minnesota.

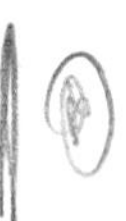

I was interested in Santana because Andrés had described his projection in glowing terms, and if he made it to the big leagues, he would be the first player from the mountainous Andean region of Venezuela to do so. An associate scout at the ceremony, Orlando Fernández, combed the towns of the Andes looking for prospects for Houston and invited me to accompany him on a trip. Unlike eastern Venezuela where prospects are in abundance, they are very scarce in the Andes. I was anxious to go with Fernández to a real backwater on the frontier of scouting.

8

Maracuchos y Gochos

Scouting in Maracaibo and the Andes

Orlando Fernández made the six-hour drive from his home in San Cristóbal, on the Colombian border, to pick me up in Maracaibo in July 2001. I tagged along as he visited his baseball contacts in Maracaibo, and then went on a scouting trip with him through the Andes. Earlier in the year, Fernández had taken an early retirement from his job as sports instructor and was hired as a full-time scout by the Astros to cover the western Venezuelan states of Barinas, Mérida, Táchira, Trujillo, and Zulia. It's not easy to discover baseball players in a region where soccer is the dominant sport. But it was nothing new for Fernández who was brought on-board by Andrés after the two met in 1990 at a baseball tournament in Anaco, on the other side of the country in the oil fields of eastern Venezuela. Andrés was there looking for players and trying to set up his scouting network, while Fernandez had gone as the manager of a team of seventeen- and eighteen-year-old players from Táchira. Andrés offered Fernández, now in his early fifties, a position as an unpaid associate scout to cover the Táchira area. He accepted, and spent eleven years doing basically the same job he now has except without a salary. While Fernández has been involved with baseball most of his life, he is one of the few Astros scouts or instructors who did not play baseball professionally.

Fifteen years after my first trip to Venezuela, I finally made it to Maracaibo, a huge city with a population of more than 3 million, spread out for miles on the western shore of Lake Maracaibo. Tell a Venezuelan from anywhere else in the country that you are going to

Maracaibo, and most will say that it is hot and not worth visiting. It is indeed hot, but it also a fascinating area of Venezuela and, for a person interested in baseball, well worth taking the time to explore. *Marabinos*—or more commonly—*maracuchos*, are generally very outgoing, friendly, proud and have a great sense of humor.[1] The state of Zulia where Maracaibo is located not only has enormous petroleum resources—it produces over one million barrels of oil each day—but also is a rich farming and ranching area. Some in Zulia half-jokingly talk about becoming an independent republic separate from the rest of Venezuela.

Upon return from his studies in the United States, Juan Besson introduced baseball to Maracaibo in 1897, only two years after the first game in Caracas. Besson also formed two teams, but after three years, baseball languished, and no games are reported being played after 1900.[2] The game in Maracaibo was reinvigorated through the efforts of William H. Phelps, an immigrant entrepreneur from the United States, who sold baseball equipment in his store and organized three teams in 1912. U.S.–based petroleum companies also contributed to the spread and popularity of baseball in the Maracaibo region from the 1920s onward.

Maracuchos are proud of the young men from the area who have been successful in baseball at every level. They closely follow the progress of players in the United States at both the minor and major league levels, and the local sports pages give extensive coverage to baseball in the United States, and in winter to the local Zulia team. And they are glued to their television sets when a local team is playing in the Little League World Series in Williamsport, Pennsylvania. On two occasions, in 1994 and 2000, teams from the metropolitan area of Maracaibo won the Little League championship. To gain a better understanding for this love of and appreciation for baseball in Maracaibo, I wanted to go to the roots: the neighborhoods where kids play in organized games.

I arrived in Maracaibo a day ahead of Fernández and took the opportunity to call the parents of Astros prospect Estéban Avila. Rafael Avila and his wife, Ligia de Avila, took me to lunch and then on a tour of Coquivacoa field, the home of the 1994 Little League World Championship team that included their son. I had met Mrs. Avila three years earlier in 1998 at the academy when she was there for Estéban's first day as a professional player. Unlike many of the players who come from more humble backgrounds, the Avilas are solidly upper middle class. Rafael Avila has a master's degree in engineering from Cornell and was dean of the School of Engineering at the Universidad de Zulia for twenty years.

Orlando Fernández was the first member of the Astros' organization to see Estéban Avila, at the time fifteen years old, play in a game at the Coquivacoa field. He told Andrés that Avila was a solid prospect but would be expensive to sign because Atlanta, Toronto, and the New York Yankees were pursuing him. Avila made the five-hour journey from Maracaibo to the academy to work out. Andrés was impressed, and Avila's parents were thrilled. Because Avila was still in high school and too young to sign, the Astros sent instructors—including Pablo Torrealba, Mario González, Omar López, Jesús Aristimuño, and Wolfgang Ramos—to Maracaibo to work with him on weekends.

The Astros were among several major league organizations vying to sign Avila, and Andrés in an attempt to woo the family invited the young man and his parents to visit with the Astros during spring training in Kissimmee, Florida, in 1998.

"Here is a sixteen-year-old kid taking batting practice and watching him are Drayton [McLane], Tal [Smith], Gerry [Hunsicker], Tim [Purpura], and Harry Spellman [at the time the minor league hitting instructor]," explained Andrés. "In his first ten at-bats, Estéban was nervous and didn't do all that well. Estéban motioned to Astros coach, Iván de Jesús, who was throwing to him, and asked if he could have a minute to compose himself. He took about thirty seconds, walked around the batting cage, regained his focus and began to hit the ball well," said Andrés. "That's quite something for a young man his age."

"I was honest with the parents from the first day. I told them 'I can't give you the money that some organizations can, but we can give other things,'" said Andrés. He explained to Rafael and Ligia

Avila that the Astros would develop their son's baseball skills at the academy, that they would not rush him, and that Andrés would be there when Estéban needed someone.

"The Astros gave him a good offer, and he decided to sign with them," Mrs. Avila explained in 1998. "We have always supported and helped Estéban. We think that is one of the reasons he has been successful. We liked the Astros because they are an organization that protects its players. It doesn't put a great deal of pressure on them. We were looking out for the progress and future of our son. And they have a great staff. Señor Reiner is a fundamental reason why we liked the Astros."

On July 2, 1998, the Astros signed sixteen-year-old Estéban, giving him a bonus of $150,000. Andrés asked me not to use the figure, because he had promised the family he would not disclose the amount, but someone else in the Astros' front office volunteered the number. Mr. Avila told me another organization—he did not name it—offered them $100,000 more than the Astros did, but they believed the Astros would do a better job of taking care of their son. Although the Avilas did not tell me, I heard from reliable sources in Venezuela that the other team was the Yankees and the offer was actually double the Astros' signing bonus.

In the summer of 1998, I asked Andrés about Estéban Avila's strength. Without hesitation, Andrés put his hands together as if holding a bat and said, "His bat! He was born with good hitting mechanics; we are just fine-tuning. He has very good instincts and reflexes, and he is very intelligent." Andrés sometimes uses this word to mean smart, and others times to mean smart on the field. In this case I think he meant it in both senses of the word.

"His family will help him stay on track," Andrés also noted. Andrés believed that Estéban would develop very quickly. "By the time he is eighteen, we will see what he can do."

Fast-forward to Maracaibo three years later. "You know why Estéban bats left-handed?" Rafael Avila asked over lunch, and then answered his own question before I had time to venture a guess. "When he was four, the yard of our house was small. When Estéban hit foul balls batting right-handed, the ball would break the neighbor's window. So I taught him how to hit left-handed."

After lunch the Avilas took me to the northern part of the city to the complex of fields that host the Coquivacoa Little League. The league, with teams starting in *compota*—literally baby food—category for four- and five-year-olds and running through a sixteen- and seventeen-year-old team, was organized in the 1950s by Frank Poterajk, known affectionately in Maracaibo as "El Gringo Loco." The most famous alumnus is pitcher Wilson Alvarez, who played between 1981 and 1986.

Little League is very active in Maracaibo, but not in all of Venezuela. Criollitos—another private youth baseball organization—is strong in much of the rest of the country, and the government-funded baseball federation exists in every part of Venezuela. Coquivacoa is one of eight Little Leagues operating the in the Maracaibo region, and another league, Sierra Maestra, won the title at Williamsport in 2000. To get to Williamsport, an all-star team is selected to represent the league. That team has to win in the Maracaibo region, then the Venezuela title (which only includes a few other states besides Zulia), then the Latin American regional. There are registration costs to play in Little League, but the leagues also have sponsors—ranging from soft-drink companies to the government petroleum company. They also have raffles to raise money to improve fields.

Estéban Avila is one of five players from the 1994 World Little League championship team who signed a professional contract, but only Guillermo Quiroz, a catcher who made his major league debut with Toronto in 2004, is still active. Quiroz signed with the Blue Jays in 1998 for a $1.2 million bonus.

Avila began his professional playing career in the *liga paralela* in the fall of 1998. He spent both the 1999 and 2000 seasons playing with the Astros' team in the Venezuelan Summer League, and both were disappointing. He hit .235 the first year and .250 the next. In 2001 he played at Martinsville in the Appalachian League and hit a dismal .206. On September 13, 2001, two months after I had lunch with his parents, the Astros released Estéban Avila. Before he reached his twentieth birthday, his professional career was over. He had shown no speed nor range, did not hit for power, and had trouble just putting the bat on the ball. Signing him—especially for what by Astros standards was a high bonus—had clearly been a mistake.

Estéban's parents were very supportive of his decision to pursue a career in professional baseball but insisted he finish high school first, which he did. They went with him to Williamsport in 1994. They spent three weeks in spring training and three weeks in Martinsville during the 2001 season. While the Avila family cares a great deal for Estéban, I got the feeling from Orlando Fernández—although it was never explicitly stated—that they were overprotective. And when I spoke to Andrés about it, he stated it specifically. He thought that Estéban felt too much pressure when his parents were around.

"I tried to get the family not to come to Martinsville, but I really couldn't stop them. There was no way to convince them not to come," said Andrés. "When they arrived, Estéban was hitting around .320. After a couple of weeks, he was hitting .230."

Estéban Avila, now in his mid-twenties, is back in Maracaibo attending the University of Zulia. He is a very intelligent young man with a bright future; however, his future does not include professional baseball.

Fernández arrived the next day with one of his local contacts, Daniel Acosta. Acosta is not an associate scout nor a bird dog, but an apprentice: he learns about scouting by watching and assisting, and he is very focused and interested in learning the profession. Coincidently, Acosta also worked as an instructor for the Coquivacoa youth league. As we drove to the Sierra Maestra neighborhood located about thirteen miles south of the center of Maracaibo, I asked Fernández who he saw as the major competition for players from Maracaibo. "Atlanta, the New York Yankees, Los Angeles Dodgers, and Seattle—mainly because the Mariners have hired some of the scouts from Toronto," he said. Fernández was not bothered by competition from other organizations, which he viewed as part of the game. His main concern was the increasing presence of agents who both inflated a player's value and often took a large—30 percent or higher—cut of the bonus.

Sierra Maestra was originally part of a land takeover—an invasion of government-owned property—in the mid to late 1950s and is thought to have been named after the Sierra Maestra mountain range in Cuba where Fidel Castro initiated his guerrilla war. The Sierra Maestra team won the Little League World Championship in 2000, defeating a team from the affluent Houston suburb of Bellaire. During the games in Williamsport in 2000, reports circulated that the Venezuelan team brought only one bat and that some of the players could not afford shoes. While Coquivacoa is a middle- to upper-middle-class neighborhood, Sierra Maestra is more working class, but it is not poor and certainly not a place where kids go around shoeless, when playing baseball or otherwise.

There were about fifty adults (plus a lot of youngsters) on hand at Estadio José Díaz Papuchi in Sierra Maestra to watch a game of fifteen- and sixteen-year-olds. Parents in the stands, of course, noted the arrival of two scouts. "Go talk to the scouts, you only have about ten years before you can sign," one mom jokingly said to her five-year-old son.

When the Sierra Maestra team was in Williamsport, several hundred fans watched the games on two large-screen televisions set up in a tent near the ballpark. After the team won the championship game, neighborhood people set off fireworks and were crying with joy. The team was welcomed home from the United States at the airport by the governor of the state of Zulia, and then by President Hugo Chávez in Caracas.

I asked league president Fernando Trejo about the reports of the team having only one bat in Williamsport. "The team may have taken only five bats to Williamsport, but that is all they needed," said Trejo who explained that one of the league's principal sponsors provided bats at no cost. And all the players have baseball shoes. "Those players who can't afford the $27 (U.S.) registration fee are given uniforms—but most families can afford to pay."

While talking with Trejo, Fernández and Acosta were checking out the players. They spotted a tall right-hander, Gilberto Agono, throwing 81 mph.

"*Hay que seguirlo*—we have to follow his progress," Fernández commented. He then picked the tallest kid playing in the outfield and asked if he could see him pitch. This often occurs. A player who does not run well, does not have a position, or is big for his age will be asked to throw in case he might be converted into a pitcher. Fernández then spoke with league president Trejo about putting Agono, sixteen, on a conditioning program.

"He has to warm up every day. He should begin with a soft toss of five meters, twelve minutes a day, expanding to fifteen meters and then thirty meters. He also needs to run thirty minutes two days a week, and sprint every day," explained Fernández. "After two or three weeks he will improve. But if he does not work at improving, he will stagnate."

Fernández jotted down Trejo's cell phone number and explained that he would call to arrange a time to come back in a month to work with Agono. His return trip would give him an opportunity to determine if the player had progressed, but also to deepen his roots—and good will—in the community. This is long, difficult work with little promise of future reward, but it is the kind of task that must be done if the Astros want to be in position to sign players in an increasingly competitive market.

We were done for the day. My excursion through youth baseball in the Maracaibo metropolitan area had certainly given me a glimpse of the foundation of baseball in Venezuela. You can see the pride the kids have and can see their understanding of the game on the field. And you begin to understand why the game is being developed here in a way that it is not in the United States.

The next day we were off to the Venezuelan Andes, the northern extension of the mountain chain that extends the entire length of the South American continent through Argentina, Chile, Bolivia, Peru, Ecuador, and Colombia. Like the countries to the south, the most popular sport of the Andean states of Mérida, Táchira, and Trujillo is soccer. Of the 214 Venezuelans who have made it to the major leagues, only one, Johán Santana, is from the region. But the Astros don't want to leave any stone unturned, so they comb the area in search of prospects.

We left Maracaibo at sunrise for the four-hour drive to Trujillo and the first tryout. Crossing the massive Rafael Urdaneta Bridge at the narrowest part of Lake Maracaibo, we proceeded on the road to the Andes. Somehow, probably because we were talking nonstop, Fernández took a wrong turn just before Trujillo. As we tried to head back in the right direction, we passed through the small town of Motatán. I spotted a ballpark and pointed it out to Fernández, and he quickly pulled into the parking lot. About thirty young baseball players, mainly seventeen- and eighteen-year-olds from all over the state of Trujillo were assembled on the field. We watched them work out for a few minutes under the direction of the Cuban instructor assigned to them. There were a couple of kids who ran faster than the others, but there appeared to be no prospects. And Fernández did not expect to see any: the state of Trujillo produces very few baseball players. The presence of Cuban instructors provoked an interesting discussion. No one I spoke to in Venezuela thought bringing Cuban instructors to Venezuela was necessary, although most understood that the agreement to have them was political in nature and had little to do with baseball.

We arrived in Trujillo, the capital of the state, by midmorning. The city of 40,000 has a nice cool climate, but the tropical sun is intense at the higher altitude (3,500 feet). At the tryout site, the main stadium on the edge of town, we met three more of Fernández's "contacts." The local Trujillo connection was a woman, Alexis de Labrador. The other two were middle-aged men—whose names I never learned—from Caja Seca, a town on the south shore of Lake Maracaibo. Caja Seca is a sugarcane growing area, where the vast majority of the population is black and poor. There were seven young men on the field, four from Trujillo and three from Caja Seca. The apprentice Acosta brought out his tools—a measuring tape, stopwatch, radar gun, notepad, and pen. He carefully wrote down the names, birthdates, and positions of the players. Most were pitchers, and all were fifteen except one, Jesús Alberto Chourio, who was fourteen. Chourio was by far the most impressive of the seven and was clearly the player that attracted Fernández's attention. Chourio was tall and skinny, and looked as if he might develop into a very good pitcher.

After about twenty pitches, which ranged between 76 and 79 mph, Fernández went out to the mound and talked to him about his mechanics.

Fernández then came over to where I was sitting behind home plate and introduced me to Alexis de Labrador, in her late forties, and her son Iván, fifteen, a pitcher at the tryout. When Fernández went back on the field, Labrador asked me if it would not be a better idea if they took the players—like her son—to the academy where they would work with instructors every day and improve. I tried to explain to her that the new MLB rules stated that a player had to be sixteen years old to sign and could only stay at the academy thirty days and that no team wanted to spend the time and money to partially produce a player and then let him go to possibly sign with another team. She understood my logic but was not convinced. "But if they were at the academy, they would improve," she said—and she was correct. I told her to talk to Fernández.

"Wouldn't it motivate the kids if they got to go to the academy to improve?" Mrs. Labrador asked Fernández. "The prize is not to get to go to the academy. This is a business, and it would be a bad investment if we took every player to the academy," Fernández told her. He explained that it was expensive to house a player there and that it would take instruction time away from prospects the Astros were on the verge of signing. He told her that the motivating factor should be the desire to improve by working out here in Trujillo so that they would one day be good enough to take to the academy.

At the end of the tryout, Fernández called the players back to the partial shade of the dugout to talk with them. He thanked them for taking the time to come out and had a few general comments directed at the group. "If you're not in good physical condition, it is like trying to build a structure on a poor foundation," said Fernández. "Baseball is not easy, it requires sacrifice and hard work. We want you to stay in school. We want all of our players to at least finish high school. I'll be back in three or four months to check on your progress. Thank you all for coming. *Vamos a seguir adelante* (Let's go forward)."

Then he directed his comments to Jesús Chourio. "Freddy García was throwing 79 mph when he was your age, and look where he is now," he said. "Chourio, when I first saw you, you didn't even know how to put on a glove. I commend you for your hard work." Fernández was excited about Chourio's progress. "Six months ago the kid knew nothing about baseball. He was at zero. Now he looks good. *Yo tengo fé en ese negrito. Va a ser pelotero* (I have faith in this black kid. He's going to be a ballplayer)."

We finished the tryout in early afternoon and drove to Valera, a bustling, hot crossroads town at an altitude of 1,500 feet, and dropped off Acosta, who would take the bus back to Maracaibo. Just outside of Valera, the Transandean Highway begins its extraordinarily beautiful ascent through the Andes. After a couple of hours, the trees began to disappear as we climbed to the barren *páramo* (high plateau) and wound our way up to the Paso del Aguila at just over 13,000 feet. Then we slowly descended to 5,000 feet and arrived in Mérida, a city of 300,000 and the capital of the state of the same name. It was hard to believe we began the day at sea level in hot and steamy Maracaibo.

The game we had planned to see in Mérida the next morning was cancelled, so Fernández scheduled an impromptu tryout for a few players. But before that, we would have breakfast with Miguel Arias, president of the Mérida Baseball Federation. I asked Arias why there were so many good players from around the south end of Lake Maracaibo, while so few came from here. "Down there it is warmer, and the kids are the sons of fisherman and cane cutters," he said, obviously referring to fact that they had limited career options and were willing to work hard at baseball. "Here in Mérida, the parents complain we work their kids too hard when we ask them to run after practice. Then we have to explain that baseball is not easy." He didn't mention the obvious—that the best athletes from the state prefer to play soccer.

After breakfast we drove over to the municipal baseball stadium, and Fernández pointed out that this was the ballpark where Richard Hidalgo played his last amateur game at the end of June 1991. Fernández conducted a short improvised tryout with only two players. He timed the seventeen-year-olds running from home to first and then had both take a few swings with the bat. He met with the players and told them they needed to work hard, and we were on our way.

After an hour's drive west from Mérida, we arrived in Tovar, a city of about 40,000 in the center of Venezuela's coffee-producing region. The first stop was the stadium where Johán Santana began his journey to the major leagues. Fernández recognized a woman who was the president of the Criollitos in Tovar and asked if she knew how to get to the Santana residence. She did not, but a gentleman standing nearby offered us to lead us there. We were greeted at the door by Johán's father, Jesús "El Negro" Santana, who invited us into his home.

"Scouts were never looking for prospects here in Tovar, but with Johán's success, they are coming now," said Mr. Santana. "And now the kids here are also more motivated to play baseball." He told us that Johán calls home every day, and it was apparent that his son had also sent enough money for a considerable upgrade to the family home. Jesús Santana explained that Johán was proud to be the first player from the Andes to get to the major leagues and that he writes his nickname "*El Gocho*" inside his cap and on his glove. The word "*gocho*" is often used to describe people from the Andes and originates from an earlier period when local residents put notches in their mule's ears so that they could be easily identified when they went to the lowland areas of Venezuela. I assumed that it was a disparaging term. When I looked the word up in a dictionary, *gocho* was defined as pig or hog.

I later asked Andrés what the common meaning of the term was.

"Stupid," he replied, laughing. He also said it did not always carry a negative connotation. "Johán really is the first *gocho* to get to the major leagues."

What Johán Santana was doing by proudly claiming to be "*El Gocho*" was turning the insult on its head and using it as a display of regional pride.

"We saw Johán Santana at the junior national championships in Güigüe, a town close to Valencia in 1994. He was playing center field and first base, but we knew that he also pitched," Andrés explained, "I really liked him very much." Andrés wanted to visit Santana and his family in Tovar, but this was just before the impending Major League Baseball Players Association strike and the Astros' scouts were not allowed to spend any money.

"So I called Dan [O'Brien] and said 'I don't want to lose this kid. I need to go to Tovar. It will cost about $400 or $500 to make the trip.' He said, 'Andrés, no way. We can't spend a penny.' About two weeks later I called him again. 'Has anything changed? Can I go?'" Again scouting director Dan O'Brien said no. Andrés asked if he could speak with GM Bob Watson directly and was granted permission.

"Bob can I spend $500? I want to go to see a kid."

"Andrés, I have orders that we can't spend any money," replied Watson.

Andrés pleaded, and Watson gave him both the authorization and $500 of his own money. Andrés and his wife Carmina made the ten-hour journey by car from Valencia to Santana's home, bringing along photos of the Astros' spring training facility in Kissimmee, Florida, and an autographed baseball from the 1994 Astros team.

"Someone knocked on my door and said 'You don't know me, but I know you,'" Johán Santana told *USA Today* reporter Mel Antonen in recalling Andrés's first visit. And that autographed ball that Andrés gave him? "That ball is priceless because it makes me feel so good about baseball."

"We sat down and talked and I invited Santana to come to the academy in January [1995]. The family agreed. Then I came to Houston to spend December and January. When I got back I heard that Santana was working out with the Colorado Rockies. I said 'Wow!' So I made another trip to Tovar."

"I thought we had an agreement," Andrés asked Jesús Santana. "Yes, and we will live up to it, but they [Colorado] came here and they convinced us and we went there, but it was really just a tryout," replied Mr. Santana. Andrés then asked Johán, "So are you ready to come to the academy?" He was.

"After that I spent almost three months deciding what position he would play," explained Andrés. He was very impressed by Santana's athleticism, his great throwing arm, and his personality. "Finally, we made the decision that he would be a pitcher and that is when we signed him for $10,000," said Andrés. Santana spent almost an entire year at the academy working on his pitching with instructors Jesús Aristimuño, Oscar Padrón, Wolfgang Ramos, and Pablo Torrealba. He was also developing off the field. Luis Carmona, the English teacher, told me Johán is the best student he has taught in his almost fifteen years at the academy. He called him "super intelligent."

In his first professional season in 1996, Santana had a 4-3 record with a 2.70 ERA with the Astros' team in the Dominican Summer League. Although Santana was 0-4 with the Astros' rookie league team in Florida and the short-season club in Auburn, New York, in 1997, Andrés's enthusiasm for Santana never diminished. He was convinced from the day he signed the left-hander that he would make it to the major leagues. In 1998 Santana spent most of the season at Auburn and compiled a 7-5 record. The following year, Santana was 8-8 at Michigan in the Midwest League. Santana's manager at Michigan, Al Pedrique, had also been his manager at Magallanes during the 1998–99 winter season when Santana posted a 5-0 record and a 2.30 ERA. His performance in Venezuela attracted the interest of several scouts, including those from Minnesota. And clearly the Twins' scout covering Midwest League had seen Santana pitch. Andrés called to alert the Astros' front office in Houston that Santana was on the radar screen of other organizations. While Andrés understood it was difficult to protect an A-ball pitcher in the Rule 5 draft, he told the Astros that Santana was likely to get picked if left off the 40-man roster in 1999.

The Rule 5 draft that takes place at baseball's Winter Meetings in December allows an organization to select a player from another organization who has played four seasons in their minor league system and is not protected on the 40-man roster. If the player was nineteen or older when signed, he has to be protected after three years. With the 2006 Collective Bargaining Agreement, the periods have been lengthened to four and five years. The organization selecting the player pays the other club $50,000. A crucial factor is that the player selected must remain on the 25-man major league roster for the entire season or be offered back to the organization that lost him for $25,000.

On December 13, 1999, Santana was Florida's first pick in the Rule 5 draft. He was immediately traded to Minnesota in a prearranged deal for Jared Camp whom the Twins had selected in the draft. Santana made his major league debut with Minnesota on April 3, 2000, and recorded his first major league win on June 6, defeating the Astros at Houston. Four years later, he was the top pitcher in the American League.

We left Tovar for the three-hour drive to Fernández's home in San Cristóbal. After descending through lush tropical surroundings for a half-hour, we reached the Pan American Highway, which at this point passes through the lowlands dotted with cattle ranches, on the south end of Lake Maracaibo.

After a couple of hours, I noticed a sign for the turn off to La Fría, a small town that for several years hosted a club in the Liga de los Andes, the predecessor of the current Liga de Desarrollo or *liga paralela*—the rookie league of Venezuelan professional baseball. The Liga de los Andes started in 1985 and by 1991 was composed of four teams situated near the Colombian border: San Cristóbal, San Antonio del Táchira, Rubio, and La Fría. Andrés was a major supporter of the Liga de los Andes because he understood that the increasing number of young men signing professional contracts would not have the opportunity to develop sitting in the dugouts on the Venezuelan professional league teams. The Magallanes team—where most of the Astros' prospects were placed—was located in San Cristóbal, ten hours by car from Valencia, and it was difficult to supervise the players' progress. After a couple of years, Andrés convinced the Magallanes club to move the rookie team closer to Valencia. Caracas owner, Oscar Prieto agreed, and during the 1992–93 winter season, the four-team circuit, now called the Liga de Desarrollo, played all of its games in Puerto Cabello, thirty miles from Valencia. Another four-team division was centered in Carora, a one-hour drive from Barquismeto. In 1994 with strong input from Andrés, the Liga de Desarrollo (now composed of four teams—Magallanes, Caracas, Lara, and a New York Yankees–Aragua co-op entry) relocated to the twenty-five-mile corridor between Valencia and Maracay. By 2005 the league featured eleven teams—Magallanes, Navegantes, Caracas, Leones, Houston (composed of both Magallanes and Caracas players), Pastora, Aragua, Philadelphia, Boston, St. Louis, and the New York

Mets. But the league's purpose remained the same: to give at bats and innings to younger players.

The one area of Fernández's scouting territory that we would not be visiting on this trip was the city of Barinas in the state of the same name located across the Andes on the edge of the vast *llanos* (plains) of southern Venezuela. When Fernández held a tryout in Barinas in 1992, one of his contacts asked, "Do you remember when you pitched for the San Cristóbal team in 1976 and you faced a good hitting, left-handed first baseman from Barinas?" Fernández said that he did. "That was Hugo Chávez!" Chávez, now Venezuela's president, was twenty-two years old at the time and still dreamed of playing professional baseball. "I recall the game, but I don't remember what he did against me," Fernández told me. "At the time I didn't know who he was." Neither did the vast majority of people in Venezuela.

As we drove along the highway, now just a few miles from the border with Colombia, I asked Fernández about the players that he had recommended and that had been signed by the Astros. He rattled off a list that included Estéban Avila, Erickson Corso, Julio Salazar, Jorge Suárez, Hamilton Sarabia, and what I wrote down as Angel Bersoto. I later checked the Astros media guide and found no Angel Bersoto. The player Fernández was referring to was in fact Enyelbert Soto, named after Engelbert Humperdinck—the popular singer of the 1960s—whose name was actually Arnold George Dorsey. (The real Engelbert Humperdinck, who died in 1921, wrote the music for *Hansel and Gretel.*)

Scouts such as Fernández are the face of the Astros on the frontier of baseball. He knows his area well, is willing to work extra hard to get to that out-of-the-way game, to work with a player who might develop into a prospect, to be honest with the kids, and not to promise the parents something he can't deliver.

"We can't just go out and see a player we like and sign him. The competition is too great," Fernández explained. "*Enamoramos,*" he said. "Basically we have to make them fall in love with us." And that is exactly what he attempts to do. He explains what the Astros have to offer that makes it in the parents' interest in to sign with them rather than with another organization.

The easy-going and unassuming Fernández spends a great deal of time on the road. He needs to touch base in Maracaibo, make frequent runs through the Andes, check out Barinas, and keep a close watch on small towns in rural Zulia. During the four days I spent with Fernández, I got a good sense of his working style and an overview of his region—certainly the most beautiful of any scout's in the baseball world.

We arrived in San Cristóbal, with a population of almost 500,000, and a center of commercial activity and exchange with nearby Colombia. On the way through the center of town, we stopped at a baseball stadium to watch a few innings of the national tournament for six- and seven-year-olds. The team from Táchira was playing before a crowd of several hundred very vocal fans. I was intrigued by how much the kids looked like baseball players. The pitchers actually used a wind up, and the batters could hit. The fielding left a lot to be desired, but you could clearly see where baseball instincts are developed at such a young age. On our way out of the park, two cabs pulled up and the entire team from the state of Bolívar spilled out—seven players and a coach in each small car.

Fernández, who frequently crosses the border to the neighboring city of Cúcuta, Colombia, to shop or see a ballgame, is the person who convinced Andrés that Colombia was a market worth scouting. "The first time I went to Colombia I was impressed by the large number of prospects there," he said. While at a tournament in Cartagena, Fernández met Guillermo Ramírez and later introduced him to Andrés. Ramírez now runs the Astros' program in Colombia. While the Andes are on the outer fringe of scouting on the frontier of baseball, Colombia is even further out. And for Andrés, it presented an opportunity to remain one more step ahead of the competition.

9

The Talent Search Expands

Scouting in Colombia, Nicaragua, Panama, and Beyond

Competition for players in Venezuela intensified in the mid-1990s, with bonuses going through the roof, and Andrés saw the necessity to further expand his search to untapped smaller markets in the Caribbean. Major league clubs with limited scouting budgets, he believed, had to find new talent pools in order to gain an advantage over deep-pocket competitors. Although none of these underscouted markets would produce the quantity of players coming out of the Dominican Republic or Venezuela, Andrés wanted to make sure he was aware of the next Fernando Valenzuela (Mexico), Dennis Martínez (Nicaragua), Mariano Rivera (Panama), Edgar Rentería (Colombia), Andruw Jones (Curaçao), or Sidney Ponson (Aruba). And when MLB implemented new regulations in Venezuela at the end of the decade that limited the Astros' ability to develop players at the academy, he became even more vigorous in his move into the hinterland of baseball scouting where there were fewer rules.

Andrés started a scouting program and opened a mini-academy in Panama in 1992 and operated a facility in Mexico for a short time in 1997 before diverting those resources to Colombia and Nicaragua a few years later. He had scouts in Aruba and Curaçao, and in 2002 he even signed a player from Brazil, Neil Massaki. When I visited with Massaki at the Venezuelan academy in the summer of 2003, he showed me one of his prize possessions, a baseball card of another Brazilian, José Pett.

In 1992 José Pett—then a sixteen-year-old pitching prospect—provoked a feeding frenzy among scouts.[1] Many, including Florida Marlins director of international scouting Orrin Freeman, descended on soccer-crazy Brazil. While going through airport security in São Paulo, a guard looked inquisitively at Freeman's radar gun. "What's this?" he asked. Freeman explained that the instrument measured the speed of a baseball. The guard, still puzzled, then asked, "What's a baseball?"

Andrés made two trips to Brazil to see the 6-6, 190-pound Pett. "He will be a very good pitcher. He has an excellent arm and is very aggressive on the mound," Andrés told me after his first trip. By the time Andrés returned to Brazil for Pett's formal tryout, five teams—the Astros, Florida, Atlanta, Los Angeles Dodgers, and Toronto—were still in the running to sign him.

Astros scout Paul Weaver joined Andrés in Brazil, and the two met with José's father, Adjimar Pett, who told them they could sign his son if the Astros would match or top the other offers. Weaver called Houston scouting director Dan O'Brien and expressed his amazement that the Astros were still in the discussions but added, "Dan, I don't think we have enough chips to stay in the game." When Weaver and Andrés informed O'Brien that it would cost at least $500,000 to $600,000 to sign Pett, they were told they could not bid that high but to see the process through until the end. So the two scouts stayed in Brazil, but it was as if they were shopping at Neiman Marcus with the Wal-Mart budget given them by the Astros.

Toronto's delegation to Brazil, headed by GM Pat Gillick, a former Astro, walked away with the prize, signing Pett for a bonus of $760,000 (tax-free due to an agreement between Brazil and Canada). There was no way the Astros were going to spend almost $1 million to top Toronto's bid. Earlier that summer the Astros had the number-one selection in the June draft and had the opportunity to sign a seventeen-year-old Michigan high-school player named Derek Jeter. The Astros' scout in the region, former major league pitcher and Hall of Fame member Hal Newhouser, reported that Jeter—who wanted a $1 million bonus—would be a franchise player. But the Astros passed on Jeter choosing instead to sign Phil Nevin for $700,000.

The Pett signing set the pace for high-price international signing bonuses. In 1993 the Atlanta Braves paid $700,000 for Australian shortstop Glen Williams (who finally made his debut twelve years later with Minnesota). Within a few years, million-dollar signing bonuses, although not common, were being paid in both in the Dominican Republic and Venezuela.

After signing with the Blue Jays, Pett played on the Brazilian team at the World Junior Championships in Monterrey, Mexico, in August 1992, where I had the opportunity to visit with the young man and his father. He was a real joy to watch pitch, and like Andrés and Toronto, I just assumed that in a few years Pett would be a major league star. It was indeed disappointing that Pett never made it past Triple-A.

It was also at the World Junior Championships in Monterrey in 1992 that I first met Aníbal Reluz, the person Andrés hired to run the Astros' Panama program. Reluz had been working as a bird dog for the New York Yankees in Panama, and his boss, Herb Raybourn, unable to offer a full-time job, recommended him to Andrés. Raybourn, a native of the Canal Zone and one of the real pioneers in Latin American scouting, had previously worked for Pittsburgh under Howie Haak and is the person responsible for putting Panama on the scouting map after discovering Manny Sanguillen, Rennie Stennet, and Omar Moreno. He moved on to work with the Yankees and in 1990 signed superstar closer Mariano Rivera. While in Monterrey in 1992, Raybourn signed eighteen-year-old pitcher Rafael Medina to a Yankees contract for a $165,000 bonus—ten times higher than any other Panamanian player had ever received. Several years later, prospects in Panama were still talking about getting "Medina money" to sign.

David Rawnsley, then in charge of the Astros' international programs, interviewed Reluz in Monterrey and said he would call him after consulting with the front office in Houston. After a few hours, when Reluz had not heard anything, he approached me and said: "Tell David I have another *novia* (girlfriend)," meaning other teams were interested. The Astros did hire Reluz, and he soon began scouring the country looking for players.

In March 1993 Reluz and Andrés signed Manuel Barrios, who made his major league debut with the Astros on September 16, 1997. Less than two months later Barrios and two other players were traded to Florida for Moisés Alou. Barrios was the second Panamanian scouted and developed by the Houston organization to play with the franchise. In the early 1960s, scout Tony Pacheco signed outfielder Iván Murrell, who made his debut with the Colt .45s on September 28, 1963.

The next time I saw Reluz was in 2000 when he picked me up at the airport in Panama City. As he negotiated the maze of streets and traffic on the way to my hotel, Reluz was constantly greeting people or stopping to chat. He seemed to know everyone in the city and that was not far from wrong. Reluz, in his late forties, had driven a taxi for fifteen years. He had also made the roster of Panama's national amateur baseball team when he was seventeen, was selected as captain two years later, and played for seventeen years. He never signed with a U.S. organization, and there was no professional league in Panama during the time he played. So Reluz played amateur baseball and made his living driving a taxi in Panama City. He brought to the Astros not only an intimate knowledge of Panama but also access and credibility in the country's baseball world. Reluz converted his home in Chame, a small seaside town about an hour by road east of Panama City, into a residential facility for players. He even constructed a small dormitory to accommodate a dozen young men. Players from Panama, Nicaragua, and Colombia worked out at Chame, which became a satellite of the Astros' Venezuelan academy. Reluz also had an agreement with the city of Chame to use the municipal field, known as El Hogar de los Astros en Panama, located a few blocks from his home.

Baseball is the most popular sport in Panama and has been played there for well over one hundred years. The first recorded game was in 1883 while Panama was still part of Colombia. In the early 1900s, as the United States increased its presence with the construction of the Panama Canal, baseball became more important and established itself as the national sport. Panama had professional baseball from the 1940s until 1972 and participated in the Caribbean Series between 1949 and 1960, winning the event in 1952. The series was suspended in 1961, and when it resumed, Panama and Cuba had been replaced by the Dominican Republic and Mexico.[2]

Older fans remember touring big league teams that often visited during spring training. In 1946 the New York Yankees spent three weeks in Panama, playing eleven games against local teams. Panamanians were thrilled to see Joe DiMaggio play in every game. In 1947 the Brooklyn Dodgers and their Triple-A franchise the Montreal Royals traveled to Panama for exhibition games for two weeks. Hall of Famer and six-time American League batting champion Rod Carew heads the list of the more than forty-five Panamanians who have played in the major leagues. But the first Panamanians to get to the big leagues were Hector López (Kansas City) and Humberto Robinson (Milwaukee Braves) in 1955. Other outstanding native sons include Manny Sanguillen, Omar Moreno, and Rennie Stennett, who all played for Pittsburgh; Ben Oglivie, who in 1980 at Milwaukee tied (with Reggie Jackson) to lead the American League in home runs with 41; Juan Berenguer, who pitched for fifteen years in the big leagues; and Mariano Rivera.

While many major league organizations scout in Panama, and the Yankees do an outstanding job, only the Astros had an academy. The plan was to have Reluz bring players to Chame and work to develop them. Andrés would visit every few months and decide who was worth pursuing. I caught up with Andrés on one of his crosschecking trips to Panama in 2000, and we went to La Chorrera, located just outside of Panama City, to evaluate a dozen or so prospects. At the tryout, Andrés discussed the prospects with Reluz and shot video to take back to Houston. He was only interested in a few players, and two of them, Christian Ríos from Panama City and Faran Dometz from Bluefields, Nicaragua, both sixteen-year-old left-handed pitchers, were signed a month later.

One player, fourteen-year-old Colombian infielder, Deivis Rivadeneira, appeared totally comfortable on a baseball field. "He is bright, eager, and wants to learn. I'm quite sure he will one day be a big league player, maybe even a star," I jotted down in my notebook. But it would be two years before Rivadeneira could sign, and a few months later, Andrés sent him back to Colombia. In July 2002 he signed with Atlanta and played four years in the Braves minor league system before being released after the 2006 season.

Between 1992 and 2002, the Astros signed twenty players in Panama, with one (Barrios) making it to the big leagues. But in late 2002 faced with budget cuts imposed by Astros owner Drayton McLane, Andrés decided to eliminate the program in Panama and let Reluz go. Because Reluz had done such outstanding work, Andrés found it very difficult to inform him that he no longer had a job. Reluz, however, landed on his feet: he was hired to scout for Cincinnati and worked as a coach for the Panamanian baseball federation. In 2006 he was selected to manage the Panamanian team in the World Baseball Classic. By that time, there were no prospects from Panama remaining in the Astros' minor league system.

I was surprised when the Astros announced in March 1997 that they would open an academy for signing and developing players in Mexico. The Houston franchise had never allocated a great deal of energy, nor money, to scouting in Mexico. The Astros had working agreements with the Monclova team of the Liga Mexicana de Béisbol Profesional (LMBP)—the Mexican league—in the late 1980s, and the now defunct Monterrey Industriales in the early 1990s, but no Mexican player signed and developed by Houston has ever played for the organization.

I knew Andrés was not too interested in scouting in Mexico. Most of the country's top athletes prefer to play soccer, and the Mexican league owns the rights to all native baseball players, making it difficult to sign promising prospects at less than inflated prices. But Andrés believed he could nonetheless find players there. The Astros reached an agreement for an academy with an LMBP team, the Olmecas de Tabasco, and utilized the team's scouts and field in Villahermosa in the southern part of the country. The academy, which was the first in Mexico run directly by a major league organization, was closed a year later, and no one was signed during that period.

But Andrés did not give up on finding players in Mexico. In 2003 on a tip from Astros' coach and Mexican native, Jorge Orta, Andrés traveled to Culiacán, Mexico, and signed shortstop Amadeo Zazueta.

Zazueta played his first two years in the Venezuelan Summer League where in 2005 he hit .313 and was selected team MVP.

The short-lived Mexican operation in 1997 and 1998 offered an opportunity for academy director, Oscar Padrón, to make the transition from player to coach and also to demonstrate his ability to run a program. Padrón, a tall power pitcher signed out of Venezuela by Andrés in 1991, played for two seasons in the United States, injured his elbow in 1994, had surgery in 1995, and never returned to play. He was released and was brought on to the Astros' Venezuelan staff as a scout and instructor in 1997.

Andrés was extremely impressed with Padrón. "Where can you find intelligence, skill, honesty, and loyalty, and a person willing to work hard?" asked Andrés rhetorically. "Padrón did a really good job, and we really didn't spend a lot of money in Mexico, but to make the academy produce it needed more money. We got to a point where Gerry and I sat down and we said OK 'How much do we need to invest in the next three or four years?' We decided it was too much, because with a lot less, you know, we ended up going into Nicaragua and Colombia."

In September 2000 the Astros announced that they planned to open a baseball academy in Nicaragua during the next year and that "the facility would follow the model of the Astros well-established baseball academy in Venezuela."[3] The Astros' academy didn't actually get off the ground until June 2002, and I went with Andrés for the official opening. Located at the Centro Don Bosco, a technical training school in Managua, it was the first baseball facility operated by a major league organization in Nicaragua. It was very modest, consisting of a playing field with dugouts and a small clubhouse and office. Players lived and took their meals in a nearby residence. Under Major League Baseball rules, the Astros could keep a player for thirty days, after which he either had to be signed or leave. Signed players would be sent to the Astros' academy in Venezuela.

"We have a plan to give young men in Nicaragua who desire to receive it the instruction and education to be not only good baseball players but also good citizens," Andrés told the three-dozen people in attendance, mainly members of the Nicaraguan media, at the dedication ceremony. "This is an historic day in Nicaraguan baseball," baseball historian and former sports editor of *La Prensa*, the country's largest newspaper, Alberto "Tito" Rondón told me. "Now we officially have an academy."[4]

Baseball was introduced to Nicaragua's isolated Atlantic coast (then under British control) by Albert Addlesberg, a businessman from the United States, in 1888. The first team on Nicaragua's Pacific coast was the Managua Base Ball Club, formed in 1891 by local elites, one of whom was Dr. Adán Cárdenas, president of the country and grandfather of René Cárdenas, the man who pioneered Major League Baseball broadcasts in Spanish. It increased in popularity over the next thirty years, and by the middle of the 1920s, baseball was Nicaragua's national sport and has remained so ever since.[5]

"Nicaraguans are separated by many things: there are Catholics and Protestants, rich and poor, black and white, and we have the geographical divide between the Pacific and Atlantic coasts," explained Rondón. "But they are united by baseball." While some young men prefer basketball or boxing, and youngsters can be seen kicking around soccer balls every four years when the World Cup occurs, baseball is far and away the most popular sport. "If you play any sport other than baseball in Nicaragua, you grow up to be a frustrated person," said Rondón.

"I wanted to open up another market," explained Andrés when I asked him why he was so interested in Nicaragua. "In 1993 I went there and through Aníbal [Reluz] got in touch with Calixto Vargas, and made him an associate scout. With the strike in 1994, there was no budget for Nicaragua, so I just stopped going for about two years." When Andrés had his budget restored, he was able to hire Vargas—a hero of the Nicaraguan national baseball team during the 1960s and 1970s—as a full-time scout. The very personable and outgoing Vargas knows Nicaragua like the back of his hand, and almost everyone in Nicaragua knows him. In addition to his work with the Astros, Vargas is the play-by-play announcer for Nicaragua's semiprofessional baseball league, and the host of a nightly radio sports talk show.

"We would fly to Bluefields, Corn Island, and Puerto Cabezas," recalled Andrés about those early scouting adventures on the Atlantic coast. "That is really tough scouting. But I saw some possibilities, so I started to go to Nicaragua every three months." Andrés convinced Gerry Hunsicker that the Astros should operate a small-scale facility in Managua that would have four or five prospects at a time and utilize Vargas's home as a residence. The Astros worked in Nicaragua in this fashion for three or four years when Andrés decided he wanted a more formal structure.

Andrés's efforts were not the first scouting venture in Nicaragua by the Astros. In 1975 René Cárdenas was returning home to Managua and thought he might be able to spot a few prospects for Houston. Astros GM Tal Smith told Cárdenas he could be a bird dog scout and would receive a commission from the Astros—probably about $5,000—for any player he recommended who reached the major leagues.

"So I was in Nicaragua and one day I saw a young fellow about seventeen years old that I liked very much," said Cárdenas. "I talked to his father, who used to be a great ball player in Nicaragua, and I said 'I'm interested in your boy; please don't let anybody from any major league ball club talk to him. Let me talk to the Astros first.'"

"I talked to Tal Smith, and he told me he would send down two scouts—Walt Mathews, a veteran, and a young scout, Scipio Spinks," explained Cárdenas. Cárdenas met the men in Managua and had a tryout for the young prospect. "And the two scouts told me 'René, he's a great ball player. He's going make it. Oh yeah. You did a good job.'"

The scouts returned to Houston to make a report while Cárdenas remained in Managua. He waited to hear from the Astros, but no one ever called.

"I decided to come to Houston, and I talked to Lynwood Stallings, who was in charge of scouting in those years. I said 'What happened with the boy that I recommended?' And he said, 'René, Matthews, and Scipio Spinks didn't want to make you feel bad about it, but the boy has nothing. He will never make it. He doesn't have what it takes to be a good ballplayer. And they didn't tell you anything because they didn't want to make you feel bad about it.'"

Cárdenas was very upset, but there he was little he could do.

"So I told the boy's father that he was free to talk to somebody else. A few weeks later, he was signed by Milwaukee and later on sold to St. Louis. That was David Green. When I was a broadcaster with the Los Angeles Dodgers, every time David Green came out to hit, I said, 'there goes my $5,000.'"[6]

Green is one of nine Nicaraguans who have played in the major leagues. But the first and most successful was Dennis Martínez who made his major league debut with the Baltimore Orioles in 1976. Nicaraguans are proud of Martínez's twenty-three-year major league career and his 245 major league victories—the most ever by a pitcher born in Latin America. They were overjoyed on July 29, 1991, when pitching for the Montreal Expos, Martínez threw a perfect game against Los Angeles at Dodger Stadium.

Andrés was convinced that Nicaragua would produce major league quality pitchers and that is what he instructed Vargas to find. The Astros signed nine Nicaraguans between 1997 and 2001, all pitchers. The only one remaining in the Astros' system is a left-hander, Douglas Argüello, signed in 2001. Even though signing bonuses were becoming exorbitant in Nicaragua—in 2000 Atlanta gave pitcher Gonzalo López $725,000—Andrés believed he could still compete by treating both the prospects and parents with respect and by pointing to the track record the Astros had established in Venezuela.

But in late 2002, the call for budget cuts came from the front office in Houston. "I was put in a situation where Gerry said, 'Andrés we have to cut so much, you name it. How do you want to do it?'" Andrés had to project which of the three satellite programs—Nicaragua, Panama, or Colombia—might be most productive in the long run and he chose Colombia. So five months after the Houston Astros became the first major league organization to open an academy in Nicaragua, they became the first to close one, although Andrés was able to retain Calixto Vargas as a part-time scout for the Astros.

With the budget cuts in 2002, Andrés also would no longer scout in Aruba and Curaçao, two islands belonging to the Kingdom of the Netherlands and located just off the coast of Venezuela. Baseball was brought to Aruba (population 110,000) in the late 1920s and early 1930s by the Lago Petroleum Company, a United States–based corporation, which constructed a refinery to process oil from Venezuela. As was the case with baseball at sugar mills in Cuba and the Dominican Republic, baseball was a form of recreation for workers. "Baseball Game Tomorrow Afternoon—Light Oils to Meet High Pressures in Season Opener," reads the title of a story in a 1934 issue of *Pan-Aruban*, a publication of the refinery.[7]

In 1999 Andrés hired an associate scout, Milton Croes, in Aruba, and I had the opportunity to visit with him on several occasions between 2001 and 2005. During my trips, Croes showed me every baseball field in Aruba and helped me track down the little-known history of the origins of the game on the island. He also introduced me to Hedwegis "Rock" Angela, the only Aruban ever signed by the Astros.

In 1975 Astros scout Tony Pacheco went to Aruba to sign the hard-throwing Angela and gave him a $10,000 bonus. I caught up with Angela in the summer of 2005 at a Sunday-afternoon softball game and barbecue at a small stadium in the middle of the island. Angela, now in his fifties, played in the Astros' system for two years before he was released. While probably no one from the Astros can recall Angela, he vividly remembers pitching batting practice for Houston in spring training and facing José Cruz, Bob Watson, and César Cedeño.

Croes, who now works as a scout for the San Diego Padres, recommended several players to Houston, but none were ever signed. Two that I saw play were signed by other organizations, infielder Rayon Lampe with Seattle in 2003 and left-handed pitcher Conrad Orman with Baltimore in 2004.

On Curaçao (population 220,000), the Dutch, not North Americans, operated the petroleum refineries, and as a result soccer was the sport of choice for most young men. That was until Hensley Meulens signed a contract with the New York Yankees in 1985 and went on to play for seven seasons in the major leagues. With the success of Meulens, baseball quickly became the national sport of Curaçao, and with the achievements of another islander—Atlanta Braves center fielder Andruw Jones—it is not likely to change anytime soon. For several years from the late 1990s to 2003, Mark Van Zanten scouted for the Astros in Curaçao, and he and Andrés signed one local player, left-handed pitcher Rainer Martis in 1998, who played two seasons for the Venezuelan Summer League team before being released.

When Andrés suggested that I accompany him on a scouting trip to Cartagena, Colombia, in early 2000, I was surprised. Only a few years earlier, he told me that the country was too dangerous to visit and that no player was worth risking your life to sign. A couple of factors intervened to change Andrés's mind. Although the majority of Colombians are much more interested in the World Cup than the World Series, along the country's northern Caribbean coast baseball is far and away the most popular sport. And the political violence that characterizes the country did not seem to affect the center of the Caribbean region, Cartagena, a city of more than 1 million inhabitants. By 2003 Colombia was the only country in Latin America outside the Dominican Republic and Venezuela where the Astros actively scouted.

Much of the credit for the move into Colombia goes to Orlando Fernández, the Astros scout who covers western Venezuela. He had traveled to Cartagena for a tournament in the late 1990s, was impressed with the level of play, and suggested that Andrés explore scouting in Colombia. During his trip, Fernández met Guillermo Ramírez, a baseball coach who he believed might be just the right person to run a satellite facility. Andrés went to Colombia to meet Ramírez and in 1998 hired him to get the program off the ground. Ramírez, a Cartagena native, is a very soft-spoken man in his early forties and looks like a shorter—he is about 6-0—version of former NBA star Clyde Drexler. He is intelligent, very thorough, and clearly understands and embraces Andrés's vision of scouting and development.

In June 2000 I went with Andrés and Ramírez to the Astros' mini-academy at Bayunca—about fifteen miles east of Cartagena—where a security guard with an automatic rifle greeted us at the entrance. This armed presence serves as some protection from bandits, insurgents, or death squads, and certainly as a deterrent to competing organizations' scouts—a real threat to take promising players. The facility is owned by Comfenalco (Caja de Compensación de Fenalco), a business foundation in Cartagena, which among other projects operates a school for 9,000 students from pre-K through high school. Comfenalco uses the complex for weekend gatherings and to maintain a small sports program.

It was very hot, damp, and muggy and, except for the chanting of frogs after a late afternoon rain, very quiet. The area around the facility is dotted with mango trees and is devoted to cattle ranching. In fact the rudimentary baseball field where the players work out has been created out of a cow pasture. But Andrés envisioned a manicured field like the one at the Astros' academy in Venezuela.

When we went back for a game a couple of days later, the field, although still very basic, had chalk foul lines, and there were twenty-five young men in mismatched uniforms ready to play. While they called it a game, it was really just a five-inning showcase of a half-dozen pitchers Andrés wanted to see. The one prospect that emerged, right-handed pitcher Ronald Bravos, was signed a couple of months later and competed for two seasons before being released in 2003.

I was anxious to learn more about the roots of baseball in the country, and Ramírez set up a meeting with Raúl Porto Cabrales, author of *Historia del béisbol profesional de Colombia*.[8] He began by explaining that the Zúñiga brothers, Colombians who studied in the United States, are thought to have brought baseball equipment to Cartagena in 1903. But during the 1950s one of the brothers, Gonzalo Zúñiga stated in an interview that he actually returned to Colombia in 1905, not in 1903. "And that's where the errors begin," said Porto Cabrales. Another source states that two local residents returning from Cuba brought baseball to Barranquilla in 1906.[9]

But baseball could have arrived on Colombia's north coast much earlier, coming with Panamanian students studying in Cartagena in the late 1890s. Panama was part of Colombia, Cartagena had the closest good universities, and baseball was played in Panama by at least the 1880s. It was also possible, explained Porto Cabrales, that a Cuban, Francisco Balmaceda, introduced the game to Colombia in the mid-1870s. Balmaceda planted sugarcane, brought cane cutters from Cuba, and reportedly built a baseball park for workers in María la Baja about one hundred kilometers south of Cartagena.

In any event, by the early 1900s baseball was being played along the Caribbean coast of Colombia and continued to gain popularity. In 1916 there was a game between all-star selections from the two largest cities, Barranquilla and Cartagena. By 1930 there were eighteen teams in Cartagena, and the first enclosed stadium was built just in time for a visit by a team from Macon, Georgia, of the South Atlantic League, featuring future Astros GM Paul Richards. During the 1930s and early 1940s, the level of amateur play along Colombia's north coast rapidly improved and was capped with a Colombian victory over Cuba in the title game of the Central American and Caribbean Games played in Barranquilla in 1946. In 1947 Colombia beat Puerto Rico (Cuba did not participate) to win the IX Baseball World Cup held in Cartagena.

The Colombian professional league was founded in 1948 and lasted until 1958. Thirty-nine players from this era of pro ball in Colombia went on to play in the major leagues including Willie McCovey and Brooks Robinson. The Colombian league started up again in 1979 and played for seven seasons. More than sixty future major leaguers, including the Astros Glenn Davis and Bill Doran, emerged from this period.

During the 1980s, Houston scout Tony Pacheco was on the board of directors of the Colombian league, and long-time Astros employee and Pacheco disciple, Carlos Alfonso, managed there for three seasons. The Astros originally signed the Cuban-born Alfonso as a player in the late 1960s. He suffered a career ending injury in 1976 and was hired by Astros GM Tal Smith as the team's bullpen catcher and coach. During his eleven years with the Astros, Alfonso at various times also worked in group ticket sales, was the team's traveling secretary, coordinator of spring training operations, director of Caribbean scouting, and also manager at the Single-A, Double-A, and Triple-A level. Between 1987 and 2005, Alfonso worked for the San Francisco Giants in various capacities from director of player development to major league coach. In early 2006, he was hired by the Tampa Bay Devil Rays to rebuild their Latin America scouting program.

During Alfonso's first year as a manager in Colombia with the Olímpica team in Barranquilla, the batboy was a thirteen-year-old kid named Edinson Rentería. Four years later in 1985, Alfonso and Gene Clines, another Astros scout who was coaching in Colombia, signed Rentería, at that time a middle infielder, to a contract with Houston. Edinson Rentería was the last player acquired by the Astros in Colombia until Andrés started up the program in the late 1990s. Clines recalled that when the Astros signed Edinson Rentería, his nine-year-old brother Edgar was always hanging around the ballpark. "We dropped the ball," Clines told me in 2005. "Somebody could have put an academy in Colombia a long time ago."

It was Edgar Rentería's game-winning hit for the Florida Marlins against Cleveland in the eleventh inning of Game 7 of the 1997 World Series that caught the attention of Colombia and not just that of baseball fans on the Caribbean coast. And it was the 2004 World Series when shortstop Edgar Rentería (Barranquilla) of the St. Louis Cardinals faced off against Orlando Cabrera (Cartagena) of the Boston Red Sox that baseball fans in the United States became aware that baseball was also played in Colombia.

Seven Colombians, not including Luis Castro, long considered to be the first Latino major leaguer when he made his debut with the Philadelphia Athletics in 1902, have played in the big leagues. Because Castro's birthplace has recently been established as New York City, the distinction of being the first Colombian-born player in the major leagues goes to shortstop Orlando Ramírez, who played for the California Angels in 1974. Other Colombian big leaguers include middle infielders Joaquin Gutiérrez, Edgar Rentería, Orlando Cabrera; Orlando's brother, utility player Jolbert Cabrera; catcher Yamid Haad; and pitcher Emiliano Fruto. Fruto, who made his debut with Seattle on May 14, 2006, is the first Colombian to ever pitch in a major league game.

Some consider Inocencio Rodríguez the best player ever in Colombian professional baseball. Rodríguez was signed by the San Francisco Giants in the mid-1950s and sent to the United States. No one is quite sure how long he stayed, but Rodríguez got tired of the cold in early spring, did not learn English, quit, and returned home to

top: Caracas Baseball Club May 1895, the first baseball team in Venezuela. *Photo by Carlos Federico Lesmann. Courtesy of Museo de Béisbol/Salón de la Fama, Valencia, Venezuela.*

bottom: The first baseball game in Venezuela, May 1895. *Photo by Carlos Federico Lesmann. Courtesy of Museo de Béisbol/Salón de la Fama, Valencia, Venezuela.*

Pete Rose with the Caracas team during the 1964–65 winter season.
Courtesy of Museo de Béisbol/Salón de la Fama, Valencia, Venezuela.

Sixteen-year-old Bob Kelly Abreu flanked by Rubén Cabrera (left) and Dr. Lester Storey (right) in May 1990 at the Astros Venezuelan academy three months before he signed with Houston. *Photo by Mary Beckner. Author's collection.*

top: Andrés Reiner, May 1990, Valencia, Venezuela. *Photo by Mary Beckner. Author's collection.*

bottom: Andrés Reiner on his last tour of the Astros' minor league affiliates, Round Rock, Texas, June 2005. *Photo by the author.*

top: Orlando Sánchez Diago and René Cárdenas looking at a map of cities that carried Houston Astros Spanish-language broadcasts in late 1960s. *Photo courtesy of René Cárdenas.*

bottom: José Herrera made his big league debut with the Astros in 1967, becoming Venezuela's fourteenth major leaguer. Herrera was the only Venezuelan native to play for the Astros until the products of the academy began to arrive in the mid-1990s. *Photo courtesy of the Houston Astros.*

top: Melvin Mora and Andrés Reiner at the tenth anniversary of the Astros academy, Guacara, Venezuela, November 1999. *Photo by the author.*

bottom: Astros Venezuela academy at Guacara, May 2003. *Photo by Eduardo Aular. Photo courtesy of the Houston Astros.*

top: Astros Venezuelan staff, Guacara, May 2003. Left to right, Jesús Aristimuño, Ramón Morales, Pablo Torrealba, Omar López, Mario González, Wolfgang Ramos, and Oscar Padrón. *Photo by Eduardo Aular. Photo Courtesy of the Houston Astros.*

bottom: Wladimir Sutil at a tryout at the Astros academy a week before signing with Houston, May 2003. *Photo by Eduardo Aular. Photo courtesy of the Houston Astros.*

top: Roberto Petagine in Jackson Generals uniform, San Antonio, Texas, 1993. *Photo by Margo Gutiérrez. Author's collection.*

bottom: Richard Hidalgo visiting a neighborhood near Valencia very similar to the one he grew up in Guarenas, 2005. *Photo by Alcaldía de Naguanagua, Lino Benítez, photographer. From the collection of Eduardo Castillo H.*

One of baseball's hottest tickets, Caracas versus Magallanes in Caracas.

top: Bob Kelly Abreu in the visitors' dugout in Houston's Minute Maid Park, August 2005. *Photo by the author.*

bottom: Seattle Mariners players celebrate winning the Venezuelan Summer League championship, Aguirre, Venezuela, August 2002. *Photo by Jorge Jamail-Gutiérrez. Author's collection.*

top: Rafael Cariel timing a prospect at a tryout in Ciudad Bolívar, 2001. *Photo by Jorge Jamail-Gutiérrez. Author's collection.*

bottom: Prospect Douglas Salinas pitching in a showcase tryout for scouts at the Astros' Venezuelan academy, July 2005. *Photo by the author.*

top: Scouts from seventeen major league organizations evaluating Salinas at the Astros' academy, July 2005. *Photo by the author.*

bottom: Salinas and his grandmother listen to an offer from the Seattle Mariners after the tryout. *Photo by the author.*

Sixteen-year-old Salinas relaxing after his tryout. *Photo by the author.*

Cartagena. When he left, Rodríguez was ahead of Orlando Cepeda at first base in the Giants organization depth chart. Supposedly, Cepeda commented that he had to thank Rodríguez for leaving the Giants, thus giving him the opportunity to get to the big leagues quicker. While Cepeda went on to the Hall of Fame, Rodríguez played in the professional leagues in Colombia, Mexico, Nicaragua, and Cuba where Porto Cabrales noted, "He hit the longest home run ever at Havana's El Cerro Stadium."

"But Rodríguez never made it to the big leagues and ended up driving a police car here in Cartagena," said Porto Cabrales. "I believe he still lives here."

After hearing that, I realized that Rodríguez was the inspiration for a short story "El cuarto bate,"(The Clean-Up Hitter) by Colombian Roberto Montes Mathieu.[10] Written in the vernacular and slang of Colombia's Caribbean coast, "El cuarto bate" is a first-person account of an unnamed baseball player. The narrator explains that he was the best player in the country during the Golden Era of Colombian baseball in the mid-1950s. He could hit for power, was outstanding on defense, and attracted the attention of scouts who wanted to sign him and send him to a team in the United States. He was so famous that when he got on the bus, the driver would say, "You're the cleanup hitter, you don't have to pay." And the women would throw themselves at him. He was, in his own words, *el pechichón del béisbol*—roughly translated as "the hottest thing going."

The player never went to the United States, he gets older, and his skill level drops. He can still ride the buses free, but fewer people stop him on the streets to marvel at his baseball feats. He decides it's time to get out of baseball and find another way to earn a living, and realizes that he has no other skills. "That's why I had to put on this uniform. They offered me this job and I took it." His new boss tells him, "We're going to see if you are still good at hitting; that you haven't forgotten how to use the bat." *El cuarto bate* asks why he was being taken to the university where a student protest was occurring. "This is a game specifically made for you," his boss told him. "Hit them hard and let them know who is in charge." So the former baseball great, now a policeman, jumped into the fray with his club and began wielding the stick with both hands. And once again the people on the street refer to him as *el cuarto bate*.

I returned to Cartagena in the summer 2004 and inquired about meeting Rodríguez and was saddened to discover he had died sometime during the last year. But later that summer, I saw Orlando Cepeda in the lobby of the Hilton Americas hotel during All-Star Game week in Houston. If anyone could say just how good Inocencio Rodríguez was, it was Cepeda. When I approached and mentioned Inocencio Rodríguez's name, Cepeda looked surprised.

"He was one of the best I ever saw," said Cepeda looking off in the distance and recalling the memory of a player that he had probably not thought about in more than forty years. He paused for a couple of seconds and repeated, "He was one of the best I ever saw." And after another pause, "He was one of the best I ever saw." Cepeda then turned away and signed an autograph for a fan. He didn't smile, and he looked very intense. It was clear that Inocencio Rodríguez had made a lasting impression on Cepeda just as I was told in Cartagena.

Very few scouts from major league organizations devote the time or energy necessary to discover players in Colombia. Some will go to Cartagena or Barranquilla for a tryout, but few venture further afield. This is understandable as it often requires travel to areas not recommended in tourist guidebooks.

When Guillermo Ramírez and pitching coach Arnold Elles went to a town an hour south of Cartagena to check out a player, they got a bit more than they bargained for. After the two Astros scouts saw the prospect, town leaders informed them that some armed group had been there earlier in the day and had killed a young woman. Then one asked, "So, are you guys going to join us for lunch?" Ramírez and Elles politely, but quickly, declined, explaining they were kind of in a rush to get back to Cartagena.

This is part of the scouting reality in Colombia.

"Some scouts are afraid to come to Colombia. Really, I hope they all are," laughed Seattle Mariners scout Curtis Wallace. "Every time Rentería makes a catch, or one of the Cabrera brothers gets a hit, someone asks 'Do we have anyone scouting in Colombia?'" Wallace, the scout who signed Emiliano Fruto, told me, "and then they get up the courage to send someone in."

While approximately a dozen organizations have scouts based in Colombia, Seattle and Wallace provide the main competition to the Astros for signing players. The Mariners do not have a facility in Cartagena—Wallace signs players out of tryouts. I first met Wallace in Puerto La Cruz, Venezuela, while he was scouting for Seattle at the 1994 Caribbean Series, and we became reacquainted in Cartagena in 2000 and 2004. Wallace, from Elizabeth, New Jersey, signed a minor league contract with the Detroit Tigers in 1975, was injured in spring training, and released. In 1979 he was playing for San Juan in the Inter-American League, and when the league folded in mid-season, made his way to Cartagena.

During his first season playing in the Colombian league in 1979–80, Wallace was known as "El Hombre Lobo" (the Wolfman) due to his long hair and full beard. But after he displayed outstanding defensive work at third base, a cartoon in a Cartagena newspaper pictured him inside of a spider web with the caption "El Hombre Araña" (Spiderman) and that has been his nickname ever since. Wallace played and managed in the league for seven seasons, is married to a Colombian woman, and has lived in Colombia for twenty-seven years. "Everybody is trying to get out of Colombia, and I'm trying to stay," Wallace told me.

On my return visit to the Astros' facility at Bayunca in 2004, I found that the academy had undergone drastic changes in four years. There were dugouts, small grandstands along the first-and third-base lines, a clubhouse, training room, and office, and the playing field was manicured. There were no mismatched uniforms: the fifteen players working out—ranging in age from fourteen to seventeen—were all wearing black shorts and white T-shirts, both with a small Astros logo, and dark blue Astros caps. Because MLB regulations do not apply in Colombia, prospects as young as fourteen can be recruited and may stay for a year. Ramírez and his staff work to develop the prospects in Bayunca, and Andrés or a scout from the Venezuelan academy visits three or four times each year to decide which players will be sent to Valencia. Then Ramírez brings in another group of players and the process starts over.

In addition to improving the physical layout of the complex, Ramírez has expanded his extensive network of contacts throughout Colombia. He, of course, scouts the baseball hotbeds of the north coast—Cartagena, Barranquilla, Montería, Sincelejo, Santa Marta, San Andrés, and Providencia—but he also has tryouts in the soccer strongholds of Cali and Medellín. Ramírez usually brings Astros caps and some new baseballs as giveaways in an effort to spread goodwill and pave the way for future contacts. He is aided by the fact that the Astros are the only organization to have an academy in the country. "This gives us an advantage over other teams: players want to sign with the Astros," Ramírez explained. It is reminiscent of the Astros' early days in Venezuela in 1990–91.

Andrés's decision to remain in Colombia while abandoning scouting programs in Mexico, Nicaragua, and Panama was based upon his belief that this was the most cost-efficient way to produce the maximum number of players. Thus far, he appears to have been correct. There are thirteen Colombians still with the Astros, including right-handed pitcher Rodrigo Escobar, who was selected to the Carolina League All-Star team in 2006. Three others—Steve Brown, Carlos Ladeuth, and Ronald Ramírez—were playing in rookie or A-ball in the United States, and eight players—one fourth of the roster—of the 2006 Astros' Venezuelan Summer League team were from Colombia. All began their journey at Bayunca, the Colombian filter to entry into the Astros' minor league system.

10

Refining the Product

The Venezuelan Summer League

When the Astros traveled to Valencia for a two-game spring training exhibition series against the Cleveland Indians in March 2001, Richard Hidalgo was asked to take on added duties. He not only assumed his regular position in center field for both contests, but before the second game he also carried the lineup card to the umpires and, along with Cleveland shortstop and fellow Venezuelan Omar Vizquel, joined local recording artist Mirla Castellanos in singing their country's national anthem. Hidalgo—who received thunderous applause when he was introduced before the games—was coming off a season in which he had a .314 batting average with 44 home runs and 122 RBI, all career marks. And only two months earlier, he had signed a $32 million, four-year contract with Houston. Clearly the Astros had high expectations of Hidalgo.

It seemed like a no-brainer for Astros owner Drayton McLane to make the three-hour flight from Orlando to visit the source of so much of his organization's talent. He had never been to the Astros' academy, but he was conspicuously absent on this trip. GM Gerry Hunsicker did, however, accompany the team for the games in Valencia.

"It was extremely important for us to be down there because of our academy and the foothold that we have. Venezuela has been vital to our development efforts," Hunsicker told me. "The fact that we could take our major league team would do nothing but reinforce and improve our popularity down there. It is also important for the kids in Venezuela to see our major league players just to show them what the dream is all about."

The kids Hunsicker was referring to were the four-dozen young men at the academy under contract to the Astros, and all of them were provided with tickets to attend one of the games. While in Valencia, Hunsicker took the opportunity to visit the academy. Although the Astros had improved the field, built a clubhouse with spartan office facilities, and added a batting cage, the facility had remained basically the same as when I first visited in 1990. That changed significantly in November 2002 when construction was completed on the new living area and a second playing field. Andrés had convinced Hunsicker and Tal Smith to invest $600,000 to build a state-of-the art facility. The organization was spending over $300,000 a year to house and feed players in a motel, and Andrés explained that the new building would pay for itself in about three and a half years. The Astros had long been the frontrunner in academies in Venezuela, and the improvements elevated the complex to one of, if not the best, in all of Latin America. In 2003 the facility received a nineteen out a possible twenty score by Major League Baseball in its annual inspection of academies in Venezuela and the Dominican Republic.

The impressive two-story building is located along the left-field line of the main playing field. In the past players lived in a house rented by the organization, stayed with local families, or resided in a motel. Those arrangements proved either unsatisfactory or too expensive. On the top level of the new building there are twenty-four rooms that can accommodate forty-eight players. Each room is air-conditioned, has a private bath, and is equipped with cable television. Because the players will be housed in this type of arrangement when they begin their minor league careers in the United States, Andrés believed it would be a good idea to get them accustomed to it in Venezuela. Between the two wings of rooms is a recreation area with picture windows overlooking both playing fields.

The first floor has an office, conference room, clubhouse for Astros coaches, small gymnasium, classroom used for English lessons and lectures, and a dining area. The food is excellent and nutritionally balanced. I can attest to that: I spent a week there in May 2003 sleeping in one of the rooms and taking my meals with the players while gathering information for a story I was writing for the *Astros Magazine*.

That visit was my third opportunity to experience the living arrangements of the Astros' prospects. In 1997 I spent a couple of nights in a room in a modest house with a local family in the Valencia suburb of Ciudad Alianza where some of the players were lodged. The rooms were small but adequate, the family atmosphere nurturing, and the meals very good. But Andrés was looking for an experience that more closely approximated the life the young men would lead once sent to the United States. In 2000 he arranged to house the prospects at the Motel La Cabaña, only a couple of miles from the academy. The players lived three to a room and received their meals in a dining hall. I stayed at the motel in 2000 and 2001 and ate with the players. It was comfortable and the food acceptable. It was clearly an improvement over the prior living arrangements but not precisely what Andrés wanted, and it was also expensive. The move to the new building at the academy represented a significant change in the players' comfort level.

But the most important aspect of the Astros' Venezuelan program—the staff—has remained remarkably stable for more than sixteen years. Jesús Aristimuño, Wolfgang Ramos, Pablo Torrealba, Rafael Cariel, Orlando Fernández, and Dr. Lester Storey are still onboard, and younger instructors and scouts Mario González, Omar López, and Oscar Padrón were added to the staff at the end of the 1990s.

Mario González, in his early thirties, is a scout and the manager of the Astros' Venezuelan Summer League team. Hired by Andrés as a scout and instructor in 1998, González, from Puerto Ordaz, was a promising middle-infield prospect with the Texas Rangers' organization in the early 1990s before an injury cut short his career. He learned the scouting trade from his father, also named Mario, and by traveling in eastern Venezuela with Rafael Cariel.

Omar López is a scout, serves as the infield and hitting coach of the Astros' Venezuelan Summer League team and also works in the administrative aspects of the academy. López, in his late twenties, was signed as a middle infielder in 1994 by the Chicago White Sox and after two seasons in the low minors, was selected in the Rule 5 minor league draft by Arizona, and then released after only two months. Frustrated, López returned home to Valencia in the summer of 1998 and dropped by the academy to see if Andrés would give him a contract. Andrés told him that he had not projected him as a prospect in 1994 and did not want to sign him now, but he would help him get a job as a coach. López went to the academy every day, worked with the instructors, and took notes. Andrés was impressed and convinced the Astros to hire him for the 1999 season. He has been a rising star in the Houston organization ever since, and his ability to communicate in both English and Spanish has facilitated his progress. In 2000 López was asked to fill in for an injured coach at Auburn in the New York–Penn League, and in the fall of that year, he was a manager in the Astros' instructional league.

After spending just over a year working in the Astros' Mexican program, Oscar Padrón returned to Venezuela and served as both scout and instructor at the academy and as the pitching coach of the summer league team.

With the opening of the new building in 2002, several other new employees were added to the payroll. Ramón Fereira—whose son was an Astros prospect in the late 1990s—runs the kitchen and dining room and provides three hot meals a day for the players. Pedro Franceschi, the building administrator, not only is responsible for keeping everything in order and the complex spotless but also makes sure the players get back to academy by the 9:00 p.m. curfew each evening.

Most players are up early and breakfast is served at 6:30 a.m. Some will report to the batting cage for extra work at 7:30 a.m., while the others will be on the field shortly after 8:00 a.m. Five days a week at 5:00 p.m., there are English classes. After the evening meal at 6:00 p.m., many players go to a nearby shopping mall to make phone calls or use the Internet. They are all back at the residence by 9:00 and begin to shut down for the evening around 10:00 p.m. Players from cities and towns close by often go home on the weekends.

The academy is open most of the year. Players recovering from injuries begin to return from their Christmas break in mid-January, while the rest arrive on February 1. After those players going to the United States have left, the focus of the academy becomes the Venezuelan Summer League. Those thirty-five players remaining at the academy are assigned to the Astros' team in the Venezuelan Summer League that plays a seventy-game schedule beginning mid-May and lasting through early August. After the completion of league play, the academy closes for six weeks. In early October play begins in the *liga paralela*. This is another busy time of the year for the facility with prospects that played in the United States during the summer joining with those who remained in Venezuela. In mid-December, the academy again shuts down for six weeks.

In addition to players under contract to the Astros, the academy also hosts young men who are being evaluated. According to rules established by Major League Baseball, a player may remain at the academy for only thirty days, after which time he must be signed or leave. About once a month, a few players are brought to Guacara by the Astros' scouting staff for a tryout, an event that Andrés described as "the final filter."

When I was there in May 2003, two Astros associate scouts, Nestor Marrero and Euclides Vargas, arrived with four young men they had seen in their pursuit of players in central Venezuela, including the metropolitan Caracas area. The four players were readily distinguished from the Astros' prospects by their mismatched uniforms. As in the tryouts I had seen all over the country, the would-be Astros, all position players, were observed running, throwing, hitting, and fielding.

The fifty-year-old Marrero, who was born and lives in the Caracas suburb of El Hatillo, has been an associate scout with Houston for almost fifteen years, covering Caracas and the nearby coastal states of Miranda and Vargas. I had visited with him on several occasions, both at Guacara and at El Hatillo. I had an open invitation to go scouting with him but had not done so partially because of time constraints and also because I was a bit hesitant to visit some of the areas of Caracas in his territory. I remember him telling me that he even went into 23 de Enero barrio in Caracas. I was intrigued because it is considered one of the roughest residential areas in the city. A place he will not enter due to concerns about his physical well-being is a neighborhood called MOP (Ministerio de Obras Públicas)-Zona 7 in Catia, the barrio adjacent to 23 de Enero. This area, named after a public-works project that was once located there, may be producing prospects but Marrero will leave them for other organizations to pursue.

At the tryout, one prospect, a very slender young man who ran sixty yards in 6.65 seconds, stood out. "It's a good time for just entering the academy," commented Dr. Storey, "but he can improve to 6.3." Andrés told me that he had a tremendous arm and that because of his age—almost 19—he could be signed for a very low bonus. I never even heard the young man's name. A week later when I was in Houston, Andrés said he had signed the skinny kid, Wladimir Sutil, a 134-pound shortstop from Guatire in the metropolitan Caracas area. Sutil's signing represented a change in Andrés's philosophy and strategy in the Venezuelan market: instead of focusing exclusively on young players, Andrés was now also interested in the eighteen-to-nineteen-year-old group. These players had been passed over by scouts, but had improved since they were first seen and were willing to sign for much lower bonuses. Andrés was not giving up on signing the sixteen-year-olds; he was simply adjusting to an ever-increasingly expensive market.

One fact that Andrés understood early on was that the young prospects he was signing needed at-bats and innings under game conditions. Knowing that most players would not be ready, or would be unable to obtain visas to go to the United States, he believed that the best way to get playing time for them would be to establish a rookie summer league in Venezuela, and he looked into ways to set it up from the moment he opened the academy in 1989. In November 1991 Astros assistant GM Bob Watson, manager Art Howe, minor league director Fred Nelson, and scouting director Dan O'Brien toured baseball parks in several small towns close to Valencia that could serve as sites for summer league teams. Representatives from several major league organizations, propelled by the Astros and the New York Yankees, met with Venezuelan sports officials to discuss the creation of a summer league and in early 1992, the MLB commissioner's office was given a detailed report outlining the need for the new circuit. "The lone remaining step is for the league to be officially sanctioned and an administrator hired to handle the initial scheduling and finances," concluded the report. But the proposal was put on hold due to demands for cutting costs industry wide and that remaining "lone step" would not be taken for over four years.[1]

Sal Artiaga, currently director of Latin American operations for the Philadelphia Phillies, picked up the ball. In 1984 when he was the head of Minor League Baseball (then called the National Association), Artiaga was instrumental in the founding of the Dominican Summer League. In August 1996 while working for the Chicago White Sox, he put together a proposal endorsing the new Venezuelan league based on the earlier MLB report. By November MLB general managers gave Artiaga's outline for the league the green light. "I'm amazed the concept moved so quickly," Artiaga told me. The league would begin in 1997.

At the time, there was an exiting Liga de Verano (Summer League) in Venezuela that had started up in the 1980s. The rosters of the eight-team league—which was not sanctioned by Major League Baseball—were a mix of veterans, released players, and rookies who spent most of their time on the bench. The new Venezuelan Summer League (VSL) would be official and exclusively for rookies. And it would be efficiently run: the person in charge, Saúl González, is one of the most well-liked and knowledgeable men in Venezuelan baseball. In 2004 González received the Warren Giles Award, the top baseball honor given to a league executive by Minor League Baseball.

With majestic mountains in the background, the Estadio José Pérez Colmenares in Maracay provided a beautiful setting for a Venezuelan Summer League game in early June 1997. On the field the midday tropical sun was relentless, making the ninety-degree temperatures seem even hotter. But in the stands, the shade, and an occasional breeze, tempered the heat. Although no admission was charged, most of the 15,346 seats at the stadium, home of the Tigres de Aragua of the Venezuelan Professional Baseball League, were empty. The noon weekday starts limited attendance mainly to scouts, instructors from the organizations involved, and friends and families of the players. But the league was not designed to attract fans or make money. Its purpose was to develop players, and the Venezuelan Summer League has become the base of the pyramid of minor league baseball. That first year the league played a sixty-game schedule with six co-op teams representing twenty-one major league organizations. Houston's co-op team included fourteen Astros, ten players from Montreal, and six from Toronto. Of the ten pitchers on that team, nine were from the Astros and seven were left-handers including Carlos Hernández.

Although the majority of the players are from Venezuela, league rules also permit participants from all Spanish-speaking countries or nations excluding the Dominican Republic and Puerto Rico. In addition to native players, young men from Aruba, Brazil, Colombia, Curaçao, Ecuador, Mexico, Nicaragua, and Panama can be found on the thirty-man VSL rosters.

Andrés was excited to finally see the league in operation but tempered his enthusiasm in his initial comments as we sat at that game in Maracay in 1997. "This is not exactly what I had envisioned, but it is a starting point," said Andrés. He was pleased that the young players were getting game experience, and he was very happy that they were doing it in Venezuela. "It is better for a young player to live in his own country. To go to the Dominican Summer League, they have to make dramatic cultural adjustments. And none of those adjustments will help them to achieve their final goal of playing in the United States," said Andrés.

The issue of Venezuelans going to play in the Dominican Republic was discussed in the 1992 report.

"The cultural differences and adjustments required of a young player going from Venezuela to the Dominican Republic, aside from the common language, is sometimes as imposing as when the young player goes from Venezuela to the United States because of the negative socio-economic differences between the two countries," the report noted. In other words, the Dominican Republic is poorer, and its population less educated than that of Venezuela.

Further, many Venezuelan parents did not want their sons to go the Dominican Summer League. Of course, they desired to see them play in rookie leagues in the United States, but short of that they wanted them in Venezuela. Once the Venezuelan Summer League was up and running, the fact that Andrés could tell a family that it was very unlikely their son would be sent to the Dominican Republic was an important recruiting tool.

I was there for the first league game in 1997 and attended games in seven of the first ten seasons. As Andrés had envisioned, the league expanded, reaching its high point in 2001 with twelve teams representing nineteen major league organizations. During my visits, I saw the league develop into an integral part of minor league baseball, visited many of the academies of other major league organizations, and saw two outstanding Astros prospects at the beginning of their careers: Carlos Hernández in 1997 and Héctor Giménez in 2001.

It took several years to overcome the budget cutbacks due to the 1994 strike, and it was not until 1997 that the Astros' academy was again operating at full capacity. By 2001 one of the players signed in 1997, Carlos Hernández, a product of the Venoco youth league teams, was beginning to blossom. The left-hander made the trip home to Valencia to play against Cleveland, pitched an inning in each game, and was impressive. Hernández had a great spring and was selected to start for his Double-A Round Rock team when they met the Astros at Enron Field in the last exhibition game. It couldn't have been scripted any better for him. In front of 20,000 fans and the Astros' owner and front office, Hernández threw five innings of no-hit, no-run ball against the major league team's opening-day lineup.

The year before in 2000, his first as a full-time starter, Hernández compiled a 6-6 record at Michigan in the Class-A Midwest League and ended the season on a low note. In one of the final games of league play his manager, fellow Venezuelan Al Pedrique, went out to the mound when it looked like Hernández wasn't really interested in pitching and asked what was up. Hernández replied that he was fine. But between innings, Hernández told the pitching coach he did not want to go back into the game. Pedrique approached Hernández and expressed his displeasure with the attitude he'd displayed. If he really wasn't interested in pitching, Pedrique told him, he should miss the next game. Hernández was suspended for one start in postseason play and was sent home to Venezuela. Although Hernández was upset with Pedrique at the time, he later told him that it was a wake-up call that helped get his career on track. The suspension and the fact that Hernández had never competed above the A-ball level made it difficult for the Astros to include the twenty-year-old pitcher on the 40-man roster. But leave him off, Andrés argued, and he would probably be selected in the Rule 5 draft, just as Johán Santana had been only a year earlier. After some discussion, Hernández was protected.

In mid-August 2001 Hernández was called up from Double-A Round Rock. He was the fourteenth player from the academy to reach the major leagues but the first to have played in the Venezuelan Summer League. I had seen seven of those fourteen on their first day in the big leagues, but it was the first time Andrés had the opportunity to be with one of the young men he had signed on the day he made it to the majors.

On the day the young pitcher arrived, I accompanied Andrés to the Astros clubhouse at Enron Field in early afternoon and encountered Hernández standing in front of his locker in his street clothes still a bit dazed by the turn of events. Less than twenty-four hours earlier, he had pitched one inning of a game in Round Rock. As we approached, Lance Berkman went over to Hernández and said, "Welcome to the big leagues, I'm glad you're up here."

A few minutes later, with Hernández dressed in his Astros uniform, Andrés pointed out that in the big leagues things were done differently than in the minor leagues. "Tell Larry [Dierker] why you like to wear your hair long," said Andrés. And he reminded Hernández to tell the bullpen coach how long it took him to warm up before going into the game (he had been a starter for two years but would likely be used in relief). The young man listened intently, and when he went out to the field a few minutes later, I noticed him talking to manager Larry Dierker, holding his hat a few inches over his head so the manager could see the length of his hair.

A few days later, Hernández made his first major league start and pitched seven innings of shutout baseball in a game against

Pittsburgh. In fact he did not allow a run in his first two big league starts—thirteen innings in total. But his season ended less than two weeks after it started when he suffered a partial tear of his rotator cuff while diving back into second base. He finished the year with a 1-0 record and a 1.02 ERA.

In 2001, the fifth year of the league, I watched the Astros' summer league team play five games. It was the first time the Astros had fielded a complete summer league team. (Cleveland was the only other organization with a full squad in the twelve-team league). I had the opportunity to see highly touted catching prospect Héctor Giménez, then eighteen years old, who had been described as an outstanding defensive player with tremendous arm speed and power from both sides of the plate. I watched as he hit a home run and threw out three opposing runners trying to steal in a game against the Seattle/Colorado team at Guacara. The next day at Cagua, home to the Cincinnati/Montreal entry, he had a triple and a single. But the most impressive performance by Giménez was at San Joaquín in the following game, on the Fourth of July, against a co-op team composed of prospects from Boston, Milwaukee, and Minnesota. In the eighth inning, with the game tied at 2–2, Giménez threw out a runner trying to steal second. In the ninth inning with two men on and no one out, Giménez picked a runner off first base. In the eleventh inning with the Astros leading 3–2, Giménez hit a three-run double to ensure the Astros' 6–2 win. "He will be something special," commented Andrés.

Although there were only between thirty and forty fans in the stands at San Joaquín, there was a guy with a microphone announcing players and providing a running commentary. "La Summer," was the way he referred to VSL. "Remember when you look at these prospects—*nosotros los vimos primero* (we saw them first)."

The Astros—led by series MVP Giménez—won the VSL championship in early August, defeating Cleveland in a best-of-three series. "It was the most exciting baseball series I have watched in maybe twenty years," Andrés told me.

In August 2002 I saw both games of the Venezuelan Summer

League finals between Cleveland and Seattle, two of the Astros' strongest competitors in Venezuela. Seattle won the first game 5–1 on Cleveland's home-field in San Felipe. The second game in the best two-of-three series was at Seattle's academy near Aguirre, about halfway between Valencia and San Felipe. The facility is located at Agua Linda, the family farm of Luis Blasimi, now an agent but previously the traveling secretary of Magallanes and the person who arranged my road trip with the team in 2000. The family built the complex in 2001 and has a five-year agreement with Seattle. Blasimi gave me a quick tour of the impressive facility, which has two complete fields, one infield, and four batting cages. The players are housed in a dormitory that can accommodate about two dozen players. There is a common bathroom area shared by all players.

Only a few days before I arrived, the academy had been robbed and I asked Blasimi about the incident. After expressing some concern about the negative publicity, he explained that fifteen armed men arrived at Agua Linda and took the players—between twenty and twenty-five of them—into the communal bathroom and then brought them out one by one and asked for their jewelry and watches. While the incident at Agua Linda was the most alarming, at about the same time, players at the Colorado Rockies academy in Valencia and at the Chicago Cubs' facility at Puerto Cabello were also robbed. Blasimi said they added additional security to prevent future robberies, but he also acknowledged that it is difficult to guarantee security. I thought to myself that the owners would need a small military unit to assure protection from fifteen armed men.

Seattle won the game 4–1 and the Venezuelan Summer League title, and I subsequently had the opportunity to visit with the Cleveland manager Henri Centeno, the first player I spoke with on my first visit to the Astros' academy in 1990. Although Centeno never made it to the major leagues, he played six years in the Astros' minor league system reaching Triple-A. He also played eight seasons of winter ball with the Caribes in Venezuela and has made a successful career in baseball. After working with Cleveland's program in Venezuela and managing their Venezuelan Summer League team to the finals two consecutive years in 2001 and 2002, Centeno was named the Indians' Venezuelan scouting supervisor in 2003. He attributes much of his success to his early training at the Astros' academy.

"In Guacara, I learned a great deal. When you come from a small town like I did, you have never experienced what you learn there. Working with Andrés Reiner and Jesús Aristimuño, I learned that there is always a positive road, despite the obstacles you encounter in professional baseball. The discipline that they taught me I believe has allowed me to do the things that I'm doing here with the Cleveland Indians," Centeno told me.

I didn't see the Astros' VSL team play in 2002, but Andrés was thrilled by the performance of an outfielder, Francisco Caraballo, that he and Cariel had signed the year before. Caraballo led the team in home runs (7), RBI (42), and hits (70) and was selected MVP. "I told Gerry [Hunsicker] that this kid will be the next Richard Hidalgo," Andrés said when Caraballo signed in early 2001.

By the end of the 2001 season, Richard Hidalgo's stock had begun to drop. His production fell off to a .275 average with 19 home runs and 75 RBI, and he was clearly overweight. And in 2002 he would bottom out. Something was not right with this former five-tool prospect.

I returned to Venezuela in 2003 a couple of days before opening day of the summer league and tagged along with Andrés and five other members of the Astros' staff to a meeting with representatives of the thirteen major league organizations and officials from MLB to go over the basic rules for the upcoming season. One of the participants was the legendary Epy Guerrero, then working with Milwaukee. Guerrero started his scouting career with the Astros in 1967, when he and Pat Gillick signed César Cedeño, and then followed Gillick to Toronto where he spent most of his career. Guerrero stood out at the meeting because he interrupted on several occasions, usually to complain about a rule or regulation. He asked about suspended games and, not satisfied with the explanation, said sarcastically, "You are in charge, do what you want to do." I wrote in my notes: "Epy is a loud guy who wants to dominate and you can see where it would be easy to dislike him," and I added, "Two scouts could not be more different than Epy and Andrés."

There were discussions about transportation, uniforms, and equipment, but much of the meeting was devoted to security issues. Several speakers commented on *la situación del país* (the situation of the country), a reference to both the political unrest and related economic downturn. But for league officials, the main concern was the issue of personal security.

"When players drive around in new cars wearing gold chains, this attracts thieves. We need to work to prevent this," commented one scout. Again, he mentioned *la situación del país*. League administrator Saúl González explained that the league would provide security guards to ride on buses with players and to be stationed at stadiums. A representative from Seattle announced that because of the robbery the previous year, a twelve-foot fence had been constructed around the complex, and visitors would be met at the gate by armed guards. Further, he added, all vehicles would be searched upon entering and leaving the complex.

A couple of days later I arranged to go with Ramón Fereira, the VSL coordinator, on his rounds of stadiums to make sure that the playing fields were ready for opening day. Before that, Fereira, whose day job was running the Astros' dining facility at the academy, had to make sure that everything was ready for lunch. He had been up since 5:00 a.m., gone to the market to buy supplies, and seen that breakfast was served without a hitch.

Our first stop was at Tronconero, a training complex now shared by the New York Mets and Philadelphia Phillies, about ten miles north of Guacara. Built in 2002 by the Magallanes club in partnership with Polar, one of Venezuela's largest beer and soft drink companies, and both state and municipal governments, the facility is larger than that of the Astros. There are four complete playing fields. Forty-eight players are housed two to a room but without private baths. Two VSL teams play here and the complex is home to four teams in the Liga de Desarrollo.

We then made our way over to Cagua, about twenty-five miles east of the Astros' complex. Cincinnati's academy is located in a building under the grandstands of the municipal stadium where league games are played. All players—at the time eighteen, but with room to expand to thirty—were sleeping in bunk beds in one large room. There was only one bathroom. There was also a dining area and TV room. It was clean, comfortable, but crowded and in no way compared to the complexes of Houston, the Mets and Phillies, or Seattle. It is clear that these four organizations, all in new and modern facilities, are the bedrocks of the league.

The league had been very successful during its first ten seasons. All the goals had been met—giving experience to players, relieving pressure of having a limited number of visa slots, and cutting costs. But it seemed that every spring, the future of the league was in doubt, and Andrés believed that MLB desired to shut it down and have all summer league activity in the Dominican Republic. That was not likely, however, because the Venezuelan Summer League had in effect become a tournament to select players to receive visas to go to the United States. That, of course, was not its main or only purpose, but without the league what would happen to the more than three hundred players who were beginning their professional baseball careers?

When the Astros and New York Mets were both pursuing Venezuelan prospect Roberto Petagine in 1990, Andrés asked the Mets scout if he was planning to sign the first baseman. No, the scout replied, the organization had no "visa slot" available. Although Andrés did not inform his competition, he had done his homework and discovered that while Petagine had lived most of his life in Venezuela, he was born in the United States and could travel there with no problem. But the Petagine case is an anomaly; the vast majority of Venezuelan players require visas to pursue their major league dream. And these are not immigrants seeking a better life in the United States, but migrant workers who must return home at the end of the baseball season.

Until 2007 the United States government strictly limited the number of foreign-born players allowed to compete in professional baseball at the minor league level. Major leaguers, including all 40-man roster players, fell under a different visa classification reserved for people of "extraordinary ability in the sciences, arts, education, business, and athletics."

The restrictions in effect through 2006 had begun in the mid-1970s with the increasing focus on scouting and signing players in the Dominican Republic. During that time, some organizations brought in large numbers of Dominicans—fifty or more—to their spring training camps in Florida, kept five or six and cut loose the others. Many of the released players did not return to the Dominican Republic and became "visa overstays"—the official government term for those who enter the United States legally but remain after their permission expires. In an effort to encourage major league organizations to be more selective in their recruitment practices abroad, the government placed limits on the number of visas allowed to the baseball industry. Over the years the visa categories changed, and the number of visas allotted grew—MLB received approximately 1200 visas in 2006, or about 40 for each organization. But the quota imposed by the government artificially limited the participation of foreign-born players in organized baseball in the United States, and the increase in visas did not keep up with the demand created by the rapid internationalization of baseball and the need for teams to recruit talent abroad.[2]

The convoluted process to obtain the necessary paperwork for a prospect to play in the United States involves three U.S. government agencies—the Department of Labor, the Department of State, and the Bureau of Immigration and Customs Enforcement [ICE] of the Department of Homeland Security)—the Office of the Commissioner of Baseball, and the thirty major league organizations. Visas issued by ICE are organized by letter—B for tourists, F for students, O and P for artists, entertainers and star athletes, and H for temporary workers. Minor league players born outside of the United required H-2B visas and were lumped together with several hundred other categories of seasonal workers. MLB submitted an application each year on behalf of the baseball industry for H-2B labor certifications. The H-2B application required an evaluation by the Department of Labor to determine that "qualified applicants in the United States are not available for referral to the employer and that employment of the alien will not adversely affect wages or working conditions of workers in the United States similarly employed." The baseball industry had to document its recruitment efforts in the United States and establish its need to import players and then the precise number of visas was negotiated.

With labor certifications in hand, the Office of the Commissioner of Baseball then informed the major league clubs of the number of visa slots each was allowed. The teams determined the countries where their allotment was to be used and the particular players they wanted to bring to the United States. After receiving their number, each organization submitted a petition to ICE for a visa on behalf of the player. When approved, ICE then notified the United States consulate in each player's home country. The consulates are staffed by the United States Department of State, the agency that actually places the visa in the player's passport—unless there are grounds for not issuing one. If a player had a criminal record or had previously entered the United States illegally, he would show up as a "hit" on the Department of State's computers. And in this game a "hit" means you don't get a visa.

The point man for the Houston Astros in the visa process is David Gottfried, Assistant General Manager of Baseball Operations. Andrés and Julio Linares in the Dominican Republic sent Gottfried lists of players they wanted to send to the United States, and Gottfried made the formal request to the commissioner's office. In 2005 the Astros asked for and received 44 H-2B visas. Gottfried then filed petitions with the ICE regional office in Lincoln, Nebraska, to obtain the visas.

Even though some organizations wanted more visa slots, for almost thirty years the process worked relatively well. In March 2004, however, there was a major glitch. The U.S. government informed MLB that all 66,000 H-2B visas for the year had been filled and that no others would be granted. The bottleneck occurred because the H-2B category includes hundreds of other occupations in addition to baseball prospects. Players were not only competing with each other for visas; they had to hope they were not edged out by ski instructors, circus workers, or those desiring a job at a bed and breakfast in Cape Cod. Under the March 2004 guidelines, if a club released a player on a visa, they could no longer use that visa slot to bring in another foreign-born player, as had been the past practice. The Astros and the other major league organizations adjusted as best they could and submitted visa requests early.

Clearly, MLB needed some adjustment in the process that would assure that their foreign-born workers would be allowed to enter the United States in a dependable manner. In a climate of anti-immigrant fear and concerns about foreign-born players taking away jobs from U.S. citizens, I was not optimistic that any reform in the visa process would occur any time soon.

But at the end of 2006, both the U.S. Senate and the House of Representatives approved legislation that President Bush signed into law that shifted minor league baseball players from H-2B to P-1 visas. Minor league players would no longer be classified as "temporary seasonal workers, but would now be considered "internationally recognized athletes." The law allows MLB teams to bring in as many foreign-born minor league players as necessary.

Ironically, the driving force behind the law, Senator Susan Collins (R, Maine), was concerned about problems that the Lewiston MAINEiacs hockey team, of the Quebec Major Junior Hockey League, was having obtaining visas for its Canadian-born players.

The main effect of the legislation for MLB is that it expands opportunities for players from Latin America, but an important provision in the law also grants P-1 visas to coaches. Previously, it proved very difficult to bring a foreign-born coach to work for minor league affiliate in the United States.

While the move to a P-1 visa status is a major advancement, foreign-born ball players will still be migrant workers, required to go home at the end of the season. No longer, however, will a minor league farm director have to decide which players receive visas, only which players are ready to compete, both on and off the field, in the United States.

With the visa in his passport, the Astros' Venezuelan prospect boards a plane for Florida and spring training. He has a superb baseball education and adequate cultural preparation, but nothing can prepare the young man for the adjustments he will face in his journey through the Astros' minor league system in pursuit of his dream.

Foreigners at Their Own Game

Welcome to the Astros' Minor League System

Every player at the Venezuelan academy is delighted when told he will travel to the United States. But for those making the trip to Kissimmee, Florida, for the first time, excitement is tempered with fear of the unknown.

"When they take the flight to come to the States, they understand that they are leaving everything behind, and they know that everything will be different when they get off the plane," explained Andrés.

And the anticipation of what will follow is so traumatic, that Andrés can't recognize some of the players. "They look like they were changed during the flight."

The phenomenon he witnessed is nothing new: it has occurred as long as players from Latin America have pursued their major league dream in the United States.

"We are strangers. I need a passport to come here," wrote Felipe Alou, a San Francisco Giants outfielder from the Dominican Republic in 1963. "Most Latin players feel they are outsiders," added Alou, who later managed the Giants, in his groundbreaking article, "Latin American ballplayers need a Bill of Rights" in *Sport* magazine in November 1963.[1]

Two years earlier, Dámaso Blanco, a nineteen-year-old middle-infield prospect from Caracas, signed with San Francisco and was sent to the Class D El Paso team in the Sophomore League that included franchises in West Texas and eastern New Mexico.

"We were playing in Hobbs, New Mexico, a very small town, and because I was black, I was not allowed to eat in the same restaurant with the white guys. It was a cultural shock for me; in Venezuela we were able go wherever we pleased," recalled Blanco, now a baseball radio and television commentator in Venezuela.

"The owner of one restaurant said to our manager, George Genovese, 'If I let your black guys come and eat, I'm going to lose all my white customers' business.' So they had an agreement: any time one of us black guys was going to eat, we would have to be in the company of one of the white players," recalled Blanco. When Blanco was hungry, he had to convince his white roommate, fellow Venezuelan Luis Peñalver, to go with him. "But Peñalver was trying to save money and he didn't want to eat, so I had to be begging him all time so I could go eat in that place in Hobbs."

Because Hobbs only drew 15,482 fans for sixty home games in 1961, more people probably remember Blanco from the diner than from the ballpark. He survived that humiliating experience and spent twelve years in the San Francisco minor league system before he made his debut with the Giants on May 26, 1972, becoming the twenty-first Venezuelan to reach the major leagues.

There is no doubt that racism affected the performance of the Latin players in the 1940s, '50s, and '60s and accounted for the failure of many to play up to their potential. But there are no statistics in the *Baseball Encyclopedia* on Latin players who returned home broken by racism. While discrimination based on skin color hasn't disappeared, it is now subtler and presents nowhere near the obstacle it did for the early migrant players. The problems that Latin players face today are mainly those of misunderstanding and insensitivity: the coach who angrily yells, "Look me in the eye," when the young player's cultural upbringing won't permit it; the prospect whose shoes are too tight, but who refuses to ask for a new pair for fear of being labeled a problem player; the beat writer who gets his information—or misinformation—about a player from another beat writer. Latin players today often confront stereotypes that portray them as childlike, hot tempered, ignorant because they are not fluent in English, or somehow less than serious about baseball.

Players from Latin America, whether by design or neglect, have had to struggle a bit harder than native-born players to attain their dream. There is no question that physical skills are what draw U.S. scouts to Latin America, but it is the player's ability to adjust mentally to adverse situations that allows him to survive, to bounce back from a poor performance, to accept criticism from coaches, and to maintain confidence in himself and make it to the major leagues. The adjustments for any baseball player are difficult. For the young men signed out of high school in the United States, it means being away from home for the first time, maintaining an apartment, balancing a bank account, learning how to cook, and building relationships with others. Often the player has been pampered since he was twelve and finds it difficult not to be the center of attention. The determination, perseverance, patience, discipline, and love for the game that spell success for the United States–born player are also necessary for those from Latin America who must also overcome a formidable language barrier, cope with the absence of a close-knit family and community, eat new foods, and struggle to survive in a new culture in a new country where they are often considered foreigners at their own game.

The preparation for players coming from Latin America today is light-years better than it was only thirty years ago. "*Cuando vas al norte, nada es fácil*" (when you go up north, nothing is easy), was the way Rafael Cariel put it. He received little or no orientation to help him through the transition when he signed with Minnesota in the early 1970s and English classes were nonexistent.

While the current Astros prospects receive instruction and game experience at the Venezuelan academy that help them adjust to playing in the United States, it is in the area of off-field preparation on which Andrés has focused special attention.

"I was always convinced that Venezuelan players needed to be prepared—very well prepared—before going to the United States. No other organization had ever done this in Venezuela before the Astros," Andrés told me in the mid-1990s.

"The main reason why our players do not have a hard time adjusting is that they started working hard here in Valencia. The players are dreaming of making millions. You have to tell them that baseball is not so easy and that they will have to make tremendous sacrifices and will miss out on many experiences that normal young men between fifteen and twenty years old will have. I explain to each player before he goes to the United States for the first time that he is an ambassador for other Venezuelan players."

That philosophy has not changed. Players at the academy clearly understand that no matter how much they improve their game on the field, until they learn the basic skills for coping with playing professional baseball in a foreign country, they will not progress in the Astros' minor league system.

Among the hundreds of players from Latin America (including several dozen signed by the Astros) I interviewed over a twenty-year period, the overwhelming majority agreed that the language barrier was the most difficult adjustment to make to be successful in baseball.

Most Latin players quickly learn English well enough to communicate on the field and to get something to eat after the game. An unwritten rule for young Latin players is never be first in line for an instructional drill. Instead, they watch closely what the player ahead does. They don't feel comfortable expressing themselves in a foreign language to reporters firing off questions. This discomfort explains in part some Latin players' reticence to talk to the press. They are not kidding when they say they would rather face a Randy Johnson fastball than a reporter in the locker room after the game. While Latin players are not invisible, they are often inaudible. Because their English is not perfect, most reporters don't seek out Latin players for the ten-second soundbite or the good, crisp quote.

The Houston organization's first attempt to ease the adjustment of players from Latin America began in the late 1960s.

"I think we were the first ones to really conduct language classes," said Tal Smith. "Tony [Pacheco] did this himself in spring training. He would start with the basics so the young Latin players would be able to order food in restaurants and be able to hail a cab and understand baseball terminology. Tony would work up his own dictionary of basic terms, and he would be the instructor. We would meet three nights a week for a couple of hours in the conference room in spring training."

When the Astros opened an academy in the Dominican Republic in the 1980s, English lessons were part of the program, and one of the academy's products is Washington Nationals manager Manny Acta. His bilingual skills coupled with his baseball experience have enabled him to become a very effective coach and manager.

"I took English in high school, but as you know, that won't teach you much. As soon as I signed, I said to myself 'I'm going to the United States and I'm going to have to adjust to them; they are not going to adjust to me,'" explained Acta.

He studied diligently in the English classes at the academy and also bought a book titled *Basic English*. "It only has eight hundred words, but it helps you communicate. And after that, I just learned with my teammates because I was never afraid to talk. Then I would read and watch TV and that helped me learn how to write in English."

Most baseball academies in Latin America have an English-language instruction program, but only the Astros have retained the same teacher for sixteen years. I met Luis Carmona on of one my first trips to Venezuela in the early 1990s, shortly after he started his classes, and I've visited with him on a regular basis.

"My father and Andrés have been friends since they were teenagers. So Andrés has known me for forty years—since I was born," Luis Carmona tells me in perfect, unaccented English. "I went to Houston during the 1980s and lived there for seven or eight years. While I was in Houston, Andrés moved there with his family." Carmona took classes at North Harris Community College in Conroe and worked an assortment of odd jobs.

"Andrés told me, 'If a dream that I have comes true, I want you to do a job for me,'" said Carmona, who did not know what Andrés was referring to until they both moved back to Venezuela in the late 1980s and the academy became a reality.

"We started the English lessons back in the clubhouse in Magallanes stadium, and from there we went to the Hotel Nacional, and then to a couple of houses that Andrés rented," explained Carmona. Since 2003 Carmona has had his own classroom in the new building at the academy. His one-hour class is held five days a week, and attendance is mandatory. The students have materials they are asked to study including a diagram of a human body as well as one of a baseball diamond—both with English terms listed. Carmona calls on students at random, and he corrects—and encourages them—as he moves along. It is not a uniform group: some have been at the academy for several months, others have just arrived; some have studied English in high school, while for others this is their first exposure; some are from urban backgrounds, others from rural settings; some study and prepare, and others don't. Often, he will hold separate classes for more advanced students.

In one class I attended, Carmona outlined a very detailed baseball diamond on the blackboard. One student pointed out that he had left out the batter's boxes.

"Where do people sit?" Carmona asked.

"The stands," responded a student.

"What do we call people who sit in the stands?" asked Carmona.

"The fans," several answered.

The similar sounds of the words, "stands" and "fans," often confuse those new to the language, and Carmona explained the importance of pronouncing words in English correctly. Another ten minutes were devoted to baseball terms: "bunt," "groundout," "cutoff," "warmup," "bases loaded," "strikeout," "screwball," and "home run." In the more advanced class I attended, Carmona had the students translate phrases such as "The batter hit the ball out of the park because I left a curve ball hanging over the plate."

Carmona shifted gears, pointed at a student, and asked, "What aches?"

"I have a stomachache," the young man replied, while another added, "I have a toothache."

"What is this?" asked Carmona holding up his thumb.

"My tumb," replied a player. Carmona corrects the young man's pronunciation without embarrassing him—or at least not too much. He would rather have a student feel a bit uncomfortable here in the classroom than in his first season in the United States in Greeneville, Tennessee.

"I always come in with high expectations," Carmona told me. "My main goal is for them to arrive in the United States able to understand basic instructions, get something decent to eat, get around, catch a bus, check into a hotel—the regular stuff."

Carmona really enjoys visits from his students who have made it to the major leagues, including Richard Hidalgo, Bob Abreu, Johán Santana, and Melvin Mora, and he takes great pride that he played a part in their development.

But preparation at the academy is not limited to English classes. Another key staff member in helping players adjust to the United States is Francisco Ruiz. Ruiz, a psychologist who was hired in 1996, has a degree in psychology from the Universidad de Monterrey (Mexico). A very congenial man in his mid-forties, he works quietly and does not attract a great of attention.

"Andrés found me when I was working in an organization that focused on drug-abuse problems and brought me into the sports world," Ruiz told me as we watched a game in Round Rock, Texas, in 2004.

"I basically work full-time for the Astros. I have my private clinic, but I don't have much time to devote to it because of the travel and the energy I have to put into the baseball work. You have to get out on the field, or go down in the dugout to talk with players. You can't just spend time behind your desk in the office," explained Ruiz.

Three mornings a week, Ruiz is at the academy meeting with prospects.

"I talk about cultural issues, legal matters in the United States, and family issues. I tell them how to act in hotels, what to expect in restaurants, and about STDs," Ruiz said. "I also talk about concentration in baseball. Players have to have a positive attitude if they are going to be successful."

Andrés was so impressed with the impact that Ruiz was having at the academy that he convinced the Astros front office to expand Ruiz's role to include players in the Dominican Summer League and those in the United States. In 2004 he was dealing with forty players in United States, twenty-eight in the Dominican Republic, and thirty-six in Venezuela: approximately half of all the players under contract to the Astros. Ruiz makes at least four trips to the United States during the season. While he will visit Triple-A Round Rock and Double-A Corpus Christi franchises, there are more players at the two A-ball teams in Salem, Virginia, and Lexington, Kentucky, the short-season team at Troy, New York, and the rookie team in Greeneville, Tennessee.

I asked Ruiz what he did on those visits.

"The same thing I do in Venezuela—attending to the psychological needs of the players: *cómo andan* (how they're doing), *qué hacen* (what are they up to), *cómo juegan* (how they're playing). Also, I want see how the players are living and speak with each of them individually."

One of the main challenges the players face is learning how to live in a group with other young men from different backgrounds. While there is no precise way to measure what Ruiz's intervention has meant to a player struggling and needing someone to talk to, clearly he has been able solve problems when they arise and diffuse potential ones even before the Astros front office becomes aware of them.

The Astros give all minor leaguers from Latin America a concise and informative handbook in Spanish that explains what is expected of them and lists phone numbers for people in the organization who can be of assistance. In addition to Francisco Ruiz, another person often called is Astros assistant director of baseball operations Carlos Pérez—not the former major league pitcher from the Dominican Republic. This Carlos Pérez has worked as a liaison with Astros' programs in Venezuela, the Dominican Republic, and Colombia, in addition to being involved in other player-development and scouting issues since 2003. Pérez, bilingual, bicultural, highly motivated, and congenial, was born in Bogotá, Colombia, and came to Houston in September 1981 just before his fifth birthday. He completed three years toward a degree in business at the University of Houston, before pursuing his real love: working in sports. He was an intern in media relations for the Houston Rockets in 2001 and with the Astros in 2002. At the end of 2002, Pérez applied for a full-time opening with the new National Football League franchise, the Houston Texans, in Hispanic outreach marketing. On the way to his interview with the Texans, Pérez ran into Andrés, who asked why he was wearing a suit and tie. At the time, Andrés was looking for someone to replace his assistant in the Houston front office, and the two talked for over an hour. When Pérez got back from his interview with the Texans, he had two phone messages: one extending him an opportunity to work for the football team, the other offering him a position with the Astros.

In his office in Houston, Pérez can often be found talking on two phones at the same time—resolving a visa issue for a player in Venezuela while simultaneously arranging for the shipment of baseball equipment to Colombia. He spends several weeks each spring in Kissimmee, Florida, helping in the transition of players arriving from the academies. While he also works on more general issues involving development and scouting, Pérez's presence in Houston has greatly facilitated coordination between the Venezuelan academy and the front office. Every organization serious about getting the most out of its investment in the region should attempt to find someone like Carlos Pérez.

In addition to working to ease the cultural and linguistic adjustment of the Venezuelans coming to the United States, Andrés was also concerned with the continued development of his academy products on the field. He wanted to have, and his promotion to special assistant to GM Hunsicker in 1997 gave him, a hand in the development of his players. But this also brought him into conflict with those inside the Astros' minor league system who believed the role of a scout was to discover a player and turn him over to the development side. Andrés was bothered by the slow development of his players once they reached the United States and the seeming lack of communication between players and staff.

In the academies in Venezuela and the Dominican Republic, the fact that there are fewer players allows the staff to spend more time with each player than in spring training. "This helps to develop a close personal relationship with the instructors and brings a comfort and confidence level where communication between players and instructors comes easy and open," Andrés noted.

All-Star shortstop Carlos Guillén addressed this issue with me as early as 1997 when he was playing for the Astros' Double-A Jackson team in the Texas League.

"In Venezuela, there is a very well-organized schedule. I believe we worked harder there than here," said Guillén. "When we get over here, we are more prepared in the basics and both physically and mentally ready to play."

"In Venezuela, we get more instruction and people telling us what we are doing wrong," said Guillén. "Maybe it's because there are fewer players that we get more attention. Over here, you may be having a problem, for example, you aren't hitting well. Here in the United States the coaches may not say anything to you because they want to see how you will do over the season. In Venezuela, a coach might even tell you during a game what you are doing wrong."

Since the mid-1990s, Andrés had been lobbying for better selection of coaches and instructors—especially at lower levels—in the Astros' minor league system. He believed it was difficult for a middle infielder to receive proper defensive instruction from a manager and hitting coach who had never played at shortstop or second base.

You couldn't blame Guillén for being a bit frustrated at Jackson in 1997. It was the first time he played every day after four injury-filled seasons. His manager had been a catcher in the major leagues, and there was no hitting coach or infield coach on the team. Guillén felt like he was ready to blossom and was yearning for someone to help him improve. He was thankful that at least the pitching coach, Jim Hickey, was bilingual and someone in whom he could confide.

In 1998 Guillén was elated not only to be promoted to Triple-A New Orleans but also to have a manager, John Tamargo, who spoke Spanish, and to be reunited with Jim Hickey. Guillén worked on improving his infield skills with a new addition to the Astros' organization, hitting coach Al Pedrique, and with teammate and former major league shortstop Luis Rivera. Guillén also benefited from the visits of roving infield coordinator, Iván de Jesús, and was thriving and growing both on and off the field.

Then in late July, Guillén, along with Freddy García and a player to be named later (John Halama) was traded to Seattle on July 31, 1998, for Randy Johnson. Six weeks later Guillén made his major league debut with the Mariners and played in ten games before a knee injury ended his season.

Many fans will recall Jim Hickey as the handsome, articulate pitching coach in the Astros dugout that Fox broadcasters turned to for comments during the 2005 play-offs and World Series. Hickey was drafted by the Chicago White Sox in 1983 and pitched for eight seasons in the minor leagues, reaching Double-A Columbus, an Astros affiliate in 1989. In 1991 Hickey began his career as a coach in the Astros' system with stops in Burlington, Asheville, and Jackson, and seven years at Triple-A New Orleans before being named Astros major league interim pitching coach on July 14, 2004. The interim was removed at the end of the season.

In addition to being a very good pitching coach, Hickey's ability to speak Spanish has greatly added to his effectiveness in dealing with players from Latin America.

"To be able to walk up to someone and speak to them in their language has a big impact when working with younger players at rookie and Class-A," explained Hickey.

While his bilingual skills are useful, they are not as critical in the major leagues where most players from Latin America are conversant in English. Hickey took Spanish in the seventh grade, improved his language skills by practicing with some of his teammates at Pan American University in south Texas, and picked up a little more Spanish at each step of his career, which included playing winter ball in Mexico and serving as the pitching coach for Magallanes.

Alfredo Pedrique, special assistant to Astros GM Tim Purpura, is a very personable and well-respected baseball man both in the United States and in his native Venezuela. Pedrique is bilingual and bicultural, intelligent, and low-keyed but aggressive when necessary. Pedrique, who played for three seasons in the major leagues with the New York Mets, Pittsburgh Pirates, and Detroit Tigers in the late 1980s, has various duties with the Astros, one of them being evaluation of the Astros' programs and players in Latin America.

Pedrique coached and managed in Houston's minor league system for three years between 1998 and 2000 and was chosen as the Astros' Player Development Man of the Year in 2000. But with his prospects for career advancement with the Astros blocked, Pedrique moved on to manage Arizona's Double-A team in El Paso in 2001, and then was promoted to head the Triple-A Tucson club in 2002 and 2003. Pedrique also managed in the Arizona Fall League in 2002.

In 2004 he was named the third base coach with Arizona's major league team and served as the team's interim manager when Bob Brenly was fired late in the season. When the Diamondbacks decided not to rehire Pedrique as full-time manager in 2005, he jumped at the opportunity to work with the Astros once again. While he enjoys his front office work, he is itching to get back into a uniform and would be thrilled to have another opportunity to manage in the major leagues. The 2005 season was the first that Pedrique had not been on the field in the United States since he signed a professional contract to play in the New York Mets minor league system in 1978. He returned to Venezuela for the 2005–6 winter season and led Magallanes to the best record in the league and was selected as the manager of the year.

While the Venezuelan prospects thrived on the instruction from bilingual coaches and managers such as Pedrique, Hickey, Iván de Jesús, Jorge Orta, and others in the Astros' minor league system sensitive to needs of players (managers Jackie Moore and Tim Bogar, pitching coach Charlie Taylor, and hitting coordinator Sean Berry among them), they were rarely prepared to deal with coaches who treated them unfairly because they were from Latin America. All baseball organizations—not only the Astros—have a fundamental flaw in this respect: the inability of some coaches, managers, minor league coordinators, and others in the front office to see beyond their own cultural limitations. The result is that some players from Latin America are released before they have an opportunity to develop their potential, or they are promoted too slowly.

GM Hunsicker was well aware of the problem. "We need to constantly remind ourselves that with all the Latin kids we can't make the assumption that the language isn't a problem and because you get a head nod that they understand what you say," Hunsicker told me.

"We need to be communicating effectively with these kids, and if we aren't, we take the steps to make sure we are. I don't care what anybody says, the communication skills many times are neglected. There is a lot lost in the translation. Kids misinterpret things that are said by staff."

"I'm pretty up front with our staff when we talk about this stuff. To bury our heads in the sand and suggest that there aren't prejudices and stereotypes throughout our personalities is neglecting the problem, because there are. I just think sometimes there are implicit prejudices that people don't even realize. Prejudice is maybe too strong a word. They don't mean anything by it, but it's just there. Just because somebody talks different, acts different, their body language many times can get misread, and you start making assumptions about kids based on those kinds of things that turn out to be untrue, and you can ruin a kid's career that way. So I'm very sensitive to that."

There were, of course, players from Venezuela who would complain about discrimination when in fact it did not exist. But for too many players the bias was real, and Andrés believed this could cause them to lose self-confidence, self-esteem, and the chance of fulfilling their big league dreams. Thus it was important to carefully choose the staff at the lower levels of the minor leagues, being especially cautious to hire instructors who treated all players with respect. Ideally, a bilingual manager or coach would be placed where there was a large group of players from Latin America. A rookie team manager did not necessarily need to be a good manager, but it was essential that he be a good teacher. During the 1990s the staff at the entry-level teams in the Astros' system in the United States often met these criteria. But for the 2005 season, the Astros' rookie team in Greeneville, Tennessee, with fifteen Spanish-speaking players on the roster, had no bilingual coaches and the manager was Russ Nixon, described to me by several observers as a cynical old man—precisely what is not needed at this level.

The organization also employed other coaches, whose inability to accurately evaluate Venezuelan pitchers often drove Andrés crazy. One coach in Greeneville in 2004 had worked with young Venezuelan pitchers at the rookie club in Martinsville, Virginia, and the Class-A team in Kissimmee, Florida, for fifteen years. Andrés ran out of patience dealing with him in the summer of 2004 when the two had a disagreement over the progress of right-handed pitcher Levi Romero. The coach was highly critical of Romero after a bad outing. Andrés had heard similar negative evaluations from the coach about pitchers Carlos Hernández and Johán Santana and insisted that Romero was coming along just fine.

"All my pitchers have gone through your hands," Andrés told him. "I know how you do your job and I don't like it. You are not a good evaluator." Andrés believed the coach had always looked for the negative in his pitchers without giving them much positive reinforcement.

Levi Romero finished the season 8-0, tied for the Appalachian League lead in wins (with Venezuelan teammate Juan Gutiérrez) and his 2.19 ERA was tops in the league. The coach in question retired after the 2004 season. But unfortunately, there were other coaches and instructors scattered throughout the Astros' minor league system who were also poor evaluators—and not just of players from Latin America. Some simply did not believe that a player signed for $10,000 in Venezuela could be as good as a player drafted in the second round with a $500,000 bonus. The question is why they were hired in the first place and why they kept their jobs. Andrés chalked it off to "politics," his manner of referring to the old-boy network.

A player Andrés believes was released prematurely is Ernnie Sinclair, a right-handed pitcher from Bluefields, Nicaragua. I first met Sinclair at the academy in Venezuela in 1998 and had the opportunity to visit with his parents in Nicaragua in 2002. Sinclair had a career 29-14 record in five seasons, and I expected to see him at Double-A Round Rock in 2004. I was shocked when Andrés told me that he had been released before the season started. Andrés had not been consulted and only discovered that Sinclair was no longer with the Astros when it was too late. "He was released because he was a Nicaraguan," Andrés told me. "It was easier to release him than an American player." Another Nicaraguan pitcher who was released at the same time as Sinclair, right-hander Devern Hansack, made his major league debut with the Boston Red Sox in September 2006.

As early as the mid-1990s, Andrés began to question why some of the players he had signed were not being promoted to higher levels, not having the opportunity to show their potential before they were released, or protected in the Rule 5 draft. He was becoming increasingly apprehensive about the fate of his players as they moved through the Astros' minor leagues. Andrés's blood pressure would rise over the release of an individual player, but it was the overall atmosphere of negativity in the Astros' minor league system that truly bothered him. He believed that players needed to be treated with more respect and that there existed a critical need to improve communication in the organization. While he was in control of his players' development in Venezuela, in the United States Andrés was not. He was constantly battling small fires and was unhappy about it. Some in the front office in Houston often viewed the man who brought radical innovation to scouting in Venezuela as a nuisance.

While Andrés could not protect Sinclair, he rarely had players released who he really believed still had potential, but often had to intercede directly with GM Hunsicker to save them. Although Hunsicker encouraged Andrés to fight for his players, this placed an extra burden on Andrés, required Hunsicker to use his social capital within the organization, and further annoyed those in the Astros' system who already perceived Andrés as meddling in areas where he did not belong.

"Why don't I hear about these complaints from other people in the organization?" Hunsicker asked Andrés. "You are like the president," replied Andrés, "they only tell what they think you want to hear. People are talking to me and complaining, but they are not telling you because they are afraid."

Some in the organization didn't appreciate Andrés's direct and honest style. Andrés countered that if he were not honest, the same mistakes would continue to be made and pointed out that his candid style was not perceived as anything but constructive criticism by Bill Wood, Dan O'Brien, Bob Watson, and Hunsicker—and by all of his staff in Venezuela. While Andrés was correct to criticize player development in the Astros' organization, he felt so strongly about the need for change that he came off as abrasive. He bombarded the Astros with so many suggestions for improvement that one could almost understand why the front office felt as though it was under attack from killer bees. Andrés was "rocking the boat" in an organization where the slightest ripple in the water was perceived as threatening. Andrés was well aware it would not be easy to make the types of changes he was suggesting.

In the meantime, he continued to fight for his players. Andrés clearly understood that all minor league players needed a *patrón*—someone to defend them in organizational meetings. He believed he had to be there, particularly when he might be the only person willing to speak up for them. This was especially the case when he believed many of his players were being undervalued. Parents entrusted their sons' futures to Andrés, and he felt an obligation—almost a moral responsibility—to defend them. From his perspective, this tenacity was not just good for his players; it was good for the Astros.

Andrés was also concerned that the minor league pitching and hitting coordinators and others from the front office involved in player development had not visited the academy for over three years (between late 2001 and early 2005). Prior to 2001, there had been a regular stream of visitors from Houston, which was curtailed because of a concern for their personal safety. Other major league organizations, however, continued to send on-field coordinators to Venezuela despite the political unrest. Andrés was offended by what he saw as essentially a "boycott" of his program. But more important, it resulted in reduced communication between the Venezuelan staff and those Astros staff members based in the United States. The front office in Houston seemed not to place a high value on the opinions of the Venezuelan instructors who knew the players best.

I believe that the entire issue of "undervaluing" Venezuelan players goes back to the inability of many of those evaluating players to transcend their own culture. Andrés already knew this. By the end of the 1990s, he had resigned himself to the fact that his job was to find players for the major leagues.

"I would like for a player I sign to get to the big leagues with the Astros, but I just want him to get there." No matter how much he rationalized it, it clearly hurt that the young men he nurtured would be playing with other organizations: "All those players are gone: Mora, Freddy [García], Santana, Guillén, Kelly [Bob Abreu]. I often think how nice it would be to have them all with the Astros."

12

What Happened? Where Did the Prospects Go?

Chicago White Sox pitcher Freddy García was a product of the Astros' Venezuelan academy as announcer Joe Buck noted during Game 4 of the 2005 World Series. That pipeline, he explained, "also included Johán Santana, Melvin Mora, Carlos Guillén, and Bobby Abreu, and all were signed for the Astros by Andrés Reiner."

"You could win a lot of games with those players" added his broadcast partner Tim McCarver. They did not have to point out the obvious—none were still with the Astros. By 1999 the word *despilfarrado* (squandered) accurately described how the Astros had lost some of the best players produced by their Venezuelan academy.

When I began to write about the Astros' academy in 1990, I envisioned an account describing how the Venezuelan players signed by Andrés fulfilled their big league dreams with the Astros. I never imagined that of the twenty-two players who made it to the major leagues, only twelve would make their debut with Houston or that by the time I was completing the book, only two academy alumni would be playing in the big leagues with the Astros. What happened?

As the academy players began to leave the Astros, I felt I had to explain why. My intention was not to embarrass the Astros nor to rationalize mistakes that had been made. It's easy to understand the trade that sent García and Guillén to Seattle for Randy Johnson in 1998 or earlier trades that shipped Roberto Petagine, Oscar Henríquez, Manuel Barrios, and Raúl Chávez to other organizations, but it's difficult to explain why Abreu, Mora, and Santana went on to become stars with other organizations while the Astros received almost nothing in return for them.

On November 11, 2004, Venezuelan fans, the media, and family of Johán Santana counted down the minutes as if they were anticipating the ball dropping at New York's Times Square on New Year's Eve. At 3:00 p.m., the Cy Young Award was to be announced by MLB. While all were cautiously optimistic that Santana would win, they were jubilant when they heard that the native son garnered all twenty-eight first-place votes. It was also an exciting moment for the staff of the Astros' academy that developed Santana, especially for Andrés.

"In particular I want to thank Mr. Andrés Reiner for having signed me for the Houston organization," Santana told Venezuelan reporters in one of his first interviews after receiving the award. "He believed in me when he told me I would get to the major leagues in four years. Regrettably, Houston's decision not to protect me was not in his hands, and I left there for Florida and Minnesota. But I followed his advice to work hard and I succeeded with the Twins."

I called Andrés in Houston a few hours after the announcement. He said he had been receiving phone calls from reporters wanting to know how he discovered Santana. I asked if anyone had inquired about how he felt that Santana was no longer with the Astros. One Caracas radio station had called: his response was, "We can find them, sign them and develop them. After that we can only hope that they get to the major leagues."

Santana has received almost every baseball award conceivable. He was selected the MVP of the Minnesota team. *Meridiano* named him Athlete of the Year in Venezuela. During the 2004 season, he won the first ever Premio Luis Aparicio given to the best Venezuelan in the major leagues. The governor of the state of Zulia presented him with the Orden Relámpago del Catatumbo (named after the unique lightning phenomenon in the state). The governor of the state of Carabobo gave him El Orden de la Batalla de Carabobo—in honor of one of Simón Bolivar's decisive battles for the independence of Venezuela from Spain. What Santana had done for Venezuela was described in the local media as a *gran hazaña*—a great feat—the same expression used to describe the victory of Venezuela over Cuba in 1941. Indeed, Santana's Cy Young celebration—along with the return of the *los héroes del 41*, and the induction of Luis Aparicio to the National Baseball Hall of Fame in 1984—is one of the three most important moments in Venezuelan baseball history.

In Spanish, the word *astro* has several meanings. While *los astros* could refer to the Houston organization, *los astros* is also the term used to describe galaxies or heavenly bodies. And an outstanding player is called an *astro*, as in *Andrés Galarraga es un astro*. When a Caracas newspaper referred to Johán Santana as *el Astro de los Twins*, it was clear a double meaning was intended.

I met with then Astros GM Gerry Hunsicker during the 2003 season and asked him why Santana had not been protected in the Rule 5 draft in 1999.

"That was a tough one. You know he didn't have a particularly good year in the Midwest League, and we just thought we didn't have room to protect a kid like that. And the Rule 5 is something that I have been very vocal about. I really think it is antiquated. It penalizes the organizations that do the best job of scouting. It's impossible to start protecting very many kids early in their careers because most of them aren't going to make it anyway. But more importantly, if you start protecting kids that are coming out of the Midwest League, the best-case scenario is that by the time they reach the big leagues, they are out of options. And, you know, it's tougher for a team to take a kid in the Rule 5 draft and keep him in the big leagues all year than it is to claim somebody on outright waivers and put them back in their system."

"So you are forced to make the difficult decisions with kids in A-ball especially asking the question, 'Can you really see somebody taking a kid at this point in his career and keeping him in the big leagues all year?' And the answer for $50,000—which is nothing today—is that a team that has no chance of winning certainly can claim anybody that they want and take a chance and take a roster spot. Not to mention in many cases it hinders a player's development because he is up here in the major leagues sitting on the bench. We need to make it at least $250,000. With the cost of development today—if somebody wants a kid in the Rule 5 draft, fine, but let's make the price up to standards."

Hunsicker was absolutely correct. It is very difficult to protect young players on the 40-man roster. This problem was alleviated somewhat in 2006 by the addition of one year to the time a player may remain unprotected.

Santana's first three years in the Astros' minor league system were not much to write home about: he had a combined 11-13 record. In 1999 he had an 8-8 record at Michigan in the Midwest League and was durable going 160 innings. The Astros had to decide whether to protect a twenty-year-old who had a combined 19-21 record in four years on their 40-man roster. They chose not to. Neither Andrés nor Hunsicker told me who was protected instead of Santana, but I later discovered it was Aaron McNeal. McNeal, a first baseman, was selected by *Baseball America* as one of the Midwest League's top-ten prospects, but he ended up being the only one of the ten not to reach the major leagues.

Santana made his major league debut with Minnesota on April 3, 2000, and on June 6 earned his first win. Pitching in relief, Santana beat the Houston Astros at Enron Field. During his first three seasons with the Twins, Santana had an 11-9 mark. In 2003 he went 12-3, with a 3.07 ERA and struck out 169 batters in 158.1 innings. In 2004 he was 20-6 with a 2.61 ERA and struck out 265 in 228 innings. He became the first Venezuelan to win twenty games in a season, and he was the American League Pitcher of the Month for July, August, and September. Needless to say, when he won the Cy Young Award Santana became the poster child for the upside of the Rule 5 draft.

While Andrés understands that the loss of Santana was partially a Rule 5 draft problem, he believes there was another contributing factor. "They [the Astros] can't project young Latin players, and a major issue is that they don't want to communicate with those who can."

The blunder of losing Santana cannot be undone. The question is whether we can expect another Venezuelan Astros prospect to be lost in a future Rule 5 draft. That was partially answered in November 2004, when Juan Gutiérrez, a twenty-one-year-old right-handed pitcher was added to the Astros' 40-man roster. You can bet that Andrés was a vocal proponent of the decision to protect the 6-3, 200-pound Venezuelan who had compiled an 8-2 record with a 3.70 ERA at Greeneville in the Appalachian League in 2004. In 2005 another academy product, hard throwing right-hander Felipe Paulino del Guidice joined the Astros' 40-man roster, and in 2006 another right-hander Paul Estrada was added. Even though many in the Astros' front office cringe when Santana's name is mentioned, perhaps they have learned something from his embarrassing departure.

While Santana was left unprotected in 1999, there was little doubt that another left-handed pitcher, Wilfredo Rodríguez, would be on the Astros' 40-man roster. For the first four years of their professional baseball careers, the paths of Santana and Rodríguez paralleled each other. They were born only a week apart, and the Astros signed both in July 1995. But while Santana compiled a lackluster 19-21 record during those early years, Rodríguez posted a stellar 35-16 mark. In 1999 *Baseball America* selected the twenty-year-old Rodríguez as the Astros' number-one prospect. The 6-3, 215-pound Rodríguez, from San Felix in the state of Bolívar, was discovered by Rafael Cariel, invited to the academy in June 1995, and signed a month later. His first professional season was with the Astros' team in the Dominican Summer League in 1996. Pitching exclusively in relief, he had a 1-2 record with a 2.97 ERA. In 1997 Rodríguez was converted to a starter and compiled an 8-2 record with the Astros' team in the Gulf Coast Rookie League and won team MVP honors. At Quad City in the Midwest League in 1998, he was 11-5. In 1999 he went 15-7 at Class-A Kissimmee where he was team co-MVP. He led the Florida State League in wins and strikeouts (148). Needless to say, the Astros were excited about Rodríguez.

"Wilfredo will be an impact pitcher at the major league level," said Andrés in 1999. "He has an overpowering fastball with a good sinking movement to the inside on right-handed hitters. He has an above average curve ball and a pretty good change up." Some scouts in Kissimmee clocked him at 100 mph.

But Rodríguez developed tendinitis in his shoulder that persisted for almost a year. The Astros' training staff thought part of the problem could be resolved through a conditioning program to build up the supporting muscles around the shoulder. It was successful, and his velocity returned. After three solid starts in the Florida State League in 2000, he was promoted to Double-A Round Rock. It appeared that Rodríguez was on the fast track to the big leagues.

I had heard so much about Rodríguez and was pleased that I would see him pitch on a regular basis. But at Round Rock in 2000, Rodríguez was 2-4 with a 5.77 ERA in 57.2 innings—all in a starting role—giving up 54 hits, walking 52, and striking out 55. It was painful to watch. His mechanics were awful, and he had no control. I never saw Wilfredo Rodríguez the prospect.

Returning to Round Rock in 2001, Rodríguez was used both as a starter and reliever and went 5-9 with a 4.78 ERA. He seemed confused—both in his mechanics and in his role on the team. Nevertheless, he was promoted and made his major league debut with the Astros on September 15 and gained instant notoriety a few days later when he gave up Barry Bonds's record-tying 70th home run—a monster 454-foot dinger to the right field upper deck in Minute Maid Park. Rodríguez will be forever known as the pitcher brave enough to pitch to, or foolish enough to attempt to put a fastball by, Bonds.

During the winter, Rodríguez had surgery on his shoulder, opened the 2002 season on the disabled list, and was sent on a minor league rehab assignment with Triple-A New Orleans. In July the Astros took him off their 40-man roster to make room for a player they needed on the big league club. It was a routine move, but one which made Rodríguez a free agent. Andrés and others in the Astros' front office believed they would be able to re-sign him. But Rodríguez signed a minor league contract with the Chicago Cubs, immediately went on the disabled list and was released after the season. He didn't play one inning of professional baseball during the 2002 season, and he didn't show up in Venezuela to play with Magallanes.

Rodríguez pitched only three innings in his short-lived major league career, and by late 2002 no one knew where he was. *Se lo tragó la tierra* (the earth swallowed him) was the way a Venezuelan acquaintance phrased it. After Rodríguez dropped out of sight, I asked Astros GM Gerry Hunsicker how a number-one prospect fails so miserably.

"The year he was in the Florida State League [1999], he was a tremendous prospect. I can still remember seeing him pitch that year and thought he had all the makings of a major league starter. And the next year, it started to unravel," Hunsicker told me. "I think some of the physical problems that he had were mechanics related, and it also prevented him from really having consistent control. And from there, it became mental. I think there were probably some issues with the coaching staff, where he just didn't seem to click with some of the coaches. And I am not casting blame on anybody; it's just a fact. I don't think there was much positive feedback going on between him and the coaches."

I asked Hunsicker if he believed Rodríguez was adversely impacted by all of the publicity and his rapid ascension to being the top prospect in the Astros' system.

"That's a real problem. There is no question about it. The evolution of *Baseball America* and the other publications and the increased exposure on the Internet have provided great exposure for baseball, but it's really been problematic from a development standpoint because these kids do get labeled," said Hunsicker. "This is a tough enough business to deal with everything, let alone be hit with it at an early age."

When his career started to sink, Rodríguez developed a negative attitude.

"It was partly due to the frustration of the downward spiral, the staff that he didn't relate to, the expectations that went with it and—when he wasn't able to achieve those expectations—the pressure that that created," said Hunsicker.

"He got negative, but you know what, when guys are injured, that happens a lot," then assistant GM Tim Purpura told me. "When guys don't produce, we see that often. So, he was not unlike a lot of players whose attitudes change over time because they realize they are expected to do more than just be a star in the Florida State League," said Purpura.

Whatever the reasons, it was very disappointing for Andrés to watch Rodríguez's career fail. "Wilfredo never got back to being healthy," Andrés told me in early 2003. "His arm came back, but he had no mechanics. It was only a question of time before he would break down again. And he broke down. With all the ability he had, it's really a shame."

"After reading all the things in the newspaper, Wilfredo thought he was the last Coca Cola in the desert," said Andrés. "Now, we don't even know where he is."

"They found Wilfredo," Purpura told me at the end of the 2003 season. Rodríguez had surfaced in Venezuela and was throwing in the mid-90s. "Actually," said Purpura, "Andrés even talked to me about bringing him back, but from our point of view he is a guy with bad mechanics and an arthritic elbow. So you have to weigh those risks."

Rodríguez signed a minor league contract with Montreal in 2004, and was 2-3 with Bravard in the Florida State League—the same league he had dominated five years earlier. He pitched a few innings with the Expos' Double-A and Triple-A clubs before being released in late July. On August 13, he signed with Winnipeg in the independent Northern League and pitched in one game before he was released on August 22.

While Santana was celebrating his winning the Cy Young Award at the end of 2004, it seemed that the predicted fantastic voyage of the flame-throwing Rodríguez had finally come to an end. However, in early 2005, Rodríguez signed with the Texas Rangers and was a nonroster invitee to spring training. He posted a 4-5 record with a 3.80 ERA at Double-A Frisco and was promoted to Triple-A Oklahoma City where he started two games and had a 1.42 ERA and seemed sure to receive a call-up from the Rangers before he had season-ending surgery on his arm. In 2006 the Milwaukee Brewers gave a healthy Rodríguez a spring training invite and another opportunity to demonstrate the potential that he had displayed only a few years ago. Although he was entering his eleventh professional season, Rodríguez was just twenty-seven years old.

Whatever happened to Romelio López, the super prospect I met at the academy in 1999?

"After Romelio left the academy he didn't have people to work with him, and he didn't improve. A lot of scouts came to see him, but some thought he was losing velocity," explained Rafael Cariel, who maintained contact with the López family. An agent convinced the parents they could receive a large sum of money when their son signed with a major league organization—maybe even $2 million. A story circulated in Venezuela that López was taken to the United States, reportedly offered $800,000 by a team, and turned it down. López had tryouts with several organizations and changed agents three times but did not sign a professional contract in Venezuela. Instead, he ended up, ironically, in a suburban Houston (Conroe) high school, where he hoped to find his value through the amateur draft.

When I saw Cariel in May 2003, I mentioned that Romelio had been drafted by Tampa Bay the year before. "Did I know the amount of the signing bonus," he asked. I told him that because he was selected so low in the draft, it was probably not very much.

"He was going to get a good bonus here," said Cariel.

"$200,000?" I asked.

"No, more," said Cariel.

"He needed a lot of work. *Está donde está* (he is where he is) because of the time he spent here at the academy," said Cariel. "You could see how good he was going to be."

Cariel doesn't believe the family ever sat down with the Astros and talked about money.

"Romelio didn't believe in us and he left," said Cariel. "It's sad. But at least now he is on the burro, and maybe he can get to the big leagues and find his fame and fortune."

López was selected by the Devil Rays in the eighteenth round of the June 2002 free-agent draft and received a signing bonus of $150,000—high for a player chosen so low in the draft—but at least $50,000 less than what the Astros would have given him almost three years earlier. He may be the only player to ever leave Latin America to be showcased in the United States and then get less bonus money than he would have received in Venezuela.

The 6-7, 252-pound López played in his first professional season at Princeton in the Appalachian League in 2003. He was 2-6 with a 4.37 ERA and led the team with 48 strikeouts in 57.2 innings. He repeated at Princeton in 2004 going 1-1 with a 2.96 ERA. I saw a notice in *Baseball America* in August 2004 that he had been placed on the suspended list by Tampa Bay, but there was no further explanation. In 2005 López compiled a 1-2 record with a 1.47 ERA in four starts for the Tampa Bay affiliate at Hudson Valley in the New York–Penn league. After the season, López was released. He was still only twenty-one years old. But he had fallen off the burro.

While no one in Houston had ever heard of Romelio López, nearly every Astros fan was aware of Richard Hidalgo. By early 1997 *Baseball America* rated the twenty-one-year-old Hidalgo as the Astros' number-one prospect (followed in second and third place by Carlos Guillén and Bob Abreu). I had the opportunity to speak with Hidalgo on a regular basis for eight seasons and gathered enough material write a book. Everyone who saw Hidalgo play, including me, was convinced that he possessed almost unlimited potential.

"As good as Petagine is, Abreu is going to be better, and I'm not sure Hidalgo won't be the best of the bunch," said Astros minor league director Fred Nelson in 1994.

"Hidalgo has the full package—speed, the hitting, and the defense," Rick Sweet, manager of the Astros' Triple-A club in Tucson told the *Houston Chronicle* in 1995. "Hidalgo has the chance to be one of the best players we've ever produced in this organization."

Although Hidalgo made a steady progression through the Astros' minor league system after being signed in 1991, it was in 1997 when he really blossomed. In January his outstanding play helped Magallanes defeat Caracas in the Venezuelan League finals, and he was selected series MVP. In August with Houston in the midst of a pennant race, some were surprised when the Astros called up Hidalgo and started him in center field. He responded by hitting .306 in 19 games. Hidalgo's incredible desire to improve and learn about the game impressed his teammates.

"He asks a lot of questions and wants to learn," Astros second baseman, Craig Biggio, told the *Houston Chronicle*. "He's got the best attitude I've seen in a young player in a long time. With his talent and his attitude, the sky's the limit for him."

Hidalgo faced the most difficult challenge of his career and his life in December 1997 when he came down with hemorrhagic dengue fever, a blood infection transmitted by mosquitoes. Hidalgo is believed to have contracted the potentially fatal disease in the visiting team clubhouse in Caracas earlier that month. The illness was caught at an early stage, and Hidalgo pulled through because he was in such excellent physical condition. But he spent almost two weeks in the hospital and told me later that he thought he might die. Although he was expected to miss the rest of the winter season, he returned for the playoffs in early January 1998 and opened the season with Houston. But dengue fever would only be the first of many setbacks that would plague Hidalgo's career.

= In late May 1998, Hidalgo crashed into the center-field wall at Coors Field in Denver and separated his right shoulder. He was on the disabled list for almost two months.

= In early August 1999 he was placed on the disabled list with a knee injury. He had surgery in late August and missed the last two months of the season.

= From August 24 to September 9, 2002, he was on the disabled with a right hip strain.

= On November 21, 2002, Hidalgo sustained a nine-millimeter gunshot wound to his left forearm during a robbery attempt in Venezuela.

= Between May 23 and June 6, 2003, he was on the disabled list with tonsillitis.

= With the New York Mets in 2004, Hidalgo ended the season a week early with a groin injury.

= Playing with the Texas Rangers in 2005, Hidalgo missed most of the last two months of the season with what was described as a "sore wrist."

In between his stints on the disabled list or while being slowed down by other nagging aliments, Hidalgo showed flashes of greatness, followed by prolonged slumps. He became a streaky player and perhaps most damaging to his career an inconsistent one.

The 2000 season was Hidalgo's peak. He began the year with an Opening Day grand slam at Pittsburgh and went on to hit .314 and established career highs in RBI (123) and home runs (44). After the season, Hidalgo was rewarded with a $32 million, four-year contract. "Richard has no weaknesses," commented then Astros GM Hunsicker.

In 2001 Hidalgo hit .275 with 19 home runs and 80 RBI—numbers that might have been acceptable a year earlier but clearly more was expected. Some thought Hidalgo was just coasting after his big contract. I believe it was the opposite: he was trying too hard to justify earning so much money, and he was putting a great deal of pressure on himself. Further, Hidalgo had put on too much weight, ballooning up to nearly 230 pounds. The weight gain was both slowing him down in the outfield and inhibiting his ability to swing properly.

While Andrés believed that academy players needed a great deal of his attention while making their journey through rookie and A-ball, he felt that by the time they reached Double-A, they could navigate the system by themselves. He made an exception for Richard Hidalgo. This was partially due to the fact that he saw Hidalgo at the ballpark in Houston on a regular basis, but he also understood the incredible potential that the young outfielder possessed.

During a particularly difficult period for Hidalgo in August 2001, I saw Andrés approach him in the Astros' clubhouse in Houston. "I only talked about positive things. I told him to remember where he came from and to look around and see how far he'd come," said Andrés. He reminded Hidalgo that he had been in slumps before and that he always rebounded. He told him he had seen improvement in his swing and noticed that he had lost about fifteen pounds. Finally, he counseled Hidalgo not to think too much about his poor performance but to relax and play baseball.

In 2002 Hidalgo's numbers dropped even further—a .235 batting average with 15 home runs and 48 RBI. It was difficult to watch him play that season. In addition to his poor numbers, he was sluggish in the field, looked terrible at the plate, argued with umpires, had problems with manager Jimy Williams, and in general developed a bad attitude.

Many observers in Houston began to wonder, "Why did the Astros pay this guy so much?"

I remember an incident in the Astros' clubhouse early in the 2002 season when Andrés gently prodded Hidalgo again about losing weight. "*Señor Andrés, con todo debido respeto* (with all due respect), I don't want to discuss that," Hidalgo responded. This was the first time that I had seen Hidalgo so defensive.

At the end of the season, Hidalgo requested that the Astros trade him. "He was demoralized all year," his agent Peter Greenberg told the *Houston Chronicle*. "Everybody knows this is a mental game. Maybe they need to communicate a little bit more and give him more encouragement."

Because Hidalgo is very reserved, he often appeared distant. Some observers thought his unassertive behavior was due to the language barrier, but that was only part of it. He often internalized his anger when he felt slighted by others. Hidalgo perceived Jimy Williams as disrespectful, and he was correct. The situation could have been defused if Williams had just sat down with Hidalgo in a courteous way and chatted with him about how the outfielder might improve.

Hidalgo was not traded, and as bad as the 2002 season was, the off-season would be even worse. In early November back in Valencia, Andrés asked Hidalgo to meet with him to discuss his career, which he feared was in jeopardy.

"Richard, don't be blind," Andrés cautioned Hidalgo. "You are mentally lost as a hitter and mechanically you are completely lost. And it was terrible to see you on the field."

Andrés could see that Hidalgo's pride was hurt, and he asked him what he really wanted to accomplish in baseball. "To be successful again," said Hidalgo.

"Good, now let's make a plan. You have to work your butt off and put it back together physically, mentally, and mechanically," said Andrés. "He agreed and was really happy about the plan. He worked out every day, lost about eight or ten pounds, and he looked a lot better."

Less than two weeks later, on November 21, Andrés received a call informing him that Hidalgo was injured in an attempted carjacking in Valencia. "He was shot at close range and was really lucky because the guy was pointing at his head and the glass deflected the bullet. You can't find a better place to get hit." Andrés pointed to area between wrist and elbow. "It went through without touching bone or ligament or nothing, not even muscle." But again, Richard Hidalgo had come face-to-face with his own mortality.

The day after the shooting, I received an e-mail from my friend Ibsen Martínez, a columnist for *El Nacional*, one of Venezuela's leading newspapers. "It's a risk characteristic of being a Venezuelan big leaguer in the twenty-first century: Hidalgo is a 'role model' for kids and an attractive attack target for the *malandros* (scoundrels) all at the same time. Perhaps the phenomenon merits a few paragraphs in your book."

By the start of spring training 2003, Hidalgo was fully recovered and seemed to have taken Andrés's suggestions to heart. Some speculated that the shooting was a wake-up call for Hidalgo. Whatever the reason, a rejuvenated Hidalgo appeared in 2003. He led Houston in hitting with a .309 average and had 28 home runs and 88 RBI, and led the major leagues with 22 outfield assists. He was named the Astros' MVP, and I was asked to introduce him at the awards banquet in early 2004.

"What fans don't have the opportunity to see is Richard's tremendous inner strength, and his strong character," I said. And I pointed out that rebounding from his awful 2002 season was the most difficult challenge he had faced in his career. I really believed that Hidalgo had turned the corner, made the necessary adjustments, and was finally on track to be the superstar he was projected to be.

Hidalgo started off 2004 where he left off in 2003. After the first three weeks, he was batting over .400 with 20 RBI and 4 home runs. He was selected the National League Player of the Week in mid-April. Two months later, his batting average dropped to the .250s, and he had not hit another home run. Now and then he made an outstanding defensive play in the field, but he had all but disappeared at the plate. It was clear that this would be his last season as an Astro—if he finished the year in Houston. The Astros would certainly exercise their $2 million buyout option. There was no way the team would, or should, pay Hidalgo $15 million for 2005.

On June 11 Richard was injured diving for a ball and missed a few games. When he was ready to return, he was no longer starting right fielder. Jimy Williams told Hidalgo to look at the lineup card posted in the clubhouse to find out if he would be playing. On June 17, 2004, after Hidalgo had been out of action for about a week, he was traded to the Mets for relief pitcher David Weathers. Although I clearly understood why the Astros had to make the move, I was saddened. I would miss my regular conversations with Richard.

A few minutes after the trade was announced, Andrés called me. "Did you hear that Richard was traded?" he asked. "It's the best thing that could happen to Richard. He will have Don Baylor [Mets hitting coach] at his side, and he will help Richard get his mechanics back. And it's the best thing for me. Now every time I come to the office in Houston, they won't ask 'Andrés, what can we do about Richard?'"

After three weeks with the Mets, Hidalgo had 8 home runs, double the number he had in the first ten weeks of the season with the Astros. As Andrés believed, Don Baylor had corrected the hitch in Hidalgo's swing. But after Hidalgo's initial hot streak, he became mired in another horrible batting slump, or funk, or depression, or inability or unwillingness to adjust, until finally a sore groin kept him on the bench for the final week of the season. After the season, the Mets exercised the $2 million buyout of a now very mediocre outfielder. But by that time the Astros had acquired outfielder Carlos Beltrán, who showed himself to be one of the best players in the game, and Hidalgo was completely forgotten in Houston.

Hidalgo signed a one-year contract with the Texas Rangers for $5 million, a chance for redemption, and an opportunity to work with one of the best hitting coaches in the business, Rudy Jaramillo. With the bilingual Jaramillo, there would be no linguistic or cultural misunderstandings. Hidalgo displayed occasional surges of power coupled with a propensity to strike out. Jaramillo thought Hidalgo had a mental block and that only Hidalgo himself could correct it—if he desired to do so. He ended the season in August with an injured wrist and a .221 batting average, but Rangers manager Buck Showalter had run out of patience by then and did not want him in the lineup even if he was healthy.

Hidalgo returned to Venezuela after the 2005 season and played in a few games with Magallanes. He struck out five times in nine at bats. And when manager Al Pedrique told him that he would not start in a play-off game, Hidalgo said he didn't feel good and never went back.

Injuries and cultural misunderstandings notwithstanding, ultimately it was Hidalgo himself who has to accept responsibility for not fulfilling his potential. But no matter who was to blame, the failure of Hidalgo was a major disappointment for Andrés. By the beginning of spring training in 2006, Hidalgo's value had depreciated so much that he was only able to get a minor league contract with Baltimore. A week later, he asked for and was given his release. There was talk of him pursuing offers to play in Japan. Hidalgo was just thirty years old, and maybe, just maybe, he could still remove that mental block which has prevented him from sharing the stage with Abreu, Mora, Guillén, Santana, and García.

When Bob Kelly Abreu was signed as a sixteen-year-old second baseman out of the academy in 1990, then assistant GM Bob Watson cautioned the Venezuelan staff to not change anything about his swing.

"Bob Kelly is a natural hitter. When you see a player like him come along, you say to yourself, 'Don't do anything, just let him play, let him get better by playing,'" observed Watson. Abreu, a five-tool, can't-miss prospect, converted to the outfield, proceeded step-by-step through the Astros' system, and made his major league debut with Houston in September 1996. The young man seemed to have everything going his way.

But problems for Abreu started in 1995. His manager at Triple-A Tucson, Rick Sweet encouraged Abreu to change his swing—something Abreu did not want and did not need to do. And when Abreu got to Houston, Sweet was a coach on the major league team.

In May 1997 Abreu broke a bone in his right wrist and was on the disabled list for five weeks. He returned in July but had only six at bats in two weeks before being sent to Triple-A New Orleans. Abreu was clearly not pleased when informed of his demotion to the minors and expressed his displeasure to GM Hunsicker. Some say the two had a very unpleasant conversation. When the draft was held in November 1997 to provide players for the new Arizona and Tampa Bay franchises, each of the existing twenty-eight organizations was allowed to protect fifteen players. The Astros decided to leave Abreu exposed, and he was selected by the Devil Rays then immediately traded to Philadelphia.

The standard explanation for the Astros not protecting Abreu was that a decision had to be made between Abreu and Richard Hidalgo. But the reasons for losing one of the best players in baseball were much more nuanced and complex. It was never about deciding between Abreu and Hidalgo: Hidalgo was viewed as having a hiring ceiling, and there was no way the Astros would risk losing him.

In an attempt to rationalize the decision to leave him exposed, some point to Abreu's demeanor as a factor.

"Abreu might still be an Astro if it wasn't for his attitude," shouted Astros radio broadcaster Milo Hamilton. It was Abreu's lack of intensity, Hamilton claimed, that led the Astros not to protect him. Another Astros official involved in the decision told me that Abreu was so low-keyed that he "did not have the inner fire" necessary to play the game. While it's true that Abreu is a very even-tempered, easy-going person, it is a mistake to assume that everyone is going to have a high-energy approach to the game: not all successful players function in the Pete Rose mode. And if Abreu had displayed an "inner fire" he probably would have been put in the "hot-tempered Latino" category that has dogged players such as pitcher José Lima.

In 2003 I asked Hunsicker why Abreu was left unprotected.

"We had a debate in the organization about whether to expose Derek Bell in the expansion draft and protect Abreu, and the decision was made to protect Bell. In fairness to that, Abreu was coming off a year where he gone down to Triple-A and had a bad attitude and a poor year. A lot of sentiment within the organization changed from Abreu as a front-line prospect to him just being another guy."

Although Bell had a solid year with the Astros in 1998, he was clearly on the downside of his career and was out of baseball four years later. If the Astros had left Bell unprotected, they would not have had to decide between Abreu and Hidalgo.

"We didn't have an opportunity for Abreu, and Abreu was further along developmentally than Richard. Abreu was ready to play in the big leagues; Richard was still pushing up the ladder," explained Hunsicker. "Abreu would have been an extra outfielder for us, and we felt that with Richard coming along behind him, we could take a chance."

When Andrés cautioned Hunsicker that the Astros could not afford to lose Abreu, Hunsicker responded that he was new on the job and had to rely on the advice of his staff, and at least two of them had told him that Abreu would never be a full-time major league outfielder. Andrés's response to Hunsicker was that those staff members were simply wrong.

"I would be less than honest if I told you that I thought Bobby would turn out to be the All-Star player he has," Hunsicker told *Houston Chronicle* reporter Neil Holhfeld in 2005.[1] "If we knew that back then, we wouldn't have made that decision. I don't want this to sound like I'm not accepting responsibility for it because I absolutely accept responsibility. It wasn't one of the better decisions I've ever made."

Many in the Astros organization never realized what a gem they had in Abreu. And there is no question that losing Abreu and receiving nothing in return was a huge mistake that really can't be rationalized. Abreu himself has been reluctant to discuss the issue in detail, preferring to display on the playing field why the Astros were wrong to let him go. As soon as he settled in Philadelphia, he began to demonstrate that he was not only an everyday outfielder but also a franchise player.

In eight years with the Phillies, Abreu consistently hit over .300 and averaged 23 home runs, 94 RBI, 109 walks, and 29 stolen bases per season. He has also been amazingly durable—playing in an average of 157 out 162 games over eight seasons. In 2002 Abreu signed a five-year, $64 million deal—the richest contract in team history. He made $13.5 million in 2006 and was traded to the New York Yankees in late July. His 2007 salary was $15.5 million. Not bad for a young man who signed for a $6,000 bonus in 1991.

Not only was Abreu an offensive threat, but he had also developed into a very good defensive outfielder. When Abreu was converted to an outfielder in the early 1990s, his defense was, in his own words, *pésima* (dreadful). But he put in the long hours necessary to improve. In Tucson 1995 I took him to the ballpark early so that he could get in some extra work in the outfield during batting practice. When I dropped him off, it was 107 degrees, and he was unfazed by the heat. He continued to improve each year, and in 2005, he won a Gold Glove.

Even though Abreu was one of the most consistent players in baseball for the first five years of the twenty-first century, it was not until the 2005 All-Star Game that Abreu finally got the recognition he deserved. With his spectacular performance in the Home Run Derby, Abreu emerged as a national star. He had a record-breaking 24 home runs in the first round, eclipsing the previous mark of 15 and another derby record of 41 in total. Abreu's power display brought Venezuelan baseball to the attention of the world. When he was awarded the trophy for winning the Home Run Derby, he draped a huge Venezuelan flag around his shoulders. At his side were Melvin Mora and Johán Santana and behind them stood the two other *criollos*, Miguel Cabrera and César Iztúris.

Abreu is immensely popular back home in Venezuela. And Venezuela really is his home, not just a place he visits during the off-season.

"I live in Caracas," Abreu definitively stated when I asked if he was going to Venezuela during the winter to suit up for the Leones del Caracas in 2004. "I play in Venezuela because I love these fans who don't have an opportunity to see me in the United States."

During the early 1990s, he played winter ball at home to help gain experience. And by the 1998–99 season, he was clearly the dominant player in the Venezuelan league. That year he hit .419—the highest single-season average in league history. Abreu did not need more at bats when he returned to play in the Venezuelan league in 2004. He even paid the premium on his life insurance policy out of his own pocket.

Abreu did not play during the 2005–6 winter season, but when he entered the stands of the Estadio Universitario in the fourth inning of a Caracas-Magallanes play-off game in January 2006, dressed in blue jeans and sport coat, several thousand fans seated behind home plate and along the first-and third-base lines stood and applauded. It was very touching to watch him soak in the warmth of the crowd. After conducting several radio and television interviews, Abreu went down on the field between innings to greet his friends on both teams. When the PA announcer roared "*Bienvenido* Comedulce (Welcome Sweet Tooth)," he was greeted with another thunderous ovation from the crowd of more than 20,000. Abreu stopped near home plate, waved with his left hand, and placed his right hand over his heart in recognition of the admiration. El Comedulce was home.

When I saw him down on the field I realized that he really hasn't changed much since I first met him in 1990. He has the same wonderful smile and engaging personality I saw in my numerous visits with him through his Astros minor league journey, back home in Venezuela, and in the visiting clubhouse in Houston each year when he came to town with the Phillies.

Abreu has also been a superstar off the field. In 2004 he was the winner of the Phillies Community Service award for a program he started in Philadelphia, Abreu's Amigos, where he purchases tickets for less-privileged children for most Friday night home games.

While Abreu helped to put Venezuela on the world's baseball stage, he gives a great deal of credit for his success to Andrés Reiner.

"He has been teaching me to do things the right way ever since I met him," Abreu told me in 2005. "Andrés is like a father to me, and he treats me like a son. He is a very, very important person in my life."

He still finds it remarkable that Andrés could see a skinny sixteen-year-old and tell that someday be he would be a major league star and then explain what he needed to do to get there. Abreu is correct. Andrés and his staff did a remarkable job in finding, projecting, signing, and developing players in the Venezuelan academy. But it was the follow through where the Astros' organization fell short. In addition to letting Abreu go and receiving nothing in return, Houston had lost players to trades, the Rule 5 draft (including infielders

Donaldo Méndez and Félix Escalona and pitcher Edgar Ramos in addition to Santana) and six-year minor league free agency (Melvin Mora). While some of these moves were good decisions designed to improve the organization (the García and Guillén trade for Randy Johnson is the best example) and some can be explained, most were just were bad decisions due to misperceptions or misreading players and the general "undervaluing" of players from Latin America. The cases of Santana, Abreu, and Mora are the most egregious—all three possessed special qualities that obviously the Astros did not appreciate. But it wasn't the loss of these three players that wore down Andrés: after all they went on to be successful. It was his failure to have an impact in changing the negative environment within the Astros' minor league system, an environment that he viewed as detrimental to all players, not just those from Latin America, that motivated him to consider leaving the organization.

13

Good-bye to the Astros

Andrés's Farewell Tour

When Hunsicker resigned as GM after the 2004 season, it was clear that Andrés's project with the Astros of fifteen years plus was nearing an end. With Hunsicker gone, Andrés knew that he would no longer have any impact on the organization. New GM Tim Purpura was not a risk taker, and Andrés believed that he had to leave or stay and appear he was endorsing policies that he did not support. Finally on February 28, 2005, Andrés submitted his letter of resignation, addressing it to Tal Smith, the one person with power in the organization that he still respected.

"Many years ago, I had a dream of developing the baseball market in Venezuela and wouldn't have been able to develop my dream this far without the support of the Houston Astros who believed in my dream and me," Andrés wrote. "Over the years, I never imagined that I would not end my career with the Houston Astros. However, over the last three years the philosophy of our minor league development has been changing to where now it is not in line with my philosophy. Recently, I have found myself with a great deal of passion to take my dream a step further. Therefore, rather than becoming a hindrance to the current direction that the Houston Astros organization have embarked on, I have decided to realize my dream in another organization."

But he was not going to leave the Astros' Venezuelan program hanging. "I intend to fulfill my contract and I look forward to meeting with you to arrange the transition to minimize the impact to the organization," he informed Smith.

The letter had been in the works for three years. Andrés had postponed the inevitable because he had been able to persuade Hunsicker to implement some of his ideas or intercede on behalf of some of his players, but he was tired of being the lone voice of dissent. Andrés did not want to make a big issue of his leaving the Houston organization or engage the Astros in a public fight: he was aware that many of those who remained would have to find rationales to defend themselves. The letter was a big step for Andrés, and after he sent it, he told me that felt a sense of inner peace that had eluded him for the previous several years.

I was not surprised Andrés was leaving, but the reality of the end of his tenure with the Astros was difficult to grasp. Although Andrés's departure seemed abrupt, he would turn seventy just after his contract ended in the fall of 2005, and for the past decade, he and the organization had begun to envision a Venezuelan program after he retired.

"We need to train someone else so that when Andrés steps aside the program can go on," then Astros GM Bob Watson told me in 1995. A year later, I wrote in my notes that Andrés spoke of wanting to come back to Houston so that he could spend more time with his children and grandchildren. "But," he said, "I'm not anxious to leave Venezuela. I love what I am doing." In 1997 when Andrés became a special assistant to GM Hunsicker, he was required to spend more time in the United States and began to transfer much of the day-to-day administration of the academy over to Pablo Torrealba, who had been hired in 1995.

In early 2001 Hunsicker told Andrés he wanted to discuss something with him but was not sure how to approach it. "I'm getting old, and you want to know what you are going to do in Venezuela when I'm no longer around," Andrés said, and explained that he had already moved much of the administrative work of the academy to the staff. Andrés was confident that Torrealba along with Rafael Cariel, Mario González, Omar López, Oscar Padrón, and the others would have no problem in running the academy when he left. The transition that Andrés outlined in 2001 was essentially the one he left in place when he retired.

One person he envisioned as possibly directing the academy in the long term was Oscar Padrón. The young pitching coach of the Venezuelan Summer League team was a rising star. He was not only scouting in Venezuela and working with prospects at the academy, but he also had gained additional experience running the academy in Mexico in 1997 and working as the pitching coach with two Astros minor league franchises in the United States in 2004.

On April 3, 2005, Oscar Padrón was killed in an automobile accident while driving back to Valencia from a scouting trip to Maracaibo. I really can't describe how distressed I was when I heard the news.

"It was like losing a son," Andrés told me when he called a couple of days later. "He was such a special person." Over 300 people attended the service in Valencia, including 39 players from the academy and pitcher Carlos Hernández who was there to represent all the other Astros Venezuelan players who had started the season in the United States.

"I have never seen so many grown men cry," said Andrés. "It was really hard on my staff." Obviously it was also very difficult for Andrés.

Although Padrón would be impossible to replace on the Astros' staff, Luis Yánez, twenty-eight, was selected as pitching coach for the summer league team. Yánez, the young man Rafael Cariel had spent so much time recruiting back in 1994, had pitched three years in the Astros' minor league system and was progressing well before an arm injury cut short his career. After being released by the Astros in 1998, Yánez returned home to El Tigre in eastern Venezuela and coached youth league teams. In 2001 Cariel invited Yánez to the academy where he worked as an unpaid assistant to the staff while learning how to become a coach. A couple of years later he was hired by the Astros.

This apprenticeship system of learning—Andrés prefers to call it an internship—is a good example of the academy serving as a educational institution not only for players but also for coaches. When I visited in 2005, two other former prospects, infielder Johán Maya and catcher Oscar Alvarado, were acting as interns. The previous year, the staff at the academy was so impressed with Maya that they all chipped in to pay his salary. Andrés was hopeful both could be hired as full-time coaches.

I was able to accompany Andrés on two of his last visits to Venezuela as an Astro in May and July 2005. It really was his "farewell tour" as he put it. But he was not just going through the motions, he was loyal to the last and still trying to sign the best players for Houston. And one of the top players who would be eligible to sign on July 2, the unofficial national signing day, was sixteen-year-old right-handed pitcher Douglas Salinas.

The academy was a beehive of activity in late May when Salinas worked out for Dewey Robinson, the Astros' minor league pitching coordinator. In total there were thirteen people with their eyes fixed on the young pitcher: Robinson; staff members Omar López, Pablo Torrealba, Mario González, Luis Yánez, Jesús Aristimuño, Wolfgang Ramos, Johán Maya, and Rafael Cariel; Andrés; Magallanes GM Ronnie Blanco; Douglas's grandmother; and me. Robinson worked with the young man's mechanics as the others observed. All of the staff would be asked their opinions, but Robinson's would be crucial because he reported back to the front office in Houston.

The 6-3, 195-pound Salinas and his grandmother, Emilia Salinas, who had raised him since infancy and had all the legal documents to act on his behalf, had been staying at the academy for a few weeks. I had heard Salinas would probably cost at least $200,000 to sign, but the *abuela* (grandmother) was thinking of $1 million.

"If another team offers $1 million, and the Astros offer $800,000, I'll sign with the Astros," she told me. But there was no way that Andrés would be able to get the Astros to pay an $800,000 bonus to a Venezuelan player, nor would he want to give a sixteen-year-year-old that kind of money. But if Salinas could be signed for $200,000 or $300,000, the Astros might be in the hunt. Salinas is about as close to a diamond that the Astros will ever have a chance at signing in Venezuela. Clearly with another two years to develop, when he would be on par with a U.S. high-school senior, Salinas would be a first-round pick in the June free-agent draft.

Salinas had attracted a great deal of attention in Venezuela. Bob Engle, Director of International Operations for Seattle visited the family, and the *abuela* and Douglas had gone to a tryout with the Texas Rangers in the Dominican Republic in January. Emilia Salinas told me she was also talking with Cleveland, Toronto, and Minnesota. I got the feeling that most organizations with any interest in Venezuela were aware of Douglas.

The Astros' strategy had not been to hide Salinas: Andrés offered other organizations the opportunity to come to the academy to work him out. Instead, the Astros would impress and charm the *abuela*. The facilities at the academy and the manner in which she and her grandson were treated clearly were important factors. But the Astros also had a special asset: Rafael Cariel. Cariel had been watching Douglas play since he was thirteen years old, and meeting with him and the *abuela* at their home in Ciudad Bolívar on a regular basis. Cariel is from a working-class background similar to Emilia Salinas's and found it easy to communicate and form a relationship of trust with her. She clearly was comfortable with Cariel. And during my few days at the academy in May, I often heard the other staff members ask Cariel how his *novia* (girlfriend) was doing. Cariel told me that if the Astros were willing to pay a reasonable bonus, he would reach an agreement with her that would be binding based upon his word.

Andrés was very impressed with Salinas. He told me the young man had a fastball that touched 90 mph, and he thought he would develop a good curve ball, and when he matured would be at 6-5. And he really liked his personality. I was anxious to get back for the July 2 signing date.

During the May trip, I was asked to give a talk on Caribbean baseball to a group of sports editors and writers at the offices of *El Nacional*, a leading Caracas daily. As we sat down for breakfast just before my presentation on the morning of May 23, one of my journalist colleagues received a call informing him that Alfonso "Chico" Carrasquel had died. Carrasquel had been ill, so his death was not a surprise, but none in the group of four could muster a word, and all fought back tears. I was reminded of that moment when I saw Ozzie Guillén at a press conference before Game 1 of the 2005 World Series. A reporter asked the White Sox manager a question about Carrasquel. "You're going to make me cry," replied Guillén. After a few brief comments about Carrasquel, Guillen struggled to keep his composure but was unable to continue and left the room.

It is difficult to explain to people outside Venezuela how important Carrasquel was to his country. He was immensely popular because of his accomplishments on the field and his accessibility off it both in Caracas and Chicago where after he retired he worked with the White Sox in both broadcasting and public relations. He was the living symbol, more than any other player, of Venezuelan baseball. When he died President Hugo Chávez declared two days of national mourning. The entire front page of the Caracas sports tabloid *Líder* featured only a photo of Carrasquel and the caption *"Adiós Chico, el país te llora"* (Goodbye Chico, the country mourns you).

After my talk, I attended Carrasquel's *velorio* (wake). The funeral home hall leading to his casket was filled with large floral wreaths including ones from each of the eight Venezuelan winter league ball clubs, Andrés Galarraga, and the Venezuelan military high command. That evening, I watched a couple of hours of tributes to Carrasquel on television. One reporter had interviewed him a week before his death, and Carrasquel had made three requests: donations of baseball books for his museum in his home; a desire to see musician Oscar D'León (D'León was informed and went by to visit); and finally, an appeal to the reporter. "Ask me how I want to be remembered," said Carrasquel. The reporter explained that he attempted to film Carrasquel's response several times, but each time Carrasquel broke into tears. Finally he responded that he wanted to be remembered as a good family man who shared his life with others and ended: "I am Venezuelan—100 percent proud to be Venezuelan."

I was back in Houston a few weeks later and ran into Astros Senior Director of Player Personnel, Paul Ricciarini, at Minute Maid Park. "Andrés tells me he has a really good pitcher in Venezuela," he said. I agreed and added that I thought that Salinas was in the same league with the Seattle Mariners pitcher Felix Hernández. Ricciarini commented that Salinas threw between 84 and 89. I reminded him that Salinas was only sixteen years old, and he retorted that Hernández was throwing in the low 90s at that age. I thought to myself, how much of a difference is there between 89 and low 90s? Dewey Robinson reported to Ricciarini that he really wasn't sure about Salinas, an honest response because Robinson is very seldom asked to evaluate a sixteen-year-old pitcher. Whether Ricciarini was too busy trying to sign the Astros' picks from the June free agent draft to go to Venezuela, didn't trust Andrés's evaluation, or did not understand the urgency, I detected no real interest in Salinas from him.

I saw Andrés at the ballpark in Round Rock a couple of days later on his final tour through the Astros' minor league system. He had been pleading for someone from the Astros front office to go look at Salinas and was under the impression that Ricciarini himself would soon travel to Venezuela with Ted Slowik, the Astros' national cross-checking scout.

When I returned to Venezuela on July 2, the last big signing day of Andrés's tenure with the Venezuelan academy, the Astros were still in the mix to sign Salinas. All that had to happen was for the front office in Houston to pull the trigger. But no one was ever sent from Houston to see Salinas, and it was clear that the Astros were not going to pursue the young pitcher. Because he was unable to sign Douglas, Andrés told Emilia Salinas that he would facilitate other major league organizations the opportunity to see him pitch; she could then deal with whomever she wanted. What occurred next was one of the most unusual events I've witnessed in my almost twenty years of writing about scouts in Latin America: Douglas Salinas was put on display at the academy—for other teams to see. The Astros' scouting staff informed all other major league organizations working in Venezuela that Salinas would be showcased at the Astros' academy at 2:30 p.m. on Saturday July 2. Cariel prepared a two-page handout, which included Salinas's birth certificate, a verification of its authenticity (Cariel had consulted the official government registry book), and a schedule of which pitches he would be throwing. He distributed the sheets to more than thirty scouts representing sixteen major league organizations. I recognized some of the scouts and with a bit of digging discovered they represented the New York Yankees, New York Mets, Chicago White Sox, Chicago Cubs, Seattle, San Diego,

Baltimore, Cincinnati, Texas, Pittsburgh, Los Angeles Angels, Philadelphia, Boston, Washington, Toronto, and Florida.

"Andrés, I want Douglas to sign with you. Keep trying," implored Emilia Salinas just before the tryout started. "I can't sign him, now I'm pushing for him," replied Andrés.

With a mini-army of scouts standing behind home plate watching him, Douglas Salinas was very poised. He had been instructed by Cariel and Luis Yánez to pitch like he normally did and not to try to throw harder for the tryout. He threw 25 pitches, the majority of which were fastballs varying between 88 and 90, and displayed a good curve ball and an acceptable change up. He was very impressive.

After the event was over, a very courteous and grateful Salinas approached Andrés to thank him for setting up the tryout. Meanwhile, the *abuela* talked to scouts from Boston, Washington, Texas, and Seattle. Seattle, which had earlier given her a sealed envelope with a bid for $150,000, stayed in hot pursuit and signed Salinas a few days later for a bonus of between $350,000 and $370,000. The Astros could have signed Salinas for considerably less.

While the Astros did not want to risk spending $200,000 in the Venezuelan market, they were willing to pay their eighth-round pick in the June free agent draft, Koby Clemens, son of Roger, $380,000—about four times the typical signing bonus for that round. (The Astros gave their number 5, 6, and 7 picks a total of $388,000 combined.) There was some logic to paying the younger Clemens such a high sum; it might help sway his father to return to pitch for the Astros in 2006. It was also easier for the Astros front office to justify paying a large sum to a kid who would make headlines in the local paper, while few would ever know that they had passed on a top prospect for half the price in Venezuela. There is no question that the "How do I explain to Drayton that I'm going to spend this much money in Venezuela," syndrome was a factor in not signing Salinas. This coupled with the reality that the front office in Houston was almost completely focused on the June free agent draft, and the increasing isolation of Andrés in the organization, helps to explain why Salinas got away. Ironically, while the Astros lost Salinas, their mystique in Venezuela as a first-class organization increased. Giving Salinas an opportunity to showcase his skills was a display of the kind of quality operation that Andrés had run in Venezuela for sixteen years.

"Finally a diamond appeared at the academy, and the Astros didn't want to sign him," Cariel commented. If anyone asks why Houston does not sign high-profile prospects in Venezuela such as Miguel Cabrera or Felix Hernández, it is basically because they don't choose to. But the success of the academy had not been based on signing the diamonds but instead as Cariel told me years before on, "Finding rocks which may contain diamonds." In another words, it was all about projection, a skill the Astros scouting staff in Venezuela had mastered.

On the scouting trip with Cariel to Ciudad Bolívar in 2001, we stopped to buy some trinkets from a man in a stall outside the market on the banks of the Orinoco River. During the dry season, the vendor explained, when the river would be fifty or sixty feet lower than its current level, he would dive to the bottom to gather *azabache,* a soft black stone which he then sculpted into various shapes. He said that he could envision the figures in the unfinished rock before he began carving. Cariel listened intently and then explained that scouting was similar to working with *azabache,* the difference being that he had to see a future big league player inside a raw prospect.

"Scouting has changed a great deal since I started," Cariel told me as we sat outside the academy one late afternoon in July 2005. "Today, you have to teach more; you have to be more intelligent in your scouting. We always have tryouts, but we have to travel more and see the player three or four times. And with the economic situation, everyone wants to be a scout."

And some people want to be both scouts and agents: representing players is a growth industry in Venezuela. A good example is Rafael Lara. "Larita" has been a bird dog or associate scout for the Astros since the late 1990s, but his background is in *toros coleados*—the bull running that is so much a part of the culture of the southern plains of Venezuela. Lara never played organized baseball at any level, and only became interested in the game in 1983 when his son, who was almost four at the time, was watching a Caracas-Lara game on television and said, "Dad, I want to play baseball." Lara gave his son a glove, a bat, and a ball and started a small baseball school near Barquisimeto. The school—Fundalara—produced future major leaguers Donaldo Méndez and César and Maicer Iztúris and is where Lara met Pablo Torrealba, who hired him to work as an associate scout for Houston. Players Lara has sent to the Astros' academy include third baseman Saúl Torres and right-handed pitcher Juan Carlos Gutiérrez, who is now on the 40-man roster.

While Lara still recommends players for Houston, he has recently become an agent. This enables him to survive financially and benefit from the expanded Venezuelan baseball industry. He started a new school in 2004, Los Pinos, in the Barquisimeto suburb of Cabudare, where he houses, feeds, and trains players not quite ready to sign professionally. Not constrained by MLB's thirty-day limit, Lara can work to develop players for several months. He offers his players to the Astros first, and if the organization is not interested, they go on the market. Most players not signed by Houston are almost immediately signed by other organizations. Lara's company—Baseball Machine Corporation—is officially registered with the Venezuelan government, and when a player produced by the school is signed, the corporation receives 15 percent of the bonus.

"I go where other scouts don't go," said Lara. Sometimes people he encounters in his daily activities give him tips. "For example, the guy who sells oranges in the market in Barquisimeto might tell me about a kid in a small town that he saw play. He doesn't know his name but says to ask at the general store when I get there. I go, find the kid, and invite him to a tryout. The guy doesn't show anything, but the friend he brought along with him is a pretty good player. That's how scouting works."

Because Lara goes to the small rural communities throughout the country, he has seen how much baseball has expanded in the past few years.

"Baseball in Venezuela is now like a raging river," said Lara. "You can't stop it. In every little town there are kids playing. And you'll see thirteen-year-olds playing against guys twenty-five or thirty years old. I'm not talking about small towns, I'm talking about little *case-*

ríos—small rural settlements—with five or six houses in one place and then others scattered nearby."

But Lara lamented the fact that while there are growing numbers of young men playing baseball, they often don't receive much technical training. The coaches are often just other men from the community who know what skills a player should have but really don't know how to teach them.

"They say 'throw hard,' but they don't teach them how to throw."

"They say 'run fast,' but they don't teach them how to improve their running."

"They say 'hit the ball hard' but don't tell them how to hit."

He brings those kids whose instincts impress him, or who have *chispa* (a spark) to his school and works with them until he believes they are ready to sign. Larita calls Andrés *"el gran chispa,"* roughly translated as "the big spark" of the academy.

"Astros sin (without) *Andrés o Andrés sin Astros,* either way it doesn't sound right," Lara told me. "It has taken me awhile to really believe that he is leaving."

The July trip was my last to Guacara while Andrés was still in charge. During my fifteen years of visiting the Astros' complex, I was given the opportunity to learn first-hand about scouting and managing the academy from Andrés. He allowed me to tag along as he went about doing his job. Arriving shortly after 7:00 a.m., he would engage in small talk with the staff, have a cup of coffee, and check to see if any matter needed his immediate attention. At 8:00 a.m. he'd meet with the entire coaching staff to go over the day's activities. Then he would roam around the academy watching the workouts and talking with players individually. For much of the year he would then attend a game involving Astros prospects in the Venezuelan Summer League or the Liga de Desarrolla. Occasionally, he would travel to see a prospect or to a tryout. I learned early on that if I was tagging along on a scouting trip with Andrés, I had to bring something to eat. He seemed fine being out all day with just a large bottle of water, not stopping for lunch.

I observed him meeting with prospective players and those he had signed who had gone on to become stars in the major leagues, with parents of players who were signing contracts with the Astros, with his staff, and with scouts from opposing organizations. I heard him talking to people from the Astros front office, to reporters, to the bus driver that didn't arrive at the academy to pick up players on time, and to the travel agent who arranged his trips to United States. I never saw him treat anyone in a disrespectful manner. As one Venezuelan journalist phrased it, *Andrés es todo un caballero* (he's a perfect gentleman).

On my last visit, I noticed that Andrés no longer sat in on the early morning meetings, preferring to let the staff become accustomed to working without him. And for the first time he referred to the Astros organization as "they," rather than the "we" that I had heard over the previous fifteen years. He was ready to leave the Astros and had hoped they would announce his retirement in mid-July 2005, on the sixteenth anniversary of his first contract with the organization. In early August, the Astros sent an e-mail to the other twenty-nine major league organizations stating Andrés was interested in pursuing job opportunities with another organization and anyone interested would be given permission to talk with him. The message did not state that Andrés had resigned. In fact, no announcement of Andrés leaving the Astros was ever made.

Andrés returned to Venezuela for a couple of other visits before his contract ended at the end of November. The first was in August for the finals of the Venezuelan Summer League. A very young Astros team made it to the championship round with a torrid finish to the season. This was a special team for Andrés. It was a group of youngsters not expected to win in a season dedicated to Oscar Padrón.

"We won!" Andrés shouted when he called me after the Astros had shut out Seattle 1–0 and 2–0 in a best-of-three championship series. He said that watching the Astros team win the VSL title capped off his academy adventure. In fact, the entire concept of the summer league was close to his heart. Its establishment, along with the revamped Liga de Desarrollo, were two of the major goals he wanted to accomplish in Venezuela, apart from scouting and signing players.

Andrés was back in Houston for the World Series in late October but told me he really had no interest in going to the games. The only academy player still with the Astros, Raúl Chávez, was not expected to see much playing time. One of Andrés's sons finally convinced him to go to Game 3. But he was at home the next evening watching Game 4 on television as Freddy García shut down the Astros for seven innings to win the last game of the World Series. Andrés didn't tell me, but it must have been satisfying for him to see one his academy products reach the pinnacle of baseball. In a classy move, the Astros front office brought most of the Venezuelan staff as well as scout Guillermo Ramírez from Colombia to Houston for Games 3 and 4 of the series.

Shortly after the series, Andrés returned to Venezuela for the last time as an Astro. He left all of his equipment with the Astros logo at the academy and attended a going-away dinner at the Cattlemen's Club in Valencia. "I said goodbye," Andrés told me when he returned to Houston at the end of November. "It was very emotional and I'm a little sad to leave that behind. It's not easy."

Divorce is never easy, especially when the honeymoon lasted so long. But Andrés was relieved and happy to be leaving the Astros: there was nothing else he needed to prove in Venezuela. He returned to the United States and began to pursue his other baseball dreams.

14

Andrés's Dream and the Future of the Astros in Venezuela

When Andrés left the Astros, there was no public announcement and no press release from the organization. There was no mention of Andrés's departure in the *Houston Chronicle*, no discussion of his leaving on Houston talk radio, and there was no fanfare and no celebration when he went to the Astros' offices at Minute Maid Park on the last day of November 2005 to drop off his radar gun and computer. It would have been awkward to explain the departure of the organization's highest-ranking Latino, especially when the Astros were taking heat (rightly or wrongly) for being the first team since the 1953 New York Yankees to play in the World Series with no African American players on the roster.

Although most in Houston were unaware Andrés had left the organization, he had delivered twenty-two major league players, at least two dozen quality prospects still in the Astros' pipeline, and a network of coaches, instructors, scouts, and contacts that assured a continuous flow of talent. The most notable legacy of his Venezuelan venture is, of course, the players who made it to the big leagues. In the period between January 1990 and the end of 2000, Andrés and his staff signed seventy-six Venezuelans, and by September 2007 nineteen of those players—25 percent—had played in the major leagues, including five that represented Venezuela in the World Baseball Classic.[1] (The three other big leaguers produced at the academy were Panama native Manuel Barrios, Devern Hansack from Nicaragua, and Felipe Paulino, who was born in the Dominican Republic.) When the baseball industry in general has only 5 to 7 percent of players signed that reach the major leagues, the 25 percent success rate of the Astros and Andrés was astounding. Making it even more incredible is the fact that the organization was signing young men, often just sixteen years old, who had not fully developed physically and who had no statistical record.

More academy products are on the way. Pitcher Paul Estrada is on the Astros' 40-man roster. Infielder Waldimir Sutil and pitchers Levi Romero and Enyelbert Soto are prospects in the Astros' system to watch, and Andrés believes that there are a dozen players from the 2005 Venezuelan Summer League team that have major league potential.

Success was not limited to finding, signing, and developing players for Houston. Andrés was instrumental in establishing the Venezuelan Summer League, upgrading the Liga de Desarrollo, and heightening the awareness of other major league organizations that the country could be a large-scale producer of prospects. That increased interest also brought with it an escalation in signing bonuses. Prior to the opening of the Astros' academy in 1989, most Venezuelan players were signed for sums ranging between $5,000 and $10,000. Attention focused on Venezuela in 1995 when the Yankees gave pitcher Tony Armas Jr., now playing with Pittsburgh, the largest bonus ever—$125,000—but in 1996 that was eclipsed by the $1.6 million bonus outfielder Jackson Melián received from the Yankees. In 1999 Florida topped that figure by giving $1.8 million to shortstop Miguel Cabrera. The Astros would never, and Andrés did not want to, give such extravagant bonuses in Venezuela. In fact, the total amount of the bonuses paid by the Astros to the 100 Venezuelan players signed between 1990 and early 2005 did not equal the $2 million the Yankees were willing to pay to one player—Jesús Montero, a sixteen-year-old Venezuelan catcher in July 2006. Even with the increased bonuses given by the competition, Andrés was nevertheless able to compete because some players accepted lower amounts to sign with the Astros because of the track record the academy had established.

The Astros' mystique in Venezuela was built on the manner in which players and their parents were treated by Andrés and his staff and on the fact that academy prospects had become major league stars, including Johán Santana, Bob Abreu, Carlos Guillén, Melvin Mora, Richard Hidalgo, and Freddy García. But basically it was Andrés's vision that led to the triumph of the Astros' program in Venezuela.

"Like most successful endeavors, it's all about people," Dan O'Brien told me in 2005. "It started with Andrés and his neverending creativity, his courage, his conviction, his commitment, his willingness to do something or try something that's never been done before, and obviously, his honesty and integrity."

Andrés would argue that a key to success was assembling a competent and loyal staff of scouts and instructors.

"To have a good organization, you have to start with really good young people," Andrés told me in the mid-1990s. "They work hard and improve, and if you treat them right, you have loyalty."

All of the staff was well aware of the goals that Andrés had laid out, the rules that would govern their behavior, and the need to be honest with a prospective player and his parents. There was a bond of trust, and all were on the same page. Rafael Cariel described Andrés as *un educador* (a teacher).

"Andrés is a very educated person, and it's very pleasant to work with him." Pablo Torrealba told me on my last visit to the academy in 2005, adding, "Andrés is also the soul of the Astros' organization in Venezuela."

And baseball, historian Javier González believes, is the mirror of the Venezuelan soul. In the end, Andrés will be appreciated not so much for what he did for Houston but for what he accomplished for Venezuela. Andrés is a national hero for helping to put Venezuelan baseball on the map and expanding the opportunities of *criollos* to play professional baseball. And with each new Venezuelan major leaguer, there is another kid dreaming of following in that player's footsteps.

Entering the market at the right time was one the keys to the success of the Astros' program. When Andrés left, Houston still had the most outstanding facility and staff of any major league club in Venezuela. But unlike the early years when they were almost alone in

Venezuela, other organizations were nipping at their heels, upgrading both their complexes and staffs.

The New York Mets and the Philadelphia Phillies shared an impressive new facility near Valencia. Phillies director of Latin American operations, Sal Artiaga, who was involved in the founding of both the Dominican and Venezuelan Summer Leagues, is one the most capable people in baseball. And the fact that the Mets signed Venezuela's top prospect in 2006, right-handed pitcher Deolis Guerra, for a $700,000 bonus demonstrates the commitment that both organizations have made in Venezuela.

Seattle also has both an outstanding physical complex, owing to solid direction from the front office's Bob Engle, director of international scouting (and a frequent visitor to Venezuela), and good scouting from the organization's Venezuelan coordinator, Emilio Carrasquel. And as the signings of Felix Hernández and Douglas Salinas illustrate, they are willing to pay big bucks for a top prospect.

Minnesota also has a serious interest in Venezuela. They have developed players, including shortstop Luis Rivas and pitcher Juan Rincón, and snagged Johán Santana in the Rule 5 draft. Bill Smith, the Twins VP and assistant GM, travels often to Venezuela and oversees the operation of the club's academy there.

The Chicago Cubs, Cincinnati, Detroit, Pittsburgh, St. Louis, and Tampa Bay also have academies or participate in the Venezuelan Summer League. But all thirty major league organizations have scouts in Venezuela. Some, such as Atlanta and the New York Yankees, are often the high bidders on top prospects, as in the case of Jesús Montero in 2006. Other organizations, including Arizona, Boston, and Colorado, have their scouts identify prospects that are then signed and developed at the club's academy in the Dominican Republic. Still others, including the Chicago White Sox, the Los Angeles Angels and Los Angeles Dodgers, and the Texas Rangers are keenly aware of Venezuelan prospects eligible to sign.

There are also scouts who cheat by hiding players, using false documents (both birth certificates and passports), or taking kickbacks from players' signing bonuses. Then there are scouts who "scout scouts," a term used to describe those who shadow the scouts of organizations deeply committed to the Venezuelan market, seeing which prospects they discover and then making a higher offer. And there is the increased presence of agents in Venezuela, some of whom make outrageous promises to players or take unreasonable percentages of signing bonuses.

Through all of these changes, Andrés managed to run a clean operation. "Like virginity, you can only lose your integrity once," he replied when I asked if it was difficult to maintain his honesty in the face of the intense competition.

Competition from agents and other organizations was not the only change in Venezuela after Andrés began his program. While the economic decline did, as he foresaw, create conditions favorable for signing players, two other nonbaseball issues have had negative impacts on all scouting in Venezuela: the political turmoil that accelerated in the late 1980s and the social disintegration that had begun a bit earlier.

The Astros opened their Venezuelan academy in August 1989, only a few months after one of the most traumatic political events in recent Venezuelan history. What occurred in February 1989 was a battle between the military and the desperately poor people from the hillside neighborhoods of Caracas who descended for a week of looting throughout the city. The conflict, known as the *Caracazo*, left several hundred dead. It was the beginning of the end of the political system put in place in 1958 after the overthrow of the dictatorship of Gen. Marcos Pérez Jiménez. Although the causes of the revolt are complex and deep-seated, the immediate catalyst was a slight rise in the price of gasoline and a subsequent rise in bus fares. Hugo Chávez, a career military officer and the current president of Venezuela, was not on duty during the *Caracazo*, but he was deeply affected by witnessing his fellow officers use force against mainly working-class citizens.

Chávez first became visible to most Venezuelans on February 4, 1992, when he was part of an unsuccessful attempt to oust Venezuelan president Carlos Andrés Pérez from power. Chávez eventually surrendered and appeared on television urging other officers involved in the plot to do likewise. But when explaining that the officers revolting had not met their objectives, Chávez used the phrase "*por ahora*" (for the moment). It was clear to most political observers that he would be back. Chávez was jailed for two years but emerged as one of Venezuela's most popular political figures.

In December 1998 Chávez was elected president of Venezuela, only seven years after his aborted coup attempt, and took office in February 1999. By 2002 Chávez, enormously popular at the time of his election, had lost much of his appeal and was struggling to stay in office. His ardent supporters consider him a savior from the previous forty years of corruption. But to many in the broad-based opposition movement, Chávez is the devil incarnate, intent on delivering Venezuela into the arms of Fidel Castro. His rural mannerisms and mode of speaking drive the Venezuelan elite and their supporters crazy. Whatever view one has of Chávez, his rise to power was predictable: he is the direct result of a breakdown of the traditional Venezuelan political system that had been in place since the late 1950s.

When outfielder Endy Chávez (no relation to the president) came to bat for Venezuela in the second inning of the Caribbean Series game against Puerto Rico on February 4, 2002, in Caracas, President Hugo Chávez was making a speech to commemorate the tenth anniversary of the 1992 coup attempt. The speech was carried on all radio and television stations in Venezuela and broadcast on the sound system in the stadium. As the president's voice echoed through the Estadio Universitario, the crowd booed loudly and, much to the surprise of Endy Chávez, began shouting "*Endy sí, Chávez no! Endy sí, Chávez no!*"

During the 2002–3 winter season, whenever Endy Chávez was introduced, he continued to be greeted in ballparks throughout Venezuela with a chorus of "*Endy sí, Chávez no!*" Endy, who now plays with the New York Mets, knew of course that the chants were not directed at him, but were merely an opportunity for those opposed to the other Chávez to express their discontent.

The coup against President Chávez on April 11, 2002, (and two days later, his return to power) caused several major league organizations to withdraw some of their scouts from Venezuela. The general strikes organized by the opposition to Chávez in November and December

2002, which brought a halt to Venezuelan winter baseball, compelled more teams to reexamine their involvement in the country.

There are very few things that can keep people in Venezuela from focusing on baseball during the winter season. But on December 1, 2002, two months before the end of the season, the last pitch was thrown. Initially, games were rescheduled, but eventually the season was cancelled, and to underscore the seriousness of the strikes, Venezuela did not send a team to the 2003 Caribbean Series. In the end, the strikes stopped baseball and devastated the economy, but failed to oust Chávez.

Chicago White Sox manager Ozzie Guillén, the first Venezuelan to manage in the big leagues, writes a column for *El Universal*, a Caracas daily. In early January 2003, responding to e-mails from his fans who were lamenting the cancelled baseball season and acknowledging the sad reality of Venezuelans confronting each other in the streets, Guillén wrote,

"I admit I'm ignorant about politics, because it has never attracted my attention."

Guillén, spending his first Christmas outside of Venezuela, explained that his entire life was baseball and that the game had taught him many lessons.

"When a team has everything it needs to win but doesn't, the first to be sacrificed is the manager. Is it the manager's fault that the cleanup batter doesn't hit a home run, or that the star pitcher doesn't strike out anyone? No, but in baseball, it is easier to fire one person than twenty. *Será eso lo que está pidiendo Venezuela?* (Is that what Venezuela is asking for?)"

The manager Guillén was referring to, of course, was Hugo Chávez. Chávez loves baseball and says he joined the military so that he could go to Caracas and pursue his major league dream. Chávez played for the Barinas team in his teens, pitched to Sammy Sosa during his visit to Venezuela in 1999, and is a self proclaimed Magallanes fan. The president had his own baseball analogy in responding to those who were trying to remove him from office. "To remove a president is the not the same as taking a pitcher out of a game."

The opposition pushed for a constitutionally provided referendum to remove Chávez from office before his term expired in 2006 and gathered the required number of signatures during 2003 and the first half of 2004. A referendum was set for August 15, 2004. Chávez had been critical of contributions to the opposition by the National Endowment for Democracy, financed by the United States Congress, and asserted that it was the major financial supporter of the Consenso para la Democracia (Consensus for Democracy), a document issued by opposition leaders. In a speech given weeks before the referendum, Chávez called the plan the *Consenso pa' Bush* (Consensus for Bush) and, armed with a baseball bat given to him by Sammy Sosa, said he'd hit the ball so hard that it would land in the gardens of the White House.

When Chávez supporters garnered almost 60 percent of the vote, the opposition was stunned. In the early morning of August 16, the day after the resounding victory, Chávez spoke from the balcony of the presidential palace to a throng of excited supporters chanting "home run." With the Sosa bat in his hands and assuming the batting position, Chávez acknowledged that he had indeed hit a home run. "I have been informed that the ball landed in the center of the White House, a present for Bush."

The reelection of George Bush in November 2004 assured that this contest would go into extra innings, and over the next two years administrations in Caracas and Washington had several unpleasant exchanges. A particularly ugly incident occurred in early April 2006, when the then U.S. ambassador to Venezuela, William Brownfield, went to a baseball stadium in Coche—a very poor area in the southern part of Caracas and one that I would be hesitant to visit—to hand out bats and other equipment to a youth league. Chávez supporters threw eggs and tomatoes at the ambassador's car and some on motorcycles chased his convoy for several miles. Brownfield clearly had to be aware of the risks to his safety of going into a Chávez stronghold, but the U.S. State Department accused the Venezuelan government of being too lax in its protection of a foreign diplomat. Chávez responded that Brownfield was engaging in provocative actions and threatened to declare the ambassador persona non grata and ask him to leave Venezuela. The incident blew over, and Brownfield stayed on as ambassador until his reassignment in mid-2007.

Just two weeks after Chávez was reelected president in December 2006, winning almost 63 percent of the vote, Ambassador Brownfield threw out the first pitch at a game between the Caribes de Anzoátegui and the Tigres de Aragua in Maracay, which celebrated "Baseball and Friendship Week," organized by the Aragua ball club and the U.S. Embassy. But when the ambassador stated in mid-January 2007 that the Venezuelan government needed to pay market value if it nationalized the country's main telephone company, President Chávez again threatened to have him expelled.

And the telephone companies were not the only industry over which Chávez was interested in exerting more control. In December 2006 the government proposed more restrictive regulations on the Liga Venezolana de Béisbol Profesional and on young men signing contracts with MLB organizations. One part of the proposed legislation required prospects to have the backing or support of the Instituto Nacional de Deportes (National Sports Institute) before signing a professional contract. It was unclear how vigorously these new rules would be enforced.

The worst-case scenario for MLB would be if Chávez outlawed the professional game as Fidel Castro did in Cuba in the early 1960s. But in early 2007, Chávez clearly stated that he had no intention of prohibiting professional baseball in Venezuela. And it really makes no sense for him to do so. Baseball is such an integral part of Venezuelan culture, and no matter how popular Chávez is, a move that in any way diminishes the pleasure his countrymen derive from baseball would be a political liability. And, unlike Cuba where players have been forced to leave clandestinely by boat in order to sign professional contracts, Venezuela is not an island and prospects could easily flee elsewhere to pursue their major league dreams. If too many restrictions are placed on the signing of players, top prospects will leave. And if the proposed rules were to go into effect, it could put a damper on the efforts of some scouts to beat the bushes for players.

But at least one baseball group was approaching Venezuela as a positive investment opportunity. In December 2006 Melvin Mora and the newest Cooperstown inductee Cal Ripken announced plans to construct a complex on 370 acres owned by Mora near Valencia.

The ambitious plan, which includes the involvement of the Venezuelan government, envisions at least two academies for major league organizations, several Little League fields and a 20,000- to 25,000-seat stadium that could be used for the World Baseball Classic.[2] The Baltimore Orioles have expressed an interest in the Mora-Ripken project.

"We don't want any major league teams to put the money out and build the academy, because I know they are scared about the country," Mora told the *Baltimore Sun*. "So we want to build it and rent it to major league teams."[3]

One of the first people Mora called upon for advice when he thought about investing in a baseball complex was Andrés.

Andrés told me he did not believe professional baseball was threatened in Venezuela but stressed that there was a need for dialogue and better communication between the Liga Venezolana de Béisbol Profesional, the Office of the Commissioner of Baseball (MLB), and the government. "There needs to be a plan, a project, in which all three groups participate," he said. He believed that it was especially important for someone from MLB to sit down with Venezuelan government officials and discuss how to proceed. For Andrés, MLB operations in Venezuela are a business, not a political, issue. After all, he pointed out, Bush and Chávez had traded insults for over six years, but the United States was still the largest buyer of Venezuelan petroleum.

Of course, the interest of the Venezuelan government in regulating their activities has made some MLB organizations nervous and caused them to reconsider investing or improving their facilities in the country.[4] But it was the increasing concern with the personal safety of players and staff that had organizations seriously reevaluating their involvement in Venezuela and discouraging native-born players under contract from returning home to compete in the winter league.

The social disintegration that Venezuela is experiencing did not begin with Chávez. The insecurity so prevalent in cities like Caracas and Valencia, including robberies, car jackings, and murders, has been commonplace for the past twenty years and leaves no one untouched. One of the most frequently heard words in Venezuela is *malandro* (scoundrel). Nearly everyone is concerned for his or her personal safety. The sad fact is that Venezuelan governmental authorities at every level have been incapable of providing security for its citizens.

And the baseball community has not been immune from the violence. At the 2006 Caribbean Series held in Maracay and Valencia, a half-dozen scouts from major league organizations had their pockets picked. They were just inconvenienced, others were less fortunate. Gustavo Polidor, who played in the major leagues for parts of seven seasons between 1985 and 1993, was murdered in Caracas in April 1995 in a robbery attempt. He was thirty-three years old. In late 1999 two minor league players, Roger Blanco, twenty-three, and Asdrúbal Infante, eighteen, were murdered in robbery attempts. I had seen Blanco only a few weeks earlier with the Magallanes team. In August 2001 more than a dozen prospects at the Seattle Mariners' academy near Valencia were robbed at gunpoint (robberies of two other academies received less publicity). In late 2002 Astros' academy alumnus Richard Hidalgo was shot in an attempted carjacking. In early 2003 Chico Carrasquel, arguably the most popular Venezuelan player ever, was roughed up by *malandros*. And in September 2004 four gunmen near Caracas kidnapped Maura Villarreal, the mother of major league pitcher Ugueth Urbina, and demanded a $6 million ransom. In February 2005 Venezuelan police officials rescued Villarreal, and no ransom was paid. But in November, Urbina himself was arrested and charged with attempted murder after several men accused him of pouring gasoline on them in an attempt to set them on fire.

Some major league players from Venezuela have complained that their salaries were made public by the local media, making them targets for kidnappers. But the truth is that with the Internet, it's not possible to keep salaries secret. Besides, anyone who follows baseball in Venezuela has a good idea what a star player is earning. Today, it is not unusual for Venezuelan major leaguers returning home during the off-season to live in gated communities, travel with bodyguards, and take out additional life insurance.

Rather than cut back operations in Venezuela, at Andrés's urging the Astros actually upgraded their facility at Guacara to make it the best physical plant of any major league complex in Latin America. Venezuela, he believes, will eventually produce more big league players than the Dominican Republic, and in three to four years there will be so many *criollos* ready to play professionally that there will simply be no room for them in the minor league. While some of the top Venezuelan prospects will be showcased in the United States and will be very expensive, Andrés foresees bonuses returning to the days of the late 1980s and early 1990s, when players could be signed for $5,000 or $10,000.

Of course, he is concerned about the uncertain political future of Venezuela, but he knows young men are still dreaming of playing in the major leagues. And when Ozzie Guillén led the Chicago White Sox to the 2005 World Series championship, even more Venezuelan boys began to envision themselves playing in the big leagues.

"Congratulations Oswaldo. All of us here in Venezuela are so proud of you," said President Hugo Chávez during his weekly radio program, *Aló Presidente,* after the White Sox qualified for the playoffs in 2005. "We are with you, and we'll be waiting for you when you come back, hopefully as world champion."

"*Un abrazo a todo Venezuela,*" Guillén announced to the world after the White Sox defeated Los Angeles to win the American League title and advance to the World Series for the first time since 1959. Their opponents, the Astros, the team that opened the Venezuelan market, had only one part-time *criollo* player on the roster, Raúl Chávez, and he did not play in the World Series. The White Sox were the team of Carrasquel, Aparicio, and Guillén—the first Latin-born manager in the World Series—and had Freddy García, originally signed by the Astros, pitching. It was little surprise that most Venezuelans were cheering for Chicago.

Before Game 1, Luis Aparicio threw the ceremonial first pitch to Guillén. And when the White Sox defeated Houston 4 games to 0 to win the championship, Guillén shouted at the award ceremony, "This is for Venezuela." He then took the World Series trophy—as if it were the touring Stanley Cup—back to Venezuela with him. Like the 1941 victory over Cuba, the selection of Aparicio to the Hall of

Fame in 1984, and Johán Santana's winning the Cy Young in 2004, the victory of "Los Ozzie's Boys" in the World Series was another transcendent moment in Venezuelan baseball history.

Only a month later, when Andrés left the organization, he encouraged his staff at the Venezuelan academy to remain. With his departure, however, there was no one in the front office in Houston to "defend" the academy, to fight for the budget, or to go to bat for Venezuelan players when the 40-man roster was assembled. And unless important changes are made in the Astros' minor league development process, some of the Venezuelan prospects signed by Andrés may never fulfill their potential.

During his more than sixteen years with Houston, Andrés always had the support of top baseball people in the organization including Bill Wood, Bob Watson, Gerry Hunsicker, and Tal Smith. He was particularly close to Hunsicker, for whom he was a special assistant for the last nine years of his tenure with Houston. While Hunsicker was supportive of and attentive to Andrés's concerns, he also had to put together a big league team, deal with free agency and arbitration, absorb constant budget restraints and interference from owner Drayton McLane, as well as worry about the June free-agent draft and keep an eye on their six minor league teams in the United States and a program in the Dominican Republic. Andrés was fortunate in that he got most of what he wanted in Venezuela and, with Hunsicker's assistance, protected most of the Venezuelan prospects in the Astros' system. But Hunsicker was worn down by constantly having to do battle with McLane. And one reason why the Astros' Venezuelan program did not achieve its full potential were the budget limits imposed by McLane. As a result, Andrés was not in the market for the top prospects in Venezuela; had to cut out programs in Mexico, Nicaragua, and Panama; and struggled to secure the budget for improvements at the academy.

"He [McLane] approves every dollar spent and is involved in almost every decision. His smothering presence was a large reason why Gerry Hunsicker resigned or was forced out as general manager last fall [2004]," wrote *Houston Chronicle* columnist Richard Justice.[5]

McLane is an outstanding salesperson and cheerleader, but he does not understand the crucial role that scouting—especially in Latin America—plays for the organization. The micromanaging owner never visited Venezuela or the academy and did not appreciate its significance to the organization. No one on the business side of the Houston organization, those who scrutinized the budget along with McLane, had a clue how outstanding the Venezuela program was. Although the program has saved the Astros millions of dollars in the production of quality players signed and developed at bargain basement prices, few of those who remained in the Astros front office in 2006—apart from Tal Smith and Al Pedrique—comprehended Andrés's true value to the organization. The Venezuelan academy offered Houston the chance to have a program in Latin America that was the shining jewel of its player-development system, but the Astros squandered the opportunity.

Drayton McLane and his budget restrictions were only part of the problem. While the Houston franchise has long maintained an interest in Latin America since its origins in 1962, there has been no consistent organizational record of success in the region. Changes in ownership, general managers, and scouting personnel help to explain this. Prior to the accomplishments of the Venezuelan program, the only other period of sustained success by the Houston organization in Latin America was during the 1960s and 1970s under Tony Pacheco, Pat Gillick, and Epy Guerrero. That trio was responsible for the signing of César Cedeño, the only real Latin American superstar signed and developed by the Astros who spent much of his career with the club.

Andrés had fulfilled his dream of establishing a system of recruiting and developing players from Venezuela and preparing them to go to the United States to pursue their major league dream. Although Andrés was pleased with the success of his program, he was disappointed that he did not achieve more. He believed that he had proven the viability of combining scouting and development in the Venezuelan academy and that some of these experiences could be useful in improving the Astros' minor league system in the United States. He was extremely disappointed to find that it was much more difficult than he anticipated. Andrés became a prophet in an industry reluctant to embrace change.

"I survived WWII, I lost my leg, and I made the transition to Venezuela when I did not speak a single word of Spanish," Andrés told me after making the decision to leave the Astros' organization. "This will not kill me."

He not only survived, he thrived, and he hardly missed a beat. On December 2, 2005, Andrés was named special assistant to Cincinnati Reds GM Dan O'Brien. To the surprise of most observers, Andrés would not work with the Reds in Latin American scouting. Instead, he would pursue the second part of his dream: revamping a minor league system. When O'Brien was fired just over a month later, Andrés understood that under new management his role would be limited at best, and he was not interested in just sitting at home and collecting the salary owed to him under his one-year guaranteed contract.

With a bit of intervention from his old Houston boss, Gerry Hunsicker, now Senior Vice President of Baseball Operations with Tampa Bay, Andrés ended his tenure with Cincinnati on February 16 and on February 17 was named Special Assistant to Baseball Operations with Tampa Bay. Working with Carlos Alfonso, another former Astro, who was hired as the Devil Rays' Director of International Operations to jump-start a moribund Latin American program (Tampa Bay did not have a facility in either the Dominican Republic or Venezuela), Andrés hit the ground running. And you can now add Tampa Bay to the list of organizations with a serious interest in Venezuela.

Much as he did for the Astros in 1989 when he located the academy inside the grounds of Industrias Venoco, Andrés arranged with the Pirelli Tire Company to build a field and clubhouse to host the Devil Rays' operations in Venezuela on the grounds of their facility in Guacara. And he brought former Magallanes GM Ronnie Blanco on board as coordinator of Tampa Bay's Venezuela program. The Devil Rays also reached an agreement with the Los Angeles Dodgers to share their Campo Las Palmas facility in the Dominican Republic, still one of the top-notch complexes in the country.

"We are fine in Latin America," Andrés told me after just a month on the job. He said he was getting ready to tackle the issue of working with the Tampa Bay staff to improve their minor league operations in the United States. "This will be difficult," he acknowledged.

Tampa Bay may be improving its Latin American operations, but the Astros are facing a daunting task in maintaining their outstanding scouting and development program developed in Venezuela. Not only is Andrés gone, but so are four of the people profiled in this book: baseball operations assistant Carlos Pérez, psychologist Francisco Ruiz, Colombian scout Guillermo Ramírez, and major league pitching coach Jim Hickey are no longer with the Astros.

Pérez, who as liaison with Astros' programs in Venezuela, the Dominican Republic, and Colombia was an essential component of the organization's Latin American operations, resigned at the end of January 2007 to pursue opportunities outside the baseball industry.

Ruiz, an integral part in helping the Spanish-speaking Astros prospects adjust to both life in professional baseball and the United States, left at the end of November 2006. He accepted a job with Tampa Bay, to perform the same duties, a few days later.

In late 2006, after Andrés arranged for Tampa Bay to utilize the same facilities used by the Astros in Colombia (Tampa Bay players would work out in the morning, the Astros' prospects in the afternoon), Houston decided to pull out of the complex and let Ramírez go. The Astros are looking for another location to develop their prospects and are no longer the only organization with an academy in Colombia.

Two other key part-time staffers at the Venezuelan academy, conditioning coach Dr. Lester Storey and English teacher Luis Carmona, were also hired by Andrés to work at the Tampa Bay facility located only a few blocks from the Astros' operations in Guacara. Because they are not under an exclusive contract with the Devil Rays, Storey and Carmona will be able to continue to work with the Astros.

Hickey was fired at the end of the 2006 season.

"I didn't expect it at all," said Hickey a veteran of seventeen seasons in the Houston organization and on the major league staff for two and one half years. Astros GM Tim Purpura said they had no problem with Hickey but wanted to go in a new direction. Hickey's strength is working with young pitchers, and with the Astros looking to bring top prospects Gutiérrez, Estrada, and Paulino up to the majors in the next couple of years, the bilingual Hickey would seem to be a valuable asset. Thus, the real reason was for replacing Hickey is unclear. In November 2006 Hickey was hired by Tampa Bay as a minor league pitching coach and within a week was elevated to the same position with the major league club.

Shortly after Hickey was fired, Purpura led a contingent of Astros front office personnel to Venezuela and announced that Alfredo Pedrique had been promoted to head the organization's Latin American operations, the same job that Andrés had. Omar López was named manager of the academy summer league team, a move necessitated when Mario González left the Astros' organization in the middle of the summer 2006. González was soon hired by the New York Mets to work in their Venezuelan development program. Rafael Cariel was given a new title, director of scouting for Venezuela, but in fact had been acting in that capacity for several years.

Pedrique is a good choice to run the Venezuelan program. He is intelligent, honest, patient, a very good instructor and is well respected in his native Venezuela where he led Magallanes to the playoffs in both 2005–6 and 2006–7. With Pedrique in charge, the Astros might be able to remain a major competitor in Venezuela. But with the plan that Andrés so carefully crafted for the program unraveling, it will not be easy. Pedrique will have to be aggressive in both defending his budget needs with the front office in Houston and supporting the young Venezuelan prospects on their way through the Astros' minor league system. And I don't see Pedrique's new role as baseball administrator to be long lasting. He is at his best when he is coaching and managing, and I look for him to jump at the opportunity to get back on the field in uniform.

Although the *Houston Chronicle* reported that Purpura "has traveled to Venezuela at least once a year for 13 years," the 2006 trip was actually his first visit to the country in almost five years.[6] And while Purpura made it sound as if these were significant improvements at the academy and to the club's Latin American scouting in general, actually little had changed, except that Andrés was no longer there. Clearly the Astros were still in denial about the impact Andrés had made on the organization and were unable to come up with a response as to why the man who had the vision to create the Venezuelan academy had left. The soul of the academy was gone and there was no mention of it at the press conference or in any reports in the *Houston Chronicle* or the Astros' Web site.

Andrés may attempt to devote his full-time energies with Tampa Bay on the development side, but he really is like a kid in a candy store when scouting in Latin America, and he just couldn't stay away.

In December 2006 Andrés ventured even further into the new frontier of scouting when he made a trip to Argentina—not at the top of the list of countries when one thinks of baseball—with Carlos Alfonso. Very little baseball is played in soccer-dominated Argentina, and only a couple of young men from the country have ever played in the U.S. minor leagues. But the Devil Rays signed two prospects from Buenos Aires on the trip, one a sixteen-year-old left-handed hitter, who Andrés told me "has more bat speed, bat control, and power than Bob Abreu did at that age." I could hear the same excitement in his voice that I first heard seventeen years earlier when he told me about the unlimited potential of Abreu.

In early 2007, when the New York Yankees made a trip to China in an effort to develop a new source of baseball talent, and New York Mets GM Omar Minaya led a delegation to Ghana in another effort to grow the game, Andrés went to Brazil at the invitation of government officials in an effort to establish a future base of players for Tampa Bay. Brazil, he told me, "is my new frontier of scouting." The fact is that for Andrés there are no boundaries in the search for baseball talent, only opportunities to discover players where most other scouts are unwilling to go.

15

Epilogue

In November 2006, *los héroes del 41* were inducted as a team into the Salón de la Fama in Valencia. And the 1941 trophy that had been given to Hugo Chávez during the 2004 Cy Young celebration for Johán Santana was returned to the Venezuelan Sports Federation. Hopefully, one day soon it will be on display in the baseball museum.

At the Salón de la Fama, the statue of the left-handed shortstop remains, but I discovered why the glove is on the wrong hand. Javier González, the director of the museum at the time the statue was commissioned, told me that it was his idea to have visitors see the back of the uniform and the number *13*. Thus, González did not have to choose between putting the likeness of Chico Carrasquel, David Concepción, Ozzie Guillén, or Omar Vizquel—all of whom wore that number—on the face of the statue. González didn't expect to have the glove on the shortstop's right hand, but from an artistic viewpoint it made more sense to place it there. Once the mistake was discovered, it was too late.

The stars produced by the Astros' Venezuelan academy—Bob Abreu, Freddy García, Carlos Guillén, Melvin Mora, and Johán Santana—continued to excel in 2006. Only Mora had a below-average year, hitting .274 with 16 home runs and 83 RBI.

Abreu, traded to the Yankees in late July, sparkled under the bright lights of New York and had 42 RBI in 58 games. Joe Torre called Abreu "the perfect fit for the Yankees." In November Abreu returned home to Caracas to launch his new record label, Cacao Música, to support up-and-coming Venezuelan musicians. While there, he expressed a desire to join los Leones del Caracas for a couple of weeks in January if the team made it to the post season. Caracas squeaked in during the last week of the season, but a disappointed Abreu was denied permission by the Yankees to join the team.

Freddy García went 17-9 with the White Sox and pitched two consecutive one-hitters late in the season. During the off-season, García was traded to Philadelphia.

Carlos Guillén hit a career high .320 and helped lead the Detroit Tigers to the World Series. "He is our smartest player," remarked Tigers manager Jim Leyland.

Santana led the American League in ERA (2.77), strikeouts (245), and innings pitched (233.2); tied for most wins (19); and won his second Cy Young. He was selected by *Baseball America* as the Major League Player of the Year and received so many honors back home in Venezuela that it was difficult to keep up with them. Santana also announced that he was creating a foundation to foster community development as well as promote baseball in his home state of Mérida.

Below, in alphabetical order is the progress of the other academy products that made it to the major leagues.

MANUEL BARRIOS

After Barrios's debut with the Astros in 1997, he was sent to the Florida Marlins along with Oscar Henríquez in the trade that brought Moisés Alou to Houston. Barrios pitched in two games for Florida and was traded to Los Angeles where he appeared in one game. Barrios's major league career consisted of 5 games, 6 2/3 innings and a 0-0 record. He pitched in the independent leagues until 2004. Andrés told me Barrios is now living in Illinois either in the Chicago area or in the Quad Cities.

RAÚL CHÁVEZ

Raúl Chávez, the first player signed by Andrés in Venezuela, was designated for assignment by the Astros at the end of spring training 2006 and claimed by the Baltimore Orioles. Chávez, signed in 1990, spent six years in the Astros' minor league system and was traded to Montreal in 1996. He played parts of two seasons with the Expos before being traded to Seattle in 1998 and appeared in one game for the Mariners. "Chamo" was signed by the Astros again in 2000 and played for parts of five seasons in Houston.

In early April 2006 Baltimore also designated Chávez for assignment. He appeared in seven games with the Orioles and had a .091 batting average, which further lowered his .215 career average going into the season. He returned to the Orioles in September and raised his season average to .179. With his weak hitting and his increased weight, the thirty-three-year-old Chávez should be thankful he played seventeen professional seasons and spent parts of nine of them in the major leagues. He was a nonroster invitee to spring training in 2007 with the New York Yankees.

FELIX ESCALONA

Escalona was selected from Houston by the San Francisco Giants in the Rule 5 draft in December 2001. In late March 2002 he was claimed off waivers by Tampa Bay and played a few games with the Devil Rays in 2002 and 2003. He was signed by the New York Yankees as a free agent in late March 2004 and played in fifteen major league games with the Yankees in 2004 and 2005. In August 2005 Escalona played all four infield positions for the Yankees in a span of four days. In 2006 he played at both Triple-A Columbus and Double-A Trenton in New York's minor league system.

ALEJANDRO FREIRE

Fourteen years after being signed by the Astros in 1991, Freire made his major league debut with the Baltimore Orioles on August 9, 2005. He played five years in the Astros' minor league system before he was selected by Detroit in the Rule 5 minor league draft in 1996. He spent another five years in the Tigers' minor league system and signed with San Francisco as a minor league free agent in 2002. After two years in the Giants' system, he played with Veracruz in the Mexican League in 2004, and then spent most of 2005 with Triple-A Ottawa before being called up by the Orioles. In 2006 he was back at Ottawa.

HÉCTOR GIMÉNEZ

Giménez became the twentieth player from the Venezuelan academy to reach the big leagues when he made his debut with the Astros on September 26, 2006. With the Astros still in the pennant race, Giménez got only two at bats (and no hits). He missed the entire 2007 season due to injury.

Giménez's arrival is particularly pleasing to Andrés—he believes Giménez may be the best player he ever signed. The young catcher had been highly touted for several years but never really blossomed and was not listed among the organization's top prospects in 2006. That all changed with an outstanding 2006 postseason with Round Rock when Giménez helped lead the team to the Pacific Coast League finals. His performance was reminiscent of his first start for Magallanes in a game against Caracas during the 2003–4 season when Giménez went 4 for 5 with 3 RBI and caught the attention of fans in Venezuela.

DEVERN HANSACK

At the end of spring training in 2004, the Astros released two Nicaraguan pitchers, Devern Hansack and Ernnie Sinclair. Both had good records in the minor leagues and had just completed successful seasons in high A-ball. But Andrés was told by the Astros' minor league field coordinator, "We don't see any projection in them." Andrés obviously did and thought both pitchers should have been sent to Double-A.

Hansack did not pitch in 2004—he worked on a lobster boat in Nicaragua—and played professional baseball in Holland in 2005. In December 2005 he was signed by the Boston Red Sox. When Hansack made his debut against Toronto on September 23, 2006, he became the ninth Nicaraguan to play in the major leagues. In his second start in the season-ending game for the Red Sox on October 1, Hansack pitched five innings of no-hit, no-run baseball in a rain-shortened game.

CARLOS EDUARDO HERNÁNDEZ

Carlos Hernández, the second baseman, played for seven years in the Astros' minor league system and played in sixteen major league games with Houston in 1999. He played in two games with Seattle in 2000 and bounced around the minor leagues after that. He has been a mainstay of the Magallanes club in Venezuela for over ten years. In 2006 Hernández was playing in the independent leagues.

CARLOS ENRIQUE HERNÁNDEZ

Left-handed pitcher Carlos Hernández never really recovered from his season-ending injury in 2001. He played for almost the entire season with Houston in 2002 and had a 7-5 record but was on the disabled list for six weeks with what was termed "left shoulder soreness." He made a couple of starts and then was shut down again in mid-September when an MRI revealed "an impingement in his left shoulder and rotator cuff tendinitis." He missed the entire 2003 season after undergoing surgery to repair a tear of the labrum and another in the rotator cuff on his left shoulder. Hernández spent most of the 2004 season at New Orleans trying to regain his velocity. He was only throwing in the mid-80s, nowhere near the low 90s he displayed earlier in his career. He made a few starts with the Astros at the end of the year going 1-3.

In 2005 he was 5-8 at Triple-A Round Rock, where he struggled most of the year. A medical exam showed no structural damage, and he was told he just needed to build his arm strength. Hernández was convinced there was some damage, and when he expressed his concerns, some in the organization questioned his attitude. Nonetheless, he had improved to the point where the Astros were about to call him up as soon as Round Rock's season ended, but during the team's last home game at the end of August, Hernández strained his left quadricep while rounding third base and was finished for the year.

He returned home to Venezuela during the winter and went 7-1 with Magallanes. I saw him in the playoffs against Caracas in Caracas, and he was very impressive, allowing no runs in six innings and striking out seven while walking only one batter, and he went 2-0 in the playoffs. But it was a different Hernández than I had seen five years earlier. While he had lost velocity, he had good control.

Hernández was not imagining that he was injured in 2005. An MRI during spring training in 2006 showed another partial tear of his rotator cuff and labrum, and Hernández underwent surgery and spent the rest of the season on the DL with a couple of rehab appearances at Double-A Corpus Christi. Hopefully his physical problems have been corrected, and with a lot of hard work, perhaps Hernández can regain the promise he showed in 2001 and return to the Astros' starting rotation. On opening day 2007, Hernández was still only twenty-six years old.

OSCAR HENRÍQUEZ

Andrés brought Henríquez to extended spring training with Tampa Bay in 2006, but "Manacho" did not show enough promise to warrant going through the difficult process of obtaining a visa at such a late date. He ended up playing for an independent league team.

RICHARD HIDALGO

Hidalgo, only thirty-one, did not play during the 2006 season. He worked out at his Orlando, Florida, home, lost quite a few pounds, and reported in very good shape on the first day of practice of Magallanes for the 2006–7 Venezuelan winter league season. Given the way he abruptly left the team at the beginning of the playoffs in early 2006, no one was sure which Richard Hidalgo would show up when the season started. Much to the delight of the Magallanes fans, Hidalgo was in the lineup from the very first game and had an outstanding year. He led the team in home runs with 9 and displayed his defensive talents in the field. In the postseason in early 2007, he turned it up a notch. He had 9 home runs in just 21 games, including 3 in one game, the first time that had ever occurred during the playoffs in league history. Clearly he was on a mission to return to the major leagues. Hidalgo signed a minor league contract with the Houston Astros with an invitation to spring training but was released at the end of March.

DONALDO MÉNDEZ

Méndez, a middle infielder signed by Andrés in 1996, was selected by San Diego in the Rule 5 draft in 2000 and played 46 games with the Padres in 2001. Méndez, who made the jump from A-ball to the major leagues, was obviously overmatched and hit only .153.

He played a few games (26) with San Diego in 2003 and after that bounced around the minor leagues. In 2006 Méndez appeared in 19 games with Triple-A Rochester.

FERNANDO NIEVE

Nieve made his major league debut with the Astros in April 2006, and spent most of the year with the Houston club going 3-3 with a 4.20 ERA. He started 11 of the 40 games in which he appeared. The 6-0, 200-pound right-hander would have been a call-up in September 2005, but a ruptured appendix on the last day of the season at Triple-A Round Rock prohibited that move.

ROBERTO PETAGINE

After getting fewer than 200 at bats spread over five seasons with Houston, the New York Mets, and Cincinnati between 1994 and 1998, Petagine went to Japan. During his six outstanding seasons in the Japanese Central League with the Yakult Swallows and the Yomiuri Giants between 1999 and 2004, Petagine won 3 gold gloves and 2 home-run titles and was the league MVP in 2001. He was indeed a superstar in Japan and is considered one of the best foreign-born players in the history of Japanese baseball.

Petagine returned to the United States in 2005 and signed a minor league contract with the Boston Red Sox with an invitation to spring training. His salary was $750,000 or approximately one-tenth of the $7 million he earned in Japan in 2004. After a seven-year absence from the major leagues, Petagine was called up by the Red Sox in early August 2005 and had 6 RBI in his first 6 games, and ended the year with .281 average.

In 2006 Petagine signed a minor league contract with the Seattle Mariners with an invitation to spring training. Petagine was a long shot to make the team, but his outstanding hitting during the spring—over a .400 average—catapulted him to the major league roster. Unfortunately, he saw little action with the Mariners and had only 27 at-bats, mostly as a pinch hitter. When Seattle designated him for assignment in early July, he was hitting only .185. He was released by the organization after the 2006 season.

WILFREDO RODRÍGUEZ

Rodríguez was a non-roster invitee to spring training with Milwaukee in 2006, but was assigned to their minor league camp on March 17 and did not play during the 2006 season. His entire major league career consisted of two games, three innings pitched and giving up home run number 70 to Barry Bonds.

EDGAR RAMOS

A right-handed pitcher, Ramos was taken in the Rule 5 draft in 1996 by Philadelphia and pitched in four games for the Phillies and had an 0-2 record before he was returned to the Astros' minor league system. He never made another major league appearance, but continued to make a living in baseball. He played at the Astros' Triple-A New Orleans affiliate in 1998 and then moved to the independent leagues and the Mexican League for several summers. At home in the winter, Ramos played for more than ten seasons with Magallanes before moving to Pastora, where in 2006–7 he was in his fourteenth season in the LVBP.

In early 2007 some of the more promising academy products were still in the Astros' developmental pipeline. Three, Paul Estrada, Juan Carlos Gutiérrez, and Felipe Paulino del Gudice were on the Astros' 40-man roster.

PAUL ESTRADA

Estrada, twenty-three, from Ciudad Bolívar, was discovered by associate scout Miguel Chacoa. The 6-1, 200-pound Estrada was signed as a nondrafted free agent on July 2, 1999, and spent his first two years in the Venezuelan Summer League, then two more with the rookie level team at Martinsville, Virginia. In 2004 he had a 5-2 record, a 2.81 ERA and 8 saves at Tri-City in the New York–Penn League, and in 2005 he was 6-7 with a 2.69 ERA at Lexington. The year 2006 was a breakout one for the twenty-four-year-old right-hander. He went 8-5 with 15 saves and a 3.05 ERA at Double-A Corpus Christi. Used exclusively in relief, he had 134 strikeouts in 88.2 innings and was second in the Texas League in strikeouts.

JUAN CARLOS GUTIÉRREZ

Gutiérrez was discovered by associate scout Rafael Lara who took the 6-3, 200-pound right-handed pitcher to his baseball school near Barquisimeto. Astros scout Pablo Torrealba saw Gutiérrez and told Andrés that the young pitcher was very good but would be expensive to sign. Andrés informed GM Gerry Hunsicker and offered to bring Gutiérrez to the United States for a showcase. "That's not necessary," Hunsicker told Andrés. "If you want to sign him, just sign him." After seeing Gutiérrez throw just twenty pitches on December 14, 2000, Andrés gave him a $200,000 bonus—the highest he had ever paid.

Similar to Estrada, Gutiérrez played his first four professional seasons at the rookie level, the first two in Venezuela. The twenty-three-year-old had an 8-2 record with a 3.21 ERA in 2004 at Greeneville in the Appalachian League, followed by a 9-5 mark with a 3.00 ERA at Lexington in 2005. In 2006 Gutiérrez had an outstanding season with Double-A Corpus Christi going 8-4 with a 3.04 ERA and won both of his play-off games to help lead his team to the Texas League championship. Gutiérrez started the 2007 season at Triple-A Round Rock and made his major league debut with the Astros and August 19, becoming the twenty-first academy product to reach the big leagues.

FELIPE PAULINO DEL GUIDICE

I was at the academy on July 2, 2001, when right-handed pitcher Felipe Paulino del Guidice was signed as a non-drafted free agent by the Astros. Three years earlier, Cincinnati wanted to convert the fifteen-year-old outfielder into a pitcher, but unwilling to change, Paulino went home unsigned. When the Astros invited Paulino, still an outfielder, to their academy in 2001, pitching coach Oscar Padrón explained that his future in baseball was as a pitcher, and he agreed to take the mound. The 6-2, 180-pound Paulino now tops 100 mph, and I have seen him throw 99 on two occasions. While Paulino is Dominican by birth, he is culturally *criollo*, having grown up in Venezuela.

Paulino, twenty-three, has completed five years in the Astros' minor league system where he has shifted between being a starter and reliever. In 2006 Paulino was 9-7 with a 4.35 ERA as a starter at high-

A Salem and pitched 126 innings, which was almost equal to the combined total of his previous four years of professional experience. More important, he was developing a good breaking ball to go along with his overpowering fastball. On September 5, 2007, Paulino made his major league debut with the Astros. He was the twenty-second academy alumnus to get to the major leagues and could be the Astros closer in 2008 or 2009.

Other Astros' academy products to keep an eye on include:

GERMÁN MELÉNDEZ

Signed in 1998 by Andrés and Orlando Fernández, Meléndez was a catcher for six years in the Astros' minor league system. In 2000 he hit .308 and was named MVP on the Astros' Dominican Summer League team. In 2005 Meléndez was converted to pitcher and spent most of the season at Tri-City where he went 7-0 with a 2.86 ERA. In late 2005 he was signed by Cincinnati as a six-year free agent, compiled a 0-1 record at Dayton, and was released early in the 2006 season. Meléndez, now twenty-five years old and in his eighth professional season, re-signed with the Astros and was 2-0 with a 1.32 ERA and 7 saves at Lexington before being promoted to high-A Salem where he was 1-1 with a 3.15 ERA and 6 saves.

WLADIMIR SUTIL

Sutil, the skinny kid I saw in a tryout at the academy, quickly moved "from zero to prospect," a phrase Andrés is fond of using when describing young men who improve rapidly at the academy. Within a week of his signing in May 2003, he was playing for the Astros' Venezuelan Summer League team. In 2004 playing shortstop, he hit .298 at Greeneville in the Appalachian League and in the winter returned home to Venezuela to play for the Magallanes team in the Liga de Desarrollo. Early in the season before the veteran players arrived, Magallanes manager Marc Bombard wanted to take a look at some of the younger players and asked that they report at 8:00 a.m. When Bombard arrived at 7:30 a.m., Sutil had already been there for half an hour. A few days later, Bombard started Sutil in a regular-season game for Magallanes. In 23 games with Magallanes, Sutil hit for a .281 average.

In 2005 Sutil spent most of the season at Tri-City where he had .329 batting average and was selected to the New York–Penn League all-star team. In 2006 he was slowed by a hamstring injury and split time between low-A Lexington (60 games) where he hit .272 and high-A Salem (29 games) where he had a .227 average. But keep an eye on his movement through Houston's minor league system. In addition to his exceptional defense and speed on the bases, the Astros have been impressed with his strong leadership both on and off the field and his incredible passion for the game.

ENYELBERT SOTO

The left-hander got off to a solid start in his professional career with a 5–0 record and a 2.14 ERA in the Dominican Summer League in 2002. Because of injuries, he did not pitch in 2001 and 2002. The twenty-four-year-old pitcher was converted to a full-time reliever in 2004 and had a 2–3 record with a 1.75 ERA at high-A Salem in 2006. He could be a pleasant surprise prospect.

LEVI ROMERO

The pitcher the Astros almost released in 2004 had a 5-5 record with a 5.43 record as a starter at low-A Lexington in 2006. Only twenty-three, Romero still has the potential to pitch at the major league level.

CÉSAR MAYORA

The 6-3, 200-pound right-hander had an outstanding year in 2006. Used exclusively in relief, the twenty-three-year-old Mayora, in his fourth professional season, was 1-1 with a 0.84 ERA at Greeneville and 1-0 with a 1.98 ERA at Tri-City.

VÍCTOR GÁRATE

After three seasons in the Venezuelan Summer League and one at rookie Greeneville, the twenty-two-year-old left-hander had an outstanding year at short-season Tri-City going 4-0 with a 0.92 ERA and eight saves. He could be another unexpected surprise for the Astros.

CÉSAR QUINTERO

Andrés reminded me not to leave Quintero off the list of those who still have a chance to reach the major leagues. Although he saw limited playing time at Tri-City in 2006, the middle infielder from Puerto Cabello, Venezuela, has a .345 career batting average in his first four professional seasons. In 2005 he was named the Astros' Dominican Summer League MVP as well as being selected to the DSL all-star team and winning all-star game MVP honors.

RICARDO BONFANTE

Andrés overheard what I had told scout Rafael Cariel about the Astros not making an effort to sign top prospect Douglas Salinas—who signed with Seattle and went 4-0 with a 2.94 ERA at Peoria in the Arizona Rookie League in 2006—and said, "I signed a diamond today: the kid from Colombia."

He was referring to shortstop Ricardo Bonfante. Andrés had invited me be at the academy July 2, 2005, as Bonfante would be the last player he signed for the Astros. The first thing I noticed was how skinny Bonfante was (137 pounds) and that he appeared younger than sixteen years old. I could not see the projection that Andrés did. But that's why I write and not scout. And I was reminded of what Bob Abreu told me a couple of years ago: "Andrés is a genius. In the body of a skinny kid like me, he could see a major league player."

I had not thought much about Bonfante until I ran into him in Houston in late September 2006. He had been named the MVP of the Astros' Venezuelan Summer League. Don't look for him tomorrow in Houston, but maybe in four or five years, you might see him playing in Minute Maid Park.

And Bonfante was not the only Colombian in the Astros' system with a chance to make it to major leagues. Shortstop and second baseman Ronald Ramírez from Cartagena was named as the MVP at Greeneville in 2006. His .314 average was seventh in the Appalachian League, and he was named to the all-star team. Two other Colombians had outstanding seasons at Greeneville. Steve Brown from Baranquilla, hit .306, and right-hander Carlos Ledeuth from San Antero, a small town southwest of Cartagena, was 1-1 and had a 0.84 ERA in 21 games.

Acknowledgments

No words can describe the gratitude I have for everyone in Venezuela who helped make this book possible. *Un abrazo fuerte* to Andrés Reiner and his staff, including Jesús Aristimuño, Rafael Cariel, Luis Carmona, Eduardo Castillo, César Cedeño, Miguel Chacoa, Pedro Franceschi, Ramón Fereira, Orlando Fernández, Mario González, Rafael Lara, Omar López, Nestor Marrero, Ramón Morales, Juan Oliveros, Wolfgang Ramos, Francisco Ruiz, Lester Storey, Pablo Torrealba, and Euclides Vargas, for being guides and teachers on my many visits to Venezuela. Two staff members, Rubén Cabrera and Oscar Padrón, died before this book was completed.

I also want to express my appreciation to my Venezuelan journalist friends who made me feel at home in their country, especially Giner García, Iván Medina, Ibsen Martínez, Humberto Acosta, and Dámaso Blanco; to all of the Astros' prospects who so generously shared their time, but specifically to Bob Kelly Abreu, Henry Centeno, Raúl Chávez, Carlos Guillén, Richard Hidalgo, and Melvin Mora, and to the many Venezuelans who took time from their busy schedules to visit with me, particularly Rafael and Ligia Avila, Ronnie Blanco, Pedro Caro, John Fitzgerald Castro, Javier González, Saul González, Mikel Pérez, Oscar Prieto, and Jesús Santana.

Two individuals provided crucial assistance in helping me make the transition from the classroom to the clubhouse when I began my baseball research in 1987: Rob Matwick, then with the Houston Astros and now vice president of communications for the Detroit Tigers, and John Blake of the Texas Rangers, now vice president for media relations with the Boston Red Sox. Thanks Rob and John for providing press credentials and making Houston and Arlington my windows to major league baseball.

My traveling companions through Latin American baseball, Alan Klein and Tim Wendel, were always ready to offer advice, expertise, and encouragement at every stage of the project. Thanks guys. Also special thanks to Mary Beckner whose photos appear in the book.

I owe a debt of gratitude to my outstanding editors including Ivy McLemore (*Houston Post*), John Royster (*Baseball America*), Paul White and Margaret McCahill (*USA Today Baseball Weekly*), and Joel Horn (*Diamondbacks Magazine*), who always improved on the copy I sent them. I was deeply saddened by John Royster's untimely death in 2003.

I also want to thank Rob Taylor and Joeth Zucco, my editors at the University of Nebraska Press, for their help and guidance.

Thanks to Carol Ness of the *San Francisco Chronicle* for teaching me how to write for a general, nonacademic audience. Other journalists and colleagues who were unselfish in offering assistance include Joe Arbena, Kevin Baxter, Rod Beaton, Bill Brown, René Cárdenas, Murray Chass, Neil Hohlfeld, Rick Lawes, Will Lingo, Gerry Martin, Tom Miller, Boris Mizrahi, John Morthland, Jim Myers, Eric Nadel, Jorge Ortiz, José de Jesús Ortiz, Bill Plaschke, Michael Point, Tracy Ringolsby, Phil Rogers, Alberto Rondón, Adolfo Salguiero, Billy Sample, and Alan Truex.

Thanks to the players, scouts, coaches, managers, general managers, and player development people who so graciously shared their baseball insights. It is impossible to name all of them, but the following deserve particular mention: Manny Acta, Carlos Alfonso, Sandy Alomar Sr., Felipe Alou, Rubén Amaro Sr., Rubén Amaro Jr., Luis Aponte, Sal Artiaga, Ralph Avila, Dick Balderson, Enrique Brito, Al Campanis, Fred Claire, Milton Croes, Mel Didier, Larry Dierker, Arnold Elles, Orrin Freeman, René Gayo, Pat Gillick, David Gottfried, Luchy Guerra, Roland Hemond, Jim Hickey, Gary Hughes, Gerry Hunsicker, Sandy Johnson, Deacon Jones, Tommy Jones, Tom Kayser, Buzzy Keller, Winston Llenas, Julio Linares, Omar Minaya, George Moreira, Fred Nelson, Junior Noboa, Dan O'Brien, José

Oquendo, Willie Paffen, Alfredo Pedrique, Tony Peña, Carlos Pérez, Tim Purpura, Guillermo Ramírez, David Rawnsley, Herb Raybourn, Phil Regan, Paul Ricciarini, Branch Rickey III, Tom Romanesko, Luis Rosa, Aníbal Reluz, Tal Smith, Scipio Spinks, Lew Temple, Alejandro Treviño, Curtis Wallace, Calixto Vargas, Bob Watson, Gene Watson, Paul Weaver, and Bill Wood.

Four players I interviewed very early in my research and who have all since died had a profound effect on me: Santos Amaro, Curt Flood, Víctor Pellot Pove (Vic Power), and Willie Wells. All fought the discrimination they faced through the quality of their play on the field and their incredible strength and dignity off it. They are my heroes and they continue to inspire me.

Very special thanks go to my wife Margo Gutiérrez who not only read each draft of the manuscript, but who also was there to support me in every step of the project. Without her assistance, this book would not have been possible. Also thanks to my son Gabriel, who made sure my computers were always functioning properly; and my son Jorge who was my photographer and, more important, my traveling companion for several years on trips to Venezuela, Colombia, Panama, Nicaragua, and Aruba.

APPENDIX

Astros' Academy Players in Major League Baseball

PLAYER	POSITION	BIRTHPLACE	DEBUT	TEAM
Roberto Petagine	1st Base	Porlamar, Nueva Esparta, Venezuela	April 4, 1994	Houston
Raúl Chávez	C	Guacara, Carabobo,Venezuela	August 30, 1996	Montreal
Bob Kelly Abreu	OF	Turmero, Aragua, Venezuela	September 1, 1996	Houston
Edgar Ramos	RHP	Cumaná,Sucre, Venezuela	May 21, 1997	Philadelphia
Richard Hidalgo	OF	Guarenas, Miranda, Venezuela	September 1,1997	Houston
Oscar Henríquez	RHP	La Guaira, Vargas,Venezuela	September 7, 1997	Houston
Manuel Barrios	RHP	Cabecera, Panama	September 16, 1997	Houston
Carlos Guillén	INF	Maracay, Aragua, Venezuela	September 6, 1998	Seattle
Carlos Hernández	INF	Caracas, D.F., Venezuela	May 26, 1999	Houston
Melvin Mora	INF/OF	Agua Negra, Yaracuy, Venezuela	May 30, 1999	New York Mets
Freddy García	RHP	Caracas, D.F., Venezuela	July 4, 1999	Seattle
Johán Santana	LHP	Tovar, Mérida, Venezuela	April 4, 2000	Minnesota
Donaldo Méndez	INF	Barquismeto,Lara, Venezuela	April 5, 2001	San Diego
Carlos Hernández	LHP	Yagua, Carabobo, Venezuela	August 18, 2001	Houston
Wilfredo Rodríguez	LHP	San Felix, Bolívar, Venezuela	September 21, 2001	Houston
Félix Escalona	INF	Puerto Cabello, Carabobo, Venezuela	April 4, 2002	Tampa Bay
Alejandro Freire	INF	Caracas, D.F., Venezuela	August 9, 2005	Baltimore
Fernando Nieve	RHP	Puerto Cabello, Carabobo, Venezuela	April 4, 2006	Houston
Devren Hansack	RHP	Pearl Lagoon, Nicaragua	September 23, 2006	Boston
Héctor Giménez	C	Chivacoa, Yaracuy, Venezuela	September 25,2006	Houston
Juan Gutiérrez	RHP	Puerto la Cruz, Anzoátegui, Venezuela	August 19, 2007	Houston
Felipe Paulino	RHP	Santo Domingo, Dominican Republic	September 5, 2007	Houston

Notes

1. Venezuelan Bust, Baseball Boom

1. Two articles in the six-part series were devoted exclusively to Venezuela: Milton Jamail, "Astros prospecting for Venezuelan talent," *Houston Post,* July 25, 1990, and Milton Jamail, "Venezuelan baseball academic for scout: Reiner connects early with young prospects," *Houston Post,* July 26, 1990.
2. Because this book is the result of seventeen years of meetings with Andrés Reiner, I have not cited each interview or conversation I had with him during this period—they run into the hundreds.

   For this book, I also conducted interviews with members of the Houston Astros front office between 1990 and 2006 and with hundreds of scouts, coaches, and players during that period. When I quote from one of these sources, I give the approximate time period of the interview. For example, I spent a week at the Astros' Venezuelan academy in May 2003 and met with all of the staff on a daily basis. Thus a quote from academy director Pablo Torrealba from the period would identify it only as occurring in May 2003.
3. Rabe, *The Road to OPEC,* 33.
4. A second edition of the book was published shortly after Carlos Daniel's death. Carlos Cárdenas Lares, *Venezolanos en las grandes ligas: sus vidas y hazañas,* 2nd ed. (Caracas: Fondo Editorial Cárdenas Lares, 1994).
5. Baseball language in Venezuela is a mixture of English and Spanish with a few hybrid terms. Words taken directly from English include "strike," "foul," "home run," "hit," and of course, "baseball." The same words are often found in print with phonetic spellings: "*estraik,*" "*faul,*" "*jonrón,*" and "*jit.*" Some terms are simply translated from English, e.g., a starting pitcher is an "*abridor,*" while the closer is the "*cerrador.*" Other words are

a mixture of the two languages. "*Catchear*" is one such hybrid describing what the catcher does. The sport itself, depending on the source and time period in which it was written, might be found as "*béisbol,*" "*beisbol,*" "baseball," or "base-ball."

Let's go around the diamond:

Pitcher: Venezuelans might use "*lanzador,*" "*serpentinero,*" or "pitcher."
Catcher is the same as in English but may be spelled phonetically as "*quécher,*" or "*receptor*" may be used.
First: "*primera base*" or "*inicialista*"
Second: "*segunda base,*" "*camarero,*" or "*intermedista*"
Shortstop: "short stop," "*campo corto,*" "*paracorto,*" or "*torpedero*"
Third: "*tercera base*" or "*antesalista*"
Outfielder: "*guardabosque*" or "*jardinero*"
Center field is "*centrofield,*" and the person playing there the "centerfielder," or "*centro-campista.*" The other two outfield positions are referred either as "left field" or "right field" or "*jardín izquierdo*" or "*derecha,*" and as "leftfielder" or "rightfielder."

A dictionary of Venezuelan baseball terms, *Léxico del béisbol en Venezuela* by Edgar Colmenares del Valle was published in 1977.

2. It's Their Game Too

1. Much of the account at the beginning of this chapter is based on Ramos, *Todos fueron heroes.* The quotes from Andrés Eloy Blanco are from his speech, which is reprinted in the book. There are two other books devoted to the 1941 game: Etedgui and Fuenmayor Pérez, *La hazaña del siglo* and Antero Núñez and Méndez, *Oro y glorias del béisbol venezolano.*
2. Casas, Alfonso, and Pestana, *Viva y en juego,* 52.
3. Losada, "Hace cuarenta y seis años se jugaba baseball en Caracas," 8–9. Losada interviewed Cramer in Cuba in 1941 during the World Amateur games.
4. Pérez Jr., "Between Baseball and Bullfighting," 514–15.
5. John, *Los Leones del Caracas,* 3.
6. Gutiérrez, Alvarez, and Gutiérrez, hijo, *La enciclopedia del béisbol en Venezuela.* See also Biblioteca Nacional, *El béisbol en Venezuela.*

The brief history of Venezuelan baseball included in this chapter is in no way intended to be detailed or exhaustive. I have attempted to present some basic information about the origins of the game in the country and some historical milestones to make Andrés's story more comprehendible. I consulted numerous historical sources to attempt to corroborate information I received in interviews or primary sources. I consulted records of ships such as the USS *Marietta* and the USS *Denver* to make sure that they could have possibly been in the Caribbean when their crews reportedly played games against local teams in the region. In an attempt to make the book as readable as possible, I did not cite every document I consulted. Likewise I did not cite every time I picked up the *Registro del béisbol profesional de Venezuela 1965–1985* by Leo Benítez or Ivan Medina's *Registro del béisbol venezolano* to check the statistics of a player in the Venezuelan league. I cited the material from which I took direct quotes and have included in the bibliography other resources on the history of baseball in Venezuela. In addition, there are many other sources for those with an interest in Venezuelan baseball. Each of the eight teams in the league issues a media guide—some on par with those published by major league teams in the United States. Most teams also have websites with detailed statistics. *Meridiano*, Venezuela's leading sports paper, and *El Universal*, a major Caracas newspaper, are readily available on-line and provide detailed coverage of baseball in Venezuela and Venezuelans playing outside of the country.

7. Dickson, *The Dickson Baseball Dictionary*, 330.
8. Krich writes in *El Béisbol*, 241, that the British introduced rounders to Venezuela in the 1890s when they built rail lines. González does not disagree with Krich but argues that the game arrived much earlier.
9. Losada, "Hace cuarenta y seis años se jugaba baseball en Caracas."
10. John, *Los Leones del Caracas*, 4.
11. González, *El béisbol en Venezuela*, 20.
12. Ewell, *Venezuela*, 52.
13. Johnson and Wolff, *The Encyclopedia of Minor League Baseball*.
14. Antero Núñez and Méndez, *Años dorados del baseball venezolano, 1927–1945*.
15. Rabe, *The Road to OPEC*, 36.
16. Baseball historian Rob Ruck describes some of the experiences of import players in Venezuela in "Chicos and Gringos of Béisbol Venezolana [*sic*]," 75–78.
17. There are several accounts of the history of the Magallanes ball club. Among them are Bracho and García, *Navegantes del Magallanes: la travesía*; González, *Magallaneros y caraquistas*; González, *Navagantes del Magallanes*; Mijares and Gutiérrez, *¡Magallanes para todo el mundo!*; Salas, *Los eternos rivales*.

18. Gutiérrez, González, and Gutiérrez, hijo, *Galarragmanía*.
19. Dickson, *The Dickson Baseball Dictionary*, 13.

3. The Astros Go South

1. A more detailed account of the Astros 1977 Cuba trip can be found in my book, *Full Count*, 126–27.

4. From Zero to Prospect

1. Kerrane, *Dollar Sign on the Muscle*, 18.
2. Paul White, *USA Today Sports Weekly*, December 10, 2003, 33.
3. Kerrane, *Dollar Sign on the Muscle*, 95.

5. From Tunapuy to Guacara

1. Milton Jamail, "Astros earn big save with closer prospect," *USA Today Baseball Weekly*, December 20, 1995, 19.

6. On the Road to El Dorado

1. Portions of this chapter originally appeared in Milton Jamail, "The road to Cumana: the life of a Venezuelan scout," *USA Today Baseball Weekly*, December 31, 1997, 18–19.
2. Milton Jamail, "Dodgers' prospect has come a long, long way," *USA Today Baseball Weekly*, August 9, 1991, 52.
3. Quotes from Damián Pratt originally appeared in Milton Jamail, "Talent pool stirs dreams of expansion in Venezuela," *Baseball America*, January 22, 2001, 8.
4. Paul White," Venezuelan presence pays dividends," *USA Today Sports Weekly*, July 3, 2002, 27.

7. A Dream Come True

1. Steve Fainaru, "Baseball's minor infractions," *Washington Post*, October 26, 2001.
2. House, *Necessities*, 112.
3. George Diaz, "Major leagues' child-snatching days are over in Latin America," *Cincinnati Post*, April 20, 1989.
4. Joyce, *The Only Ticket Off the Island*, 29.
5. Kerrane, *Dollar Sign on the Muscle*, 313.

8. Maracuchos y Gochos

1. The word "*maracucho*" was often intended as an insult, but today many residents of Maracaibo and the state of Zulia proudly use the term to refer

to themselves. For more detail on the words "*maracucho*" and "*gocho*"—a term used later in this chapter—see Pérez, *El insulto en Venezuela*, 37–39.

2. Besson, *Historia del estado Zuila*, 653 and Arrieta Meléndez, *Crónicas del deporte regional*, 9.

9. The Talent Search Expands

1. Milton Jamail, "Jays land Brazilian prospect." USA *Today Baseball Weekly*, July 15, 1992, 3.
2. The most extensive source of information on baseball in Panama, and where much of the information for this section is drawn, is Pérez Medina, *Historia del baseball panameño.*

   In addition to traveling with Andrés to Panama in 2000, I was able to make another excursion into the world of baseball in that country in 2003 when I was invited by the United States Embassy to go there for three days to give a series of talks on baseball. It was a fantastic experience and included dinner with the country's top baseball editors and writers in Panama City and a meeting with sports officials in the provincial capital of Chitré.
3. "Astros to Open Baseball Academy in Nicaragua in 2001," Press Release from Houston Astros, September 11, 2000.
4. No one knows more about Nicaraguan baseball than Rondón. I spent a delightful day with him in Managua in 2001 discussing baseball and taking a tour of Dennis Martínez stadium. I have since communicated with Rondón on a regular basis and have benefited from his insights into the origins of baseball in Nicaragua.
5. Federación Nicaragüense de Béisbol Asociada (FENIBA), *Reseña de cien años de béisbol en Nicaragua, 1891–1991.* See also Arellano, *El Doctor David Arrellano, 1872–1928*, 71; Arellano, *Historia básica de Nicaragua*, 156; Gobat, *Confronting the American Dream*, 63–65; and Ham, "Americanizing Nicaragua," 185–91. Tito Rondón pointed out to me that while Ham's claims that the U.S. Marines introduced baseball to Nicaragua are incorrect, U.S. military forces do deserve credit for popularizing the game in the country.
6. My knowledge of Nicaraguan baseball was greatly enhanced by regular conversations with René Cárdenas in the press box at Enron Field and Minute Maid Park in Houston between 2000 and 2006.
7. *Pan-Aruban* 6, no. 16 (April 21, 1934): 15.
8. Porto Cabrales, *Historia del béisbol profesional de Colombia.*

9. Nieto Ibáñez, *Génesis del béisbol profesional colombiano*, 19.
10. Montes Mathieu, "El cuarto bate," 29–38.

10. Refining the Product

1. Andrés showed me a draft copy of the eighteen-page report in 1992. In addition to Andrés, another key figure in compiling the report was Herb Raybourn, who at the time was the New York Yankees director of Latin American scouting.
2. Milton Jamail, "Government quota creates visa bottleneck for players." *Baseball America*, March 2, 1998, 12.

11. Foreigners at Their Own Game

1. Alou, "Latin-American ballplayers need a Bill of Rights," 21ff.

12. What Happened? Where Did the Prospects Go?

1. Neil Hohlfeld, "One loss remains tough to forget," *Houston Chronicle*, July 27, 2005.

13. Good-bye to the Astros

No notes.

14. Andrés's Dream and the Future of the Astros in Venezuela

1. To more accurately measure the success rate of players signed, 2000 was chosen as the cut-off date. Players signed after that date still retain the possibility of reaching the major leagues.
2. Dave Sheinin and Jorge Arangure Jr., "Ripken skirts McGwire, speaks of Venezuela, *Washington Post*, December 6, 2006.
3. Dan Connolly, "Mora buys Venezuelan tract for baseball," *Baltimore Sun*, December 6, 2006.
4. Chris Kline, "Political changes in Venezuela leave teams concerned," *Baseball America*, January 15, 2007, 39.
5. Richard Justice, "McLane has squandered opportunity," *Houston Chronicle*, May 16, 2005.
6. José de Jesús Ortiz, "Astros set to announce changes to Latin American operations," *Houston Chronicle*, October 17, 2006.

Bibliography

Acosta Gutiérrez, Humberto. *El Gato con Humberto Acosta*. Caracas: Fondo Editorial Cárdenas Lares, 1997.

Alou, Felipe "Latin-American ballplayers need a Bill of Rights." *Sport*. November 1963, 21ff.

Alvarez Bajares, Rodolfo, and Oscar Arango Cadavid. *Alfonso "Chico" Carrasquel: ídolo de siempre*. Caracas: Servicio Gráfico Editorial, 1986.

Antero Núñez, General José, and Alfredo Méndez. *Años dorados del baseball venezolano, 1927–1945*. Caracas: JAN Editor, 1992.

———. *Oro y glorias del béisbol venezolano*. Caracas: JAN Editor, 1991.

Arellano, Jorge Eduardo. *El Doctor David Arrellano, 1872–1928*. Managua: Edición del Autor, 1993.

———. *Historia básica de Nicaragua*, vol. 2. Managua: Fondo Editorial CIRA, 1993.

Arrieta M., Orlando. *Crónicas del deporte regional*. Maracaibo: Ediciones de la Academia de Historia del Estado Zulia, 2001.

Benítez, Leo. *Las grandes ligas, 1900–1980*. Caracas: Publicaciones Seleven, 1980.

———. *Registro del béisbol profesional de Venezuela 1965–1985*. Caracas: Gustavo Urbina H., 1986.

Besson, Juan. *Historia del estado Zulia*, vol. 4. Maracaibo: Ediciones Banco Hipotecario de Zulia, 1973.

Biblioteca Nacional. *El béisbol en Venezuela: un siglo de pasión*. Caracas: Biblioteca Nacional, 1996.

Bracho, Emil, and Giner García. *Navagantes del Magallanes: la travesía*. Caracas: Editorial La Brújula, 1997.

Cárdenas Lara, Carlos. *Leones del Caracas: crónica de una tradición*. Caracas: Fondo Editorial Cárdenas Lares, 1992.

——. *Venezolanos en las grandes ligas: sus vidas y hazañas.* 2nd ed. Caracas: Fondo Editorial Cárdenas Lares, 1994.

Casas, Edel, Jorge Alfonso, and Alberto Pestana. *Viva y en juego.* Havana: Ministerio de Cultura, Editorial Científico-Técnica, 1986.

Colmenares del Valle, Edgar. *Léxico del béisbol en Venezuela.* Caracas: Ediciones Centaro, 1977.

Díaz Rangel, Eleazar, and Guillermo Becerra Mijares. *El béisbol en Caracas.* Caracas: Círculo de Periodistas Deportivos, 1985.

Dickson, Paul, ed. *The Dickson Baseball Dictionary.* New York: Avon Books, 1991.

Dinneen, Mark. *Culture and Customs of Venezuela.* Westport CT: Greenwood Press, 2001.

Etedgui, Chiquitín, and Asdrúbal Fuenmayor Pérez. *La hazaña del siglo.* Caracas: Colección Radio Deportes 1590, 2001.

Ewell, Judith. *Venezuela: A Century of Change.* Stanford CA: Stanford University Press, 1984.

Federación Nicaragüense de Béisbol Asociada (FENIBA). *Reseña de cien años de béisbol en Nicaragua, 1891–1991.* Managua: FENIBA, 1991.

Fuenmayor Pérez, Asdrúbal. *Johán Santana.* Caracas: Radio Deportes 1590, 2005.

García, Giner, Emil Bracho, and Luis E. Sequera. *99+1: Magallanes.* Caracas: Editorial La Brújula, 1996.

Gobat, Michael. *Confronting the American Dream: Nicaragua under U.S. Imperial Rule.* Durham NC: Duke University Press, 2005.

González, Javier. *El béisbol en Venezuela.* Caracas: Fundación Bigott, 2003.

——, ed. *Magallaneros y caraquistas: cronología de sufrimientos y satisfacciones.* Caracas: s.n., 2000.

——. *Navagantes del Magallanes: 84 años de historias.* Caracas: Museo Jacobo Borges, 2001.

Guillén, Oswaldo. *¡Se los dije!* Caracas: Alfadil, 2005.

Gutiérrez, Daniel. *50 años de big leaguers venezolanos 1939–1989.* Caracas: privately printed, 1990.

Gutiérrez, Daniel, Efraim Alvarez, and Daniel Gutiérrez, hijo. *La enciclopedia del béisbol en Venezuela.* Caracas: Fondo Editorial Cárdenas Lara, 1997.

Gutiérrez, Daniel, and Javier González. *Numeritos del béisbol profesional de Venezuela 1946–1992.* Caracas: Simerca, 1992.

Gutiérrez, Daniel, Javier González, and Daniel Gutiérrez, hijo. *Galarragmanía.* Caracas: Fondo Editorial Cárdenas Lares, 1984.

Ham, Clifford D. "Americanizing Nicaragua: How Yankee Marines, Financial Oversight and Baseball Are Stabilizing Central America." *American Review of Reviews*, February 1916, 185–91.

Horenstein, Henry. *Baseball in the Barrios*. San Diego: Gulliver Books, 1997.

House, Phillip M. *Necessities: Racial Barriers in American Sports*. New York: Random House, 1989.

Jamail, Milton. "Dodgers' prospect has come a long, long way." *USA Today Baseball Weekly*. August 9, 1991, 52.

———. "Fan favorite Abreu still is the toast of Tucson." *USA Today Baseball Weekly*. April 3, 1996, 37.

———. *Full Count: Inside Cuban Baseball*. Carbondale: Southern Illinois University Press, 2000.

———. "Hidalgo focuses in on winning." *USA Today Baseball Weekly*. March 26, 1997, 22.

———. "Hidalgo's long road reaches majors." *Baseball America*. March 30, 1998, 21.

———. "Mora rises in stature and through Astros system." *USA Today Baseball Weekly*. April 17, 1996, 27.

———. "Nicaragua sees brighter future in baseball." *Baseball America*. September 2, 2002, 56.

———. "Reiner keeps talent flowing." *Baseball America*. November 26, 2001, 13.

———. "Venezuelan academy updated." *Astros Magazine*. August 2003, 32–34.

———. "Venezuelan pipeline: Astros tap into talent-rich country by operating academy for young players. *Houston Chronicle*. July 23, 1995.

———. "Venezuelan shortstop Guillen rewards Astros' faith." *Baseball America*. July 20, 1998, 11.

———."Venezuelan Summer League champions." *Astros Magazine*. October 2001, 17–19.

John, Rosa Alma, *Los Leones del Caracas*. Caracas: Editorial Cejota, 1982.

Johnson, Lloyd, and Miles Wolff, eds. *The Encyclopedia of Minor League Baseball*. Durham NC: Baseball America, 1993.

Joyce, Gare. *The Only Ticket Off the Island*. Toronto: McClelland and Stewart, 1991.

Kerrane, Kevin. *Dollar Sign on the Muscle: The World of Baseball Scouting*. Lincoln: University of Nebraska Press, 1999.

Krich, John. *El Béisbol: Travels Through the Pan-American Pastime*. New York: Atlantic Monthly Press, 1989.

Larez Granado, Francisco. *Béisbol en Margarita 1907–1944*. Nueva Esparta, Venezuela: Imprenta Oficial del Estado Nueva Esparta, 1975.

Liga Venezolana de Béisbol Profesional. *Guía del fanático '93*. Caracas: Fondo Editorial Cárdenas Lares, 1993.

Littlefield, Bill. *Baseball Days: From the Sandlots to the Show*. Boston: Little, Brown and Company, 1993.

Losada, Jess. "Hace cuarenta y seis años se jugaba baseball en Caracas," *Carteles* (Havana), November 30, 1941:8–9.

Medina, Ivan, ed. *Registro del béisbol venezolano*. Caracas: Liga Venezolana de Béisbol Profesional, 1995.

Mijares, Rubén. *Béisbol por dentro*. Mérida, Venezuela: Editorial Alfa, 1990.

———. *Hechos y hazañas del béisbol profesional en Venezuela 1946–1992*. Caracas: Grupo Editorial EGE, 1992.

Mijares, Rubén, and Daniel Gutiérrez. *¡Magallanes para todo el mundo!* Caracas: Grupo Editorial EGE, 1993.

Montes, Mari. *Por la goma 2005: Guillén y otras alegrías*. Caracas: Alfadil, 2005.

Montes Mathieu, Roberto. "El cuarto bate," In *El cuarto bate*, 29–38. Bogotá: Plaza & Janes, 1985.

Nieto Ibáñez, José. *Génesis del béisbol professional colombiano*. Baranquilla: Fondo de Publicaciones Universidad del Atlántico, 1999.

Pérez, Francisco Javier. *El insulto en Venezuela*. Caracas: Fundación Bigott, 2005

Pérez, Louis A., Jr. "Between Baseball and Bullfighting: The Quest for Nationality in Cuba, 1868–1998." *The Journal of American History* 81, no. 2 (1994): 493-517.

Pérez Medina, Ramón G. *Historia del baseball panameño*, vol. 1. Panamá: s.n, 1992.

Porto Cabrales, Raúl. *Historia del béisbol profesional de Colombia*. Cartagena: Gráficas El Cheque, 2002.

Rabe, Stephen G. *The Road to OPEC: United States Relations with Venezuela, 1919–1976*. Austin: University of Texas Press, 1982.

Ramos, Alí. *Todos fueron héroes*. Caracas: Ministerio de Información y Turismo, 1982.

Rodríguez, Luis Felipe, and others. *El Deporte en Venezuela*. Caracas: Dirección de Cultura, Universidad Central de Venezuela, 1968.

Ruck, Rob. "Baseball in the Caribbean." In *Totally Baseball*, edited by John Thorn and Pete Palmar, 605–14. New York: Warner Books, 1989.

———. "The *Chicos* of Winter." *Baseball History* 1, no. 4 (Winter 1986): 18–27.

———. "Chicos and Gringos of Béisbol Venezolana [*sic*]." *The Baseball Research Journal* 15 (1986): 75–78.

Salas H., Alexis. *Los eternos rivales: Caracas-Magallanes, Pastora-Gavilanes.* Caracas: Grupo Editorial, 1988.

———. *Momentos inolvidables del béisbol profesional venezolano, 1946–1984.* Caracas: García e hijo, 1985.

Tijerino, Edgar. *Double play.* Managua: Vanguardia, 1989.

Vené, Juan, Eleazar Díaz Rangel, and Humberto Acosta. *Un siglo de béisbol.* Caracas: Liga Venezolana de Béisbol Profesional, 1995.

Vizquel, Omar, with Bob Dyer. *Omar! My Life On and Off the Field.* Cleveland: Gray and Company Publishers, 2002.

Wagner, Eric A. "Sport in Revolutionary Societies: A Comparative Study of Cuba and Nicaragua." In *Sport and Society in Latin America,* edited by Joesph L. Arbena, 113–36. New York: Greenwood Press, 1988.